CHECKPOINTS

CHECKPOINTS

DEVELOPING COLLEGE ENGLISH SKILLS

FIRST CANADIAN EDITION

JACK PAGE
MERRITT COLLEGE

JANE MERIVALE
CENTENNIAL COLLEGE

Addison-Wesley Publishers Limited
Don Mills, Ontario · Reading, Massachusetts
Menlo Park, California · New York · Wokingham, England
Amsterdam · Bonn · Sydney · Singapore · Tokyo · Madrid
San Juan · Paris · Seoul · Milan · Mexico City · Taipei

Senior Editor: Brian Henderson
Developmental Editor: Trish Morgan
Project Coordination and Text Design: Ruttle, Shaw & Wetherill, Inc.
Cover Designer: Kay Petronio
Electronic Production Manager: Christine Pearson
Manufacturing Manager: Willie Lane
Electronic Page Makeup: Ruttle, Shaw & Wetherill, Inc.
Printer and Binder: R. R. Donnelley & Sons Company
Cover Printer: The Lehigh Press, Inc.

For permission to use copyrighted material, grateful acknowledgement is made to the copyright holders on pp. 297–298, which are hereby made part of this copyright page.

Canadian Cataloguing in Publication Data

Page, Jack
Checkpoints
1st Canadian ed.
Includes index.
ISBN 0-673-99964-5

1. English language—Rhetoric.   2. English language—Grammar.
3. College readers.   I. Merivale, Jane.   II. Title

PE1408.P34 1997   808'.0427   C96–930323–8

ISBN 0-673-99964-5

123456789–DOW–00999897

CONTENTS

PREFACE TO THE SECOND U.S. EDITION

Checkpoints is designed to help students acquire the language skills needed to succeed in all college courses that require the ability to write with clarity and precision and to read with critical understanding. Of course, these skills will continue to be valuable after college—both in the workplace and in social and family life.

A key feature of *Checkpoints* is its integration of a variety of interest-sustaining elements in each chapter. One of the most important of these is the reading that begins each chapter. The readings provide examples of writing strategies for students to emulate, as well as information and ideas that they may incorporate into their own writing. The readings also offer opportunities for improving oral communication skills through class discussions of significant contemporary topics—discussions that may help students clarify their own ideas and values. The follow-up questions under the headings "Checking Meaning and Style" and "Checking Ideas" help develop critical thinking skills.

From Paragraph to Essay

Throughout, *Checkpoints* emphasizes the need to express ideas and present information in clear, well-organized paragraphs. Students usually find it more rewarding to focus on developing paragraphs than on writing isolated sentences. In the last five chapters, students learn to build on these paragraph skills in writing short essays.

This second edition contains a number of changes from the first edition. The most significant is the increased emphasis given to an understanding of writing as a multi-stage *process,* with material in all chapters covering such phases as prewriting, revising, and editing. More models and step-by-step guides for student writing are also provided. The number of chapters has been reduced to a more manageable 15, and the chapter sequence has been strengthened.

Fundamentals Made Accessible

Each chapter again covers a particular area of grammar or mechanics and includes extensive exercises and quizzes. This instruction is designed to be accessible to students who need help with fundamentals and is presented concisely in a conversational, nontechnical way. Each brief unit of instruction is followed by a "Spotcheck" exercise to test understanding. Several related units are then reviewed in a "Doublecheck" exercise. A final "Checkpoint" quiz tests mastery of the entire section. More opportunities to reinforce this learning are afforded by the quizzes in the Instructor's Manual.

Checkpoints is a flexible text. The answers provided in the Instructor's Manual for all Checkpoint, Spotcheck, and Doublecheck exercises can be reproduced for students. This permits independent work by students and opens up class time for freewriting, group writing, revision, and other activities that may be considered appropriate. The appendices offer additional chances for classroom variety, with material on dictionary use, reading strategies, words often misused, words often misspelled, and a guide to the parts of speech. Additional suggestions for using the text can be found in the Instructor's Manual, which also contains answers and background material for the readings. Using the correction key on the inside front cover of the text, the instructor can easily direct students to appropriate pages for help with writing problems. The Instructor's Manual also includes a set of overhead transparency masters, a set of two more quizzes on grammar or mechanics for each chapter, and two diagnostic tests, one for the beginning and one for the end of the term.

Jack Page

PREFACE TO THE FIRST CANADIAN EDITION

Welcome to the Canadian version of *Checkpoints*. It is very exciting to be able to offer our students the same quality of textbook as the American edition, but within an all-Canadian context. In the Canadian edition, all but one of the readings are articles written by Canadians; the vocabulary and spelling has been Canadianized; and references throughout cover features, issues, people and historical facts relevant to Canadians from coast to coast.

The readings are a reflection of the variety and diversity of life we celebrate in our country. In the Canadian version of *Checkpoints,* articles from diverse subject areas have been chosen for their current relevance to all Canadian students, no matter what their age, background, or where they live. The readings are a selection from famous writers as well as from new—sometimes student—writers. The selected readings should all stimulate lively discussion and prompt interesting writing. The last five essays are examples of writing we find common in our daily lives. The authors use a variety of stylistic devices for impact; the models that follow the essays, however, adhere rigidly to the five-paragraph format we encourage our students to begin their essay writing with.

In general, some of the reading models follow more closely the academic essay format than others. In Chapter 1, the students' attention is drawn to the fact that some authors omit certain conventions for effect or impact. The fact that these readings do vary in their writing styles is a reflection of their interesting assortment, and there is full compensation for this variety of styles in the presentation of strictly formula writing models that the students are asked to follow.

In the Canadian edition there is a new appendix, Writing a Summary, which gives the student a writing model with the reading "Lack of English, Not Good Will, Is the Culprit" and a step by step approach to summary writing, an essential study skill. The second major change is the position of the Job Application Letter which is no longer in Chapter 12; it is in the Appendix, with a reading "Take a Close Look at Your Letter and Résumé."

I thank my dear family, Ian and Ross, for their patience and support while I couldn't play with them, and my mother for her help in research. Many thanks also to the Darlings, without whom I couldn't have completed this.

My first editor, Michael Young, was immeasurably supportive, and I am extremely grateful for Brian Henderson's great assistance during the book's completion.

Last, but not least, thanks to Jack Page for creating a book which I truly believe can teach people how to teach themselves to enjoy reading, to value discussion, and to write well.

Jane Merivale

THE PARAGRAPH

◆ READING

PARAGRAPHS WITH TOPIC SENTENCES AND SPECIFIC DETAILS

Writers often organize a paragraph with an opening topic sentence, followed by specific details that make their ideas clear and interesting to the reader. In this selection about local Newfoundland foods, Ray Guy lists all the homemade, natural treats he ate as a child, before the "trickle" of imported and, to him, tasteless food arrived. Once he has introduced a particular food, he describes it in greater detail. I wonder if they sound to you like tempting foods.

You will notice in several of the readings in this book that many experienced writers will omit writing complete sentences, or will use one-sentence paragraphs for effect. In "Outharbor Menu," pay special attention to the paragraphs that do have topic sentences followed by further, more specific details: Paragraphs 3, 4, 7, and 13.

Outharbor Menu

—Ray Guy

pod auger days old days

outports isolated fishing villages

What feeds we used to have. Not way back in the pod auger days, 1 mind you. That was before my time. I mean not long ago, just before the tinned stuff and the packages and the baker's bread started to trickle into the outports.

Out where I come from the trickle started when I was about six or 2 seven years old. One day I went next door to Aunt Winnie's (that's Uncle John's Aunt Winnie) and she had a package of puffed rice someone sent down from Canada. She gave us youngsters a small handful each. We spent a long time admiring this new exotic stuff and remarking on

emmets' eggs ants' eggs

how much it looked like emmets' eggs. We ate it one grain at a time as if it were candy, and because of the novelty didn't notice the remarkable lack of taste. "Now here's a five cent piece and don't spend it all in sweets, mind." You never got a nickel without this caution attached.

There were so many thrilling sweets to choose from. Peppermint 3 knobs. White capsules ringed around with flannelette pink stripes. Strong! You'd think you were breathing icewater. They're not near as strong today. Chocolate mice shaped like a crouching rat, chocolate on the outside and tough pink sponge inside. Goodbye teeth. Bullseyes made from molasses. And union squares—pastel blocks of marshmallow. Those mysterious black balls that were harder than forged steel, had about 2,537 different layers of color and a funny tasting seed at the centre of the mini-universe.

Soft drinks came packed in barrels of straw in bottles of different 4 sizes and shapes and no labels. Birch beer, root beer, chocolate, lemonade, and orange. There was spruce beer, which I could never stomach, but the twigs boiling on the stove smelled good. Home brew made from "Blue Ribbon" malt and which always exploded like hand grenades in

puncheons large barrels

the bottles behind the stove. Rum puncheons. Empty barrels purchased from the liquor control board in St. John's. You poured in a few gallons of water, rolled the barrel around, and the result was a stronger product than you put down $7.50 a bottle for today.

Ice cream was made in a hand-cranked freezer, the milk and 5 sugar and vanilla in the can in the middle surrounded by ice and coarse salt. I won't say it was better than the store-bought stuff today, but it tasted different and I like the difference.

cod fish
pork scruncheons crisp slices of pork fat

Rounders (dried tom cods) for Sunday breakfast without fail. 6 Cods heads, boiled sometimes, but mostly stewed with onions and bits of salt pork. Fried cod tongues with pork scruncheons. Outport soul food. Salt codfish, fish cakes, boiled codfish and drawn butter, baked cod with savoury stuffing, stewed cod, fried cod.

Lobsters: We always got the bodies and the thumbs from the can- 7 ning factories. When eating lobster bodies you must be careful to stay away from the "old woman," a lump of bitter black stuff up near the head which is said to be poisonous. I was always partial to that bit of red stuff in lobster bodies but never went much on the pea green stuff although some did.

turrs diving birds
tickleaces kind of gull

We ate turrs (impaled on a sharpened broomstick and held over 8 the damper hole to singe off the fuzz); some people ate tickleaces and gulls, but I never saw it done. We ate "a meal of trouts," seal, rabbits that were skinned out like a sock, puffin' pig (a sort of porpoise that had black meat), mussels and cocks and hens, otherwise known as clams, that squirt at you through air holes in the mud flats.

Potatoes and turnips were the most commonly grown vegetables 9 although there was some cabbage and carrot. The potatoes were kept in cellars made of mounds of earth lined with sawdust or goosegrass. With the hay growing on them they looked like hairy green igloos.

A lot was got from a cow. Milk, certainly, and cream and butter 10 made into pats and stamped with a wooden print of a cow or a clover leaf, and buttermilk, cream cheese. And I seem to remember a sort of jellied sour milk. I forget the name, but perhaps the stuff was equivalent to yogurt.

There was no fresh meat in summer because it wouldn't keep. If 11 you asked for a piece of meat at the store you got salt beef. If you wanted fresh beef, you had to ask for "fresh meat."

Biscuits came packed in three-foot long wooden boxes and were 12 weighed out by the pound in paper bags. Sultanas, Dad's cookies, jam jams, lemon creams with caraway seeds, and soda biscuits.

Molasses was a big thing. It was used to sweeten tea, in ginger- 13 bread, on rolled oats porridge, with sulphur in the spring to clean the blood (eeeccchhhh), in bread, in baked beans, in 'lassie bread. It came in barrels and when the molasses was gone, there was a layer of molasses sugar at the bottom.

The list of delights runs on in my memory. Glasses of lemon crys- 14 tals or strawberry syrup or limejuice. Rolled oats, farina, Indian meal. Home-made bread, pork buns, figgy duff, partridgeberry tarts, blanc mange, ginger wine, damper cakes. Cold mutton, salt beef, peas pudding, boiled cabbage, tinned bully beef for lunch on Sunday, tinned peaches, brown eggs, corned caplin. And thank God I was twelve years old before ever a slice of baker's bread passed my lips.

figgy duff raisin pudding
damper cakes pancakes
bully beef corned beef
corned caplin fish

CHECKING MEANING AND STYLE

1. Identify the topic sentences in Paragraphs 2, 3, and 4. What details are there in each paragraph to support its topic sentence?

2. What is the time that Ray Guy is recalling?

3. Why does he mention that puffed rice was sent down "from Canada"?

4. Guy uses one-word sentences, words like "stuff" and expressions like "eeeccchhhh." How do these add to the reader's interest?

5. What effect does the sum "2,537" have on the description of the black balls?

6. How does the last sentence seem to emphasize the point of the article?

CHECKING IDEAS

1. Ray Guy describes all the treats he ate when he was growing up. Can you remember things you ate and whether or not you liked them?

2. What we eat is often determined by our culture. Are there any foods special in your family because of where you come from?

3. Do you get the impression that Guy enjoyed his childhood and that he misses it now?

4. In this age of fast food, is there anything you miss?

◆ WRITING MODELS

A PARAGRAPH WITH A TOPIC SENTENCE AND SPECIFIC DETAILS

For good reasons, most writing is broken into paragraphs. One reason is that paragraphs help the reader follow the flow of the writer's ideas. Since a traditional paragraph discusses only one idea, a new paragraph alerts the reader that a new idea is coming up. Another reason for paragraphs is that they help the writer organize his or her thoughts. In this section, you will read three model paragraphs in which the writers' thoughts are well organized. These model paragraphs are similar to the kind you will later be asked to write.

We can recognize the beginning of a paragraph because it is usually indented. That is, it starts several spaces in from the left side of the page, as in the model paragraphs below. However, typewritten and typeset material is sometimes written in block form: A new paragraph is indicated by an extra space between paragraphs, and there is no indenting.

The selection "Outharbor Menu" has a thesis sentence in the first paragraph that establishes the focus of the whole selection:

What feeds we used to have.

Many of the following paragraphs begin with a topic sentence and describe the kinds of dishes Newfoundlanders used to eat; the reader senses Guy's nostalgia for his youth. Here is an outline of the paragraphs that have topic sentences and further details:

TOPIC

Paragraph 1—the food we used to have before the trickle

Paragraph 3—the thrilling sweets to choose from

Paragraphs 6 to 8—the kinds of fish and fowl we ate

Paragraph 10—the dishes from milk

Paragraph 14—the list of dishes is endless

These ideas could have been expressed in only one paragraph with fewer details.

FOCUS

Study the model paragraphs that follow. Observe how the opening topic sentence establishes the *focus* of the paragraph. All the other sentences add interesting details that clarify the topic sentence.

The paragraph about the candies has a topic sentence and further details about the treats:

Model Paragraph #1

The topic sentence has been underlined.

    There were so many thrilling sweets to choose from. Peppermint knobs. White capsules ringed around with flannelette pink stripes. Strong! You'd think you were breathing icewater. They're not near as strong today. Chocolate mice shaped like a crouching rat, chocolate on the outside and tough pink sponge inside. Goodbye teeth. Bullseyes made from molasses. And union squares—pastel blocks of marshmallow. Those mysterious black balls that were harder than forged steel, had about 2,537 different layers of color and a funny tasting seed at the centre of the mini-universe.

Model Paragraph #2

Notice how the details support the writer's topic sentence.

<u>Recent milk advertisements suggest that natural, nutritional products have to be given a "product identity" to sell.</u> In one advertisement, hockey player Doug Gilmour is wearing his Leafs sweater, but his legs are in the black-and-white design of a cow! The ad suggests that he gets his energy from milk; if we drink milk, we can be like him. It now has a designer image.

Model Paragraph #3

The underlined topic sentence states what the paragraph will discuss.

<u>Walking is a healthful form of exercise that avoids some of the problems in running or jogging.</u> Running places stress on the ankles and knees and can cause injury; walking is much gentler to the body. Runners often risk their lives in auto traffic, while walkers tend to stick to the safer sidewalks. The flashing legs of a runner are of much greater interest to neighbourhood dogs than is the slower stride of a walker. Runners need a shower after their workout, but walkers can take a brisk noontime stroll and return to the office without fear of offending. Doctors say that walking rapidly for a half-hour or more several times a week can be beneficial in keeping a person's heart and lungs operating efficiently.

1. State three specific advantages of walking over running.

UNIFIED

A paragraph should be *unified;* that is, it should deal with only one subject. **The topic sentence says what the main point of the paragraph is.** Putting the topic sentence first is most helpful in writing a unified paragraph.

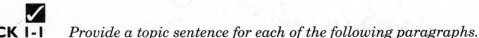

SPOTCHECK 1-1   *Provide a topic sentence for each of the following paragraphs.*

1. _____

_____

The kids use the computer mostly for playing games, such as Zoop and SimCity, but ten-year-old Billy has a program to help him with his spelling. The teenager, Sally, enjoys a program that casts horoscopes for her and her friends. My wife works out the family budget with an accounting program. I, meanwhile, try to catch up on some of my office correspondence in the evening with the word processing program—if no one else is using the computer.

2. _____

_____

We arrived at the lake early, about 9:30 a.m., when the air was still cool and the lake so still that the surrounding mountains were reflected as in a mirror. Alex suggested we go to an old miner's cabin on the opposite shore. We walked through a cool pine forest along the edge of the lake, scaring up a few ducks as we went. After a picnic lunch near the cabin, I took a nap while Alex scouted around for good photo subjects. When we got back to the car, the sun was hot, and we were glad to take a dip in the lake.

3. _____

 _____

I have liked animals since I was a little girl. While I was growing up, my pets included rabbits, snakes, guinea pigs, and a series of kittens. Another reason is that veterinarians provide a useful service in helping animals stay healthy, and they make a good living while doing it. Furthermore, the nearby state university has a respected program in veterinary medicine.

Compare your answers with those in the Answer Key before continuing. This is important; otherwise, you may just be practising making errors.

SPECIFIC DETAILS

People are not satisfied with generalities. They want *specific details*. They want to know not just that it was hot yesterday, but that the thermometer hit 35°C, that downtown office workers waded in the courthouse fountain at lunchtime, that highway traffic was snarled with overheated cars. Writing that does not get down to specifics—writing that is general or vague—is uninteresting and often unclear.

 (vague) Kevin lives in a <u>big house</u>.

 (specific) Kevin lives in a <u>14-room mansion that has 6 bathrooms, 4 garages, and an indoor swimming pool</u>.

SPOTCHECK 1-2

Rewrite these sentences to make the vague (underlined) words more specific. Your sentences will probably be longer than the originals.

1. Larry was <u>angry</u>. (Say what Larry *did* that showed anger.)

 _____

2. Yolanda has an old <u>car</u>.

 _____

3. Naomi brought a <u>snack</u>.

 _____

Compare your answers with those in the Answer Key.

◆ WRITING ASSIGNMENT

A PARAGRAPH WITH A TOPIC SENTENCE AND SPECIFIC DETAILS

The topic of a paragraph is what it is about. You could write a paragraph about bowling, reckless drivers, or your uncle Fred. Each one could be a topic of a paragraph. But you would not have a **topic sentence** until you said something about your topic that led you into the paragraph. Notice how the three topics just mentioned could become parts of topic sentences:

1. <u>Bowling</u> on the company team has helped me get along better at the office.

Now you can give specific details and examples: how you can join in your teammates' conversations at coffee break, how the boss complimented you on your 200 game Wednesday night, and so on.

2. <u>Reckless drivers</u> have taken over the highways these days.

Now tell about some of the reckless drivers you have seen on the highways lately, and add some statistics from news stories about the increase in accidents.

3. Of all my relatives, <u>Uncle Fred</u> is the most generous.

Now discuss the way he is helping you attend college, the birthday presents he gives the family, and his contributions to charity.

Be sure your topic sentences lead easily into a discussion of the topic. If you state only facts, there will be nothing to discuss. Stating an opinion leads to a more interesting paragraph. Avoid "So what?" sentences that lead nowhere, such as these:

> Our bowling team meets the first and third Mondays of each month at Bowlerama. *(So what?)*

> The insurance company magazine had an article about reckless drivers. *(Who cares?)*

SPOTCHECK 1-3   *In the blanks at the left, write **good** for effective topic sentences that would lead to fully developed paragraphs. Write* weak *for those that seem to lead nowhere.*

_____ **1.** My writing skills have improved since I started reading more books and magazines.

_____ **2.** Mayor Gallant wants to improve the city's park system.

_____ **3.** Canada's highest mountain is 5,959 metres high.

_____ **4.** Banff's mile-high altitude affects visiting athletes.

_____ **5.** There are three boys and three girls in my family.

Check the Answer Key before continuing.

Topic sentences should not be too broad; that is, they should not try to cover too much ground. After all, you are writing a paragraph, not a book. Narrow your subject so that it can be discussed in a worthwhile way in the few sentences of a paragraph.

(too broad) <u>The weather in British Columbia</u> is sometimes uncomfortable.

(better) <u>The weather in Lytton</u> is sometimes uncomfortable.

(too broad) <u>Dogs</u> are devoted pets.

(better) <u>My grandfather's poodle Fifi</u> is a devoted pet.

Further Practice in Topic Sentences

From the following subjects, narrow the topics into suitable topic sentences.

1. Using public transportation
2. Violence policies in schools
3. The fishing industry
4. Public broadcasting
5. Winter sports
6. Learning a second language

SPOTCHECK 1-4   *Rewrite the subjects at the left twice, each time making them less broad and more suitable for discussion in a single paragraph.*

EXAMPLE:

outdoor activity   <u>gardening</u>   <u>growing roses</u>

1. work   _____   _____

2. buildings   _____   _____

3. music   _____   _____

4. students   _____   _____

Compare your answers with those in the Answer Key.

Having narrowed your topic, be sure that what you say about it is *specific,* not general or vague.

(**vague**) The CBC <u>has good programs</u>.

(**specific**) The CBC <u>features the kind of news programs that I like</u>.

(**vague**) Montreal <u>is an interesting city</u>.

(**specific**) Montreal <u>has many outstanding restaurants</u>.

(**more specific**) Montreal <u>is a good place to find French cuisine</u>.

SPOTCHECK 1-5

In the blanks at the left, write **weak** *for topic sentences that are broad or vague. Write* **good** *for the others.*

_____ 1. Mr. and Ms. Howell are good people.

_____ 2. Baseball is one of Canada's favourite sports.

_____ 3. The woman at the checkout counter is nice.

_____ 4. My new pickup truck costs a great deal in loan payments, insurance, and maintenance.

_____ 5. Most of the "romance" novels sold at supermarkets are poor.

_____ 6. Running eight kilometres several times a week can improve a person's health.

Check the Answer Key before continuing.

SPOTCHECK 1-6

Turn the listed topics into topic sentences by saying something specific about each one. Ask yourself if each sentence would lead easily into a full paragraph.

    EXAMPLE: Watching professional football on TV <u>takes up too much of my time in the fall</u>.

1. My neighbourhood _____

_____

2. The neighbour's cat _____

_____

3. My cousin _____

_____

4. Shopping _____

_____

5. My English class _____

_____

Compare your answers with those in the Answer Key.

WRITE A PARAGRAPH WITH A
TOPIC SENTENCE AND
SPECIFIC DETAILS

You have read models of paragraphs with topic sentences and specific details, and you have practised these parts of a paragraph. Now you are ready to write your own paragraph. First write a topic sentence for one of the broad subjects listed below. Narrow the topic to one particular example — one relative or one sports event, for instance — and make a particular point about it.

> **EXAMPLE:** kids <u>My brother's two-year-old son was the centre of attention at Sunday's family reunion.</u>

1. relatives _____

_____

2. animals _____

_____

3. stores _____

_____

4. sports _____

_____

5. music _____

_____

Now write a paragraph that begins with one of the topic sentences you just wrote. Make sure your paragraph contains five to ten sentences.

◆ SENTENCE STRUCTURE

THE SUBJECT AND VERB OF THE SENTENCE

The Problem: Writing
Sentences with Subjects
and Verbs

To write acceptably, we have to write in <u>sentences</u>, which most of us do most of the time without thinking about it. But sometimes we may write something that looks like a sentence — that starts with a capital letter and ends with a period—but isn't a sentence. Here is an example:

> Driving into the parking lot while following a green Mercedes.

Since a complete sentence needs a subject and a verb, we need to be able to recognize these sentence parts. Recognizing subjects and verbs is not worth much in itself. But if you can do it, you will be able to deal later with some very real problems in writing: sentence fragments, run-together sentences, lack of subject–verb agreement, inconsistencies in person and tense, and errors in punctuation.

Solution #1: Finding the Subject of the Sentence

The <u>subject</u> tells *who* or *what* the sentence is about. The underlined words in the following sentences answer the question "Who?" or "What?"

> <u>Lee</u> arrived early.
>
> <u>Winnipeg</u> is the capital of Manitoba.
>
> <u>Glass</u> breaks.
>
> <u>We</u> always sing before supper.

PARTS OF SPEECH

The subject is usually a noun or a pronoun. A *noun* is the name of a person, place, or thing (*Lee, Winnipeg, glass*). A *pronoun* is a word that takes the place of a noun. *We* is an example of a pronoun. *He, she,* and *it* are other examples.

The words underlined in the examples just given are the *simple subjects* of their sentences. A *complete subject* is the simple subject plus any words that describe it. In the following example, the complete subject is underlined once and the simple subject (*car*) twice:

> The blue <u>car</u> with the damaged fender struck a tree yesterday.

In this text, the phrase *the subject* refers to the simple subject.

SPOTCHECK 1-7

*Underline the subject in each sentence. To find the subject, ask **who** or **what** the sentence is about.*

1. The electricity went out at 11 p.m.

2. Swimming is good exercise.

3. Ms. Jackson bought a new dress.

4. Our new calendar has a picture of Stanley Park.

5. The hardworking plumber finished the job.

Check the Answer Key before continuing.

Solution #2: Finding the Verb of the Sentence

There are two kinds of verbs.

1. <u>Action verbs</u> tell what the subject *does* (or did, or will do).

   Geese <u>fly</u> south in the winter.

   Maria's brother <u>attended</u> Concordia University.

2. <u>Linking verbs</u> connect the subject to words that say something about the subject.

Marcia <u>was</u> overjoyed at getting the job.
Robert <u>seems</u> tired tonight.

The verb *was* links the subject *Marcia* to information about the subject: that she was overjoyed. The verb *seems* links the subject *Robert* to the description *tired*.

One group of linking verbs consists of forms of the verb *to be*:

am   is   are   was   were   been

Another group of linking verbs contains words such as these:

seem   appear   look   become   feel   taste   smell

Some of these words can be either linking or action verbs.

Rudy <u>looked</u> happy. [linking verb]
Rudy <u>looked</u> at the magazine. [action verb]

SPOTCHECK 1-8   *Underline the verbs. In the blanks, indicate whether they are action or linking verbs.*

_____   1. The firefighters fought the blaze for two hours.

_____   2. They were happy to be home.

_____   3. The water in Lake Huron looked dirty last fall.

_____   4. The third baseman hit two home runs.

_____   5. The spectators cheered for the home team.

Check the Answer Key before continuing.

Solution #3: Crossing Out Prepositional Phrases to Find the Subject

Often it is easier to find the subject if you first cross out all prepositional phrases in a sentence. Look at this example:

~~Behind the house,~~ Mr. Olson was napping ~~in a hammock.~~

After you cross out the two prepositional phrases, *Behind the house* and *in a hammock*, it is clear that the subject is *Mr. Olson*.

IMPORTANT: A word in a prepositional phrase is never the subject of a sentence.

Prepositional phrases are groups of words that begin with a preposition and end with a noun or pronoun. Here are some common prepositions:

about	beside	of
above	between	on
according to	by	over
across	during	through
after	for	to
among	from	toward
around	in	under
at	into	upon
before	near	with

SPOTCHECK 1-9　　*Use eight different prepositions to form prepositional phrases with these words.*

EXAMPLE: <u>near</u> the window

1. _____ the two trees

2. _____ the binoculars

3. _____ the leaves

4. _____ our car

5. _____ the roof

6. _____ town

7. _____ friends

8. _____ ten o'clock

Compare your answers with those in the Answer Key.

SPOTCHECK 1-10　　*Cross out the prepositional phrases and underline the subject.*

EXAMPLE: ~~In the office~~, the <u>president</u> stood ~~near his desk~~.

1. Of the three singers, Charles is best.

2. Between the tall buildings, a tree turned to the sunlight.

3. One of the ducks on the pond is tame.

4. For some reason, the instructor gave an "A" to everyone in the class.

5. Between you and me, the award should go to Sylvia.

Check the Answer Key before continuing.

DOUBLECHECK I-I   *Draw one line under the subject and two lines under the verb in each sentence.*

1. The new neighbours have three children.
2. The prom queen removed her crown after the dance.
3. Eric's 1975 Chevy is ready for the scrap heap.
4. Your stew tastes like my mother's.
5. Lawrence was a good source of gossip at the office.

Check the Answer Key before continuing.

Solution #4: More Tips on Finding the Subject of the Sentence

The subject usually appears at the beginning of the sentence, but it may appear elsewhere.

Flitting from flower to flower was a <u>hummingbird</u>. (The usual word order: A hummingbird was flitting from flower to flower.)

Although it often starts a sentence, *there* is never the subject.

There were three books lying on the table. (*Books* is the subject of the verb *were lying*.)

A sentence can have more than one subject.

The <u>oil</u> and the <u>filter</u> need to be changed.

In sentences that express a command, the unwritten but understood subject is *you*.

[<u>You</u>] Bring home a loaf of bread after work.

Sometimes it is easier to find the subject if you pick out the verb first, then ask *who* or *what* questions.

                                                                      verb

In the spring, the poppies on the hillsides <u>appear</u> first.

SPOTCHECK I-II   *Draw a line under each subject.*

1. College athletes have little chance of joining a professional team.
2. In football, for example, only one player in 100 has a chance of turning professional.
3. There is only one chance in 500 of succeeding in the National Basketball Association.
4. Even then, the average sports career is short—4.2 years in football and 3.2 years in basketball.
5. [_____] Remember these statistics when dreaming about sports instead of doing homework.

6. Less likely than other students to complete a degree are athletes at university or college.

Check the Answer Key before continuing.

Quickcheck on Subjects of a Sentence

✓ Every complete sentence must have a subject.

✓ The subject tells who or what the sentence is about.

✓ The subject usually appears at the beginning of the sentence, but it may appear elsewhere.

✓ A prepositional phrase is never the subject.

✓ In commands, the unwritten but understood subject is *you*.

Solution #5: More Tips on Finding the Verb of the Sentence

If the subject performs more than one action, there will be more than one <u>verb</u>.

The car <u>swerved</u> to the left and <u>hit</u> a tree.

The verb may consist of more than one word. The main verb may have one or more *helping verbs*.

The hikers <u>had walked</u> ten miles before noon.

Here are some examples of helping verbs with forms of the verb *work*:

can work	does work
is working	has been working
might have been working	should have worked
had worked	will work
will have worked	will be working

NOTE: A word ending in *-ing* cannot be the verb without one or more helping verbs. A verb preceded by *to* (*to work*) is an *infinitive* and cannot be the verb.

Sometimes the verb is broken by words that are not part of the verb. Words that often separate parts of a verb are *not* (and its contraction *-n't*), *never, always, just,* and *only*.

Mr. Ochoa <u>had</u> never <u>seen</u> a redwood tree before.

The fire <u>hadn't</u> <u>been</u> <u>started</u> in the fireplace when we arrived.

Sometimes the verb has an *object*—the person or thing acted upon by the verb. The object of a verb is **never** the subject of a sentence.

       verb   **object**
The landlord <u>raised</u> the rent twice this year.

SPOTCHECK I-12 ✓   *Underline the verb or verbs in each sentence.*

1. The Barbie doll first appeared in 1958 and achieved instant popularity.

2. It was invented by Ruth Handler for the Mattel toy company.

3. Before Barbie, North American dolls had usually resembled infants.

4. Noticing her daughter's fondness for full-figured paper cutout dolls, Mrs. Handler developed a shapely adult doll.

5. As a full-sized person, Barbie would have a 39–23–33 figure.

6. A large wardrobe and other accessories for Barbie were soon offered.

7. Taking his place with Barbie on toy store shelves in 1961 was Ken.

8. Barbie and Ken were named after the Handlers' daughter and son.

Check the Answer Key before continuing.

Quickcheck on Verbs in a Sentence

✓   Every complete sentence must have a verb.

✓   Action verbs tell what the subject *does;* linking verbs tell what the subject *is.*

✓   A sentence may have more than one verb.

✓   A verb can be more than one word—a main verb plus helping verbs.

✓   To be a complete verb, a verb form ending in *-ing* always needs a helping verb.

DOUBLECHECK I-2 ✓   *Draw one line under the subject and two lines under the verb. Finding the subject may be easier if you first cross out prepositional phrases.*

1. Education in Japan is different in many ways from education in Canada.

2. For one thing, only 7 percent of Japanese students drop out.

3. In Canada, the dropout rate is much higher.

4. The quality of the Japanese education system is often credited for Japan's success in technological fields.

5. For many Japanese, education has been the only path to social and economic status.

6. Starting in the first grade, Japanese schools stress hard work, endurance, and concentration.

7. These same values are reinforced in the students' homes.

8. The status of a Japanese woman depends in large part on the success of her children in school.

9. Nearly half of the high school students attend tutoring centres after school.

10. They worry about passing the difficult college entrance exams.

11. Four hours of sleep at night is common for serious students.

12. Surprisingly, Japanese colleges often receive low marks from some Canadian observers.

13. Canadians sometimes have been critical of the emphasis in Japanese schools on memorizing facts.

14. Too much emphasis on learning facts may hamper creativity.

Check the Answer Key before continuing.

◆ WRITING PROCESS

AN OVERVIEW OF THE WRITING PROCESS

Many new college students fear they will be asked to write perfect papers on their first try. However, writing is a task that has at least five steps:

1. Prewriting—getting ready to write

2. Writing—putting down a rough draft

3. Revising—improving the first version

4. Editing—correcting errors

5. Rewriting—copying the final draft

Learning about the stages of the writing process will help you with the assignments in each chapter of this book and also with the other writing you do in college. Each chapter of this text discusses one aspect of the writing process in detail. For now, here is a quick summary:

1. Prewriting   We have all probably found ourselves with a blank piece of paper in front of us that seems matched by the blank spot in our brains where all the words and

ideas are supposed to come from. There must be an easier way to write a paper. One way to make writing easier is to do some prewriting first.

Silvia used the prewriting step of <u>brainstorming</u> when she thought about her parents' home and listed her ideas:

small   60 years old   brick   on lake

Use the prewriting step to list some ideas you might include in a sentence about your school or college.

---

2. Writing

The most important point to remember in writing the first draft of any paper is that it is just a beginning. You will not be turning in this copy, and it does not have to be perfect.

After prewriting, Silvia was able to write this first sentence about her parents' house:

My parents love there small cottage on the lake

Look at your prewriting ideas and write a sentence about your school or college.

---

3. Revising

Even skilled writers do their "assignments" more than once. In other words, they need to revise their work to make it as good as possible. Revision literally means "seeing again." Be prepared to look at your paper again and to perform major surgery.

In the revision stage, Silvia was able to add details to her one-sentence description:

My parents love there small 60 year old cottage overlooking Lake Manitoba

Revise the sentence you wrote about your school or college.

---

4. Editing

Editing your paper means finding and correcting errors in grammar, punctuation, capitalization, and spelling. Your editing skills will grow as you study those aspects of writing.

While editing her sentence, Silvia corrected some mistakes:

My parents love their small, 60-year-old cottage overlooking Lake Manitoba.

Edit your own sentence.

_____

_____

5. Rewriting   When you are ready to write the final draft of an assignment, observe the following guidelines:

Quickcheck for Handwritten Papers

✓ Use a pen (never a pencil) with black or dark blue ink. Write as neatly and clearly as you can.

✓ Use standard-lined notebook paper. Avoid the spiral-bound kind that leaves "frizzies" when you tear a sheet out.

✓ Write on every other line to leave room for corrections.

✓ Leave margins on both sides—1½ inches on the left and 1 inch on the right.

✓ Write on only one side of each sheet.

✓ Number each sheet in the upper right-hand corner, starting with the second.

✓ Before turning the paper in, proofread it and correct any errors.

Quickcheck for Papers Written on Typewriters or Word Processors

✓ Use standard white paper, 8½ by 11 inches.

✓ Double-space.

✓ Be sure your ribbon or toner is fresh enough to print clearly.

✓ Follow the last four instructions for handwritten papers.

CHECKPOINT 1-1   ✓ *Draw one line under subjects and two lines under verbs. Then enter the subjects and verbs in the blanks.*

_____   **1.** The history of advertising goes back thousands of years.

_____

_____   2. Street peddlers long ago called out the praises of their goods.

_____

_____   3. The ancient Greeks advertised the sale of cattle and slaves.

_____

_____   4. In Rome, signs on walls informed the public of upcoming gladiatorial games.

_____

_____   5. In the Middle Ages, handbills often contained pictures to help the illiterate.

_____

_____   6. The first newspaper in England was *The Weekly Newes.*

_____

_____   7. It appeared in 1622 and contained an ad for the return of a stolen horse.

_____

_____   8. During the plague of 1665, many ads for pills preventing sickness appeared.

_____

_____   9. King Charles II cracked down on the numerous signs "shutting out the air and the light of the heavens."

_____

_____   10. In Canada, the first formal ad appeared in a government publication in 1752.

_____

No answers are given for Checkpoint quizzes.

2

THE NARRATION PARAGRAPH

◆ READING

NARRATION PARAGRAPHS TELL STORIES

PRECHECK

Writing that tells a story, that relates "what happened," is called *narration*. Often the story makes a point. In the following narration, novelist Neil Bissoondath recalls his family's traditional Christmas in Trinidad.

Traditions

—Neil Bissoondath

arrowing marking the stalks for cutting

December in Trinidad, the land of my birth, meant gray skies, rain and temperatures that were chilling after the great summer heat. January would herald dry heat and the arrowing of the sugarcane stalks that preceded the cutting, but before that there was Christmas—as elsewhere, a time of family gatherings, parties and gifts around the tree. 1

Hindu person who practises Hinduism, the major religion of East India

My father, the grandson of immigrants from India, was born into a Hindu household in a society that was, at the time, largely Christian. He was not a man of many stories but this one tale of Christmas in the late 1940s has shaped itself into a fullness in my mind. His childhood memory informs mine and has become, through the vibrancy of imagination, as fully part of me as it was of him. This is how it goes: 2

His brother breathed deeply in undisturbed sleep beside him, but the boy had been awake for some time, listening to the silence of the predawn darkness, searching in vain through the darkened windowpanes for any hint of morning light. There was nothing to be seen, not the shadows of the orange tree he knew to be out there, not the outline 3 of the neighboring house that sat just beyond the tree. He pulled the blanket to his neck, burrowed more comfortably into the soft mattress.

His brother stirred. "Stop movin'," he mumbled sleepily.   4

"You think he come yet?"   5

"Pa get up for prayers?"   6

"No."   7

"Well, he ain't come yet. Go back to sleep."   8

But the question would not let him sleep: had Santa Claus come 9 yet?

Somewhere in the distance a cock crowed. Not many minutes later, 10 the floorboards creaked. His father was up. A fastidious man, he would, even on cool mornings, take a cold-water shower out back, slapping the cold away, shivering aloud. Then, he would dry himself off and, wearing his cotton shirt and dhoti, wander about the garden in search of fresh hibiscus for his prayers.

These prayers remained a mystery to the boy. His father had not 11 yet explained the rituals or their meanings, so he did not know why Krishna and Hanuman and the other gods needed to be offered fresh flowers every morning, saw only simple beauty in the flame in the holy lamp, could not fathom the Hindi words his father chanted so effortlessly.

He thought of the young American soldiers—"Hey, Joe, got some 12 gum?"—at the base not far away, wondered what they did with their time now that the war, so recently savaging Europe, was over. Were they too awake in their beds, wondering whether Santa Claus had visited yet?

The darkness outside began to break up. Shadows—the branches 13 of the orange tree, the roof of the house next door—took shape against a field of gray.

From deeper in the house came the sound of worship: the tinkling 14 of the brass bell, the musical murmur of his father's voice.

His brother, eyes blinking open, whispered, "So, he come yet?" 15 "Don't know."

They eased out of bed and quietly opened the door to the living 16 room. It was large and dark, the louvered windows glowing dull with the light outside. And there, on the lace doilies that covered the gramophone, sat proof that he had indeed come. For there, side by side, were the gifts he had left for them: an orange, an apple and a can of soda biscuits each.

The boy, my father, could not suspect it in the excitement of the 17 moment, but the years to come would bring changes bewildering in scope. All religious observance would fall by the wayside: he was never to understand the rituals, never to learn the words. He would have family of his own, and we, his children, would write letters to Santa Claus demanding impossible things, letters he would promise to mail. We would sing Christmas carols before a twinkling Christmas tree, eyes bright with longing at the stacks of colorfully wrapped boxes crowded round it.

But no gift—none of the toys, none of the games—would retain so 18 central a place in our memories as would the orange, the apple and the

---

fastidious   fussy, particular

dhoti   Indian garment for the lower body
hibiscus   bright, tropical flower

fathom   understand
Hindi   language of East India

eloquently with particular grace and force

soda biscuits in his. For none of the gifts he would give us could speak quite so eloquently of the distance traveled between generations, of the visions that inevitably came to change expectations forever.

CHECKING MEANING AND STYLE

1. The story told in Paragraphs 3 to 16 of "Traditions" has been handed down to Neil Bissoondath. How important is it to him?

2. How did Bissoondath's father feel about Christmas time in Trinidad? How do we know?

3. What influences may have prevented Bissoondath's father from ever being able "to fathom the Hindi words his father chanted so effortlessly"?

4. In what way were Bissoondath's childhood Christmas seasons different from those of his father? Which has more significance?

CHECKING IDEAS

1. Do you celebrate Christmas in any way? How different is the way Christmas is celebrated now to when your parents were young?

2. What point does the story make beyond the narration of a Christmas experience?

3. Are there traditions, rituals, or languages that your parents know, but that you don't understand?

◆ WRITING MODELS

THE NARRATION PARAGRAPH

Narration tells a story. A story is just a series of events with a beginning and an end. The story usually makes a point of some kind. The point Neil Bissoondath's story makes is that vast lifestyle changes have occurred between one generation and another. The events in the story lead up to the revelation of these cross-generational differences.

A close look at Bissoondath's narrative reveals this sequence:

1. Background about Christmas in Trinidad.
2. His father's Christmas in 1940.
3. The boys' wait for Santa Claus.
4. Christmas morning sounds.
5. The gifts Santa brought.

Bissoondath could have written one sentence about each event. He could have put the sentences together into a narrative paragraph that might have looked something like this:

Model Narration Paragraph #1

Notice how a topic sentence comes before the other sentences.

My father's story of a Christmas in Trinidad reveals just how different life is for us today. While his brother was sleeping, on Christmas Eve, he lay awake, waiting for Santa. When morning came, he heard his own father performing many Hindu rituals. He would never understand these mysteries. When the morning noises finally woke his brother, the two boys got up to see whether Santa had come yet. They found their gifts: an orange, an apple, and a can of soda crackers. No gifts that I have ever received have been as important to me as those gifts my father got from Santa, which shows clearly how much has changed in our lives.

In the two narrative models that follow, notice how the student writers develop their topic sentences with specific details about the events in their stories.

Model Narration Paragraph #2

Notice how the writer describes the events in order, saving the surprise ending for the last sentence.

[1]Children need to understand that frustration and failure are not only inevitable but often helpful. [2]Over the weekend my husband and I tried to teach my daughter to ride her new bike. [3]Each time one of us wasn't holding her up, Sue fell over. [4]After falling again and again, she became frustrated and started to cry. [5]I couldn't get her to try again. [6]Then my neighbour talked to her, and Sue decided to give it one more attempt. [7]My daughter ran over bushes and sprinklers. [8]She tried to ride up walls. [9]But by the end of the day she had a smile on her face that couldn't be wiped off. [10]Sue had learned to ride her bike.

1. What is the point of this narration paragraph?
2. What event happens in Sentence 2?
3. What event happens in Sentence 10?
4. What made the daughter successful?

Model Narration Paragraph #3

[1]When I was six years old, I decided, against my mother's advice, that I could pet bees. [2]The sun was warm on my back, and the bees were buzzing around the sweet-smelling flowers of the lemon tree. [3]Some of the bees were sitting so still that I just had to touch one. [4]The bee felt soft and furry, and I could feel its "buzziness." [5]Then I let out the loudest yell I could make. [6]I thought my finger was going to explode. [7]My mother yelled out the back door, "I told you so!" [8]She pulled out the stinger and put ice on my finger. [9]The cold ice dulled the pain, and I knew that I was going to live.

1. What is the point of this narration paragraph?

◆ WRITING ASSIGNMENT

A NARRATION PARAGRAPH

Starting in childhood, we get much of our information and entertainment through stories or narratives. The child says, "Read me a story," and the parent gets out *Winnie the Pooh* for the umpteenth time. Stories continue to entertain us as we go through life—in books and magazines, on television, and at the movies.

We require narratives of a different kind when we want to know "what happened." What happened at the neighbourhood meeting? What happened on Tom's date with Sylvia, Saturday night? We want a story that gives us information, although it may be entertaining, too.

Don't be shy about using incidents from your own life in your writing. Let us say you are writing an essay on crime in your community. The essay will be more interesting and believable if you include a short account of the time you were mugged. Or if you want to make the point that Christmas has become too commercialized, you could write about an experience you had shopping at the mall when the season was in full swing.

Tell your story in the order in which it happened. Start with the event that happened first and continue step by step to the end. Include details, but only those needed to make your point. Do not go on and on; beware of boring your audience.

WRITE A NARRATION PARAGRAPH

Write a narration paragraph—one that tells "what happened"—on one of the following numbered topics:

1. The time I tried to fix my car (or other object)

2. When a teacher embarrassed me

3. A memorable experience

4. The day I learned how to . . . (swim, drive, dance, etc.)

5. The time I learned an important lesson (Model #3)

6. A child's lesson (Model #2)

Start with a topic sentence that says what point the paragraph will make. For example:

Uncle Ed made a fool of himself at the football game Saturday.
I'll never forget my embarrassment at the senior prom.

Then develop the topic sentence with interesting details.

To help you get started, complete the following outline. (You perhaps will use more or fewer details than indicated here.)

(Topic sentence) _____

(First detail)   _____

(Second detail)   _____

(Third detail)   _____

(Fourth detail)   _____

(Fifth detail)   _____

Now, using this outline as a starting point, write a first draft of a narrative paragraph with no more than 12 sentences. Check the first draft to be sure each sentence has a subject and a verb before writing the final draft to turn in.

◆ SENTENCE STRUCTURE

SENTENCE FRAGMENTS

The Problem: Avoiding Sentence Fragments

In the last chapter you learned how to recognize subjects and verbs. Now you can put that knowledge to good use as we move on to writing sound sentences, a skill that lies at the heart of effective writing.

A complete sentence has three characteristics:

1. A sentence has a <u>subject</u> (which tells who or what the sentence is about).

2. A sentence has a <u>verb</u> (which either tells what the subject does or links the subject to words that describe it).

3. A sentence <u>expresses a complete thought</u> (makes sense by itself).

<u>Fragments</u> are pieces of sentences that look like sentences because they start with a capital letter and end with a period, but they are not sentences unless they meet the three tests just listed; for example:

The man on the white horse.

The man on the white horse is a fragment. It has a subject, *man*. (You know *horse* isn't the subject because it is the object of the preposition *on*. The object of a preposition is **never** the subject of a sentence.)

But *The man on the white horse* is not a sentence because it lacks a verb (what did the man *do?*) and because it is incomplete (it does not make sense by itself).

The man on the white horse fell.

When we add the verb *fell*, the words express a complete thought and become an acceptable sentence.

SPOTCHECK 2-1

The following paragraphs contain fragment errors. At the end of each paragraph, indicate which "sentences" are really fragments by writing the appropriate letters in the blanks. Then circle S, V, or Both to indicate whether the fragments lack a subject, a verb, or both.

NOTE: Fragments are more obvious if you read backwards—from the last sentence to the first.

1. ᴬIn the 1980s, Canadians still travelled more to the United States than to anywhere else. ᴮAccording to Statistics Canada. ᶜIn 1989, 204 visits were made to South America, compared to 56 in 1980.

   Fragment _____ lacks a: S   V   Both

2. ᴬTokyo is a very expensive city to visit. ᴮEven for an overnight stay. ᶜIn 1988, a hotel room cost an average of $742. ᴰMaking it the most expensive city in the world.

   Fragment _____ lacks a: S   V   Both

   Fragment _____ lacks a: S   V   Both

3. ᴬIn all of human history, there have been about 250 different alphabets. ᴮAbout 50 still in use today, including our own ABCs. ᶜOf the 50 alphabets, half are in one country. ᴰIndia.

   Fragment _____ lacks a: S   V   Both

   Fragment _____ lacks a: S   V   Both

4. ᴬJoe was "cool" in high school. ᴮHe usually cut classes to hang out. ᶜHe hardly ever did assignments. ᴰHe said he could attend a community college even if he didn't pass his high school courses. ᴱHe was "cool" in college, too. ᶠCutting classes and ignoring assignments. ᴳHe flunked out after one term.

   Fragment _____ lacks a: S   V   Both

5. ᴬA bicycle is a good choice if one wants cheap transportation. ᴮA good bike costs far less than a car. ᶜUses muscle power instead of expensive and polluting gasoline. ᴰIt also promotes good health.

   Fragment _____ lacks a: S   V   Both

Check the Answer Key before continuing.

SPOTCHECK 2-2

The following paragraphs contain fragment errors. At the end of each paragraph, indicate which "sentences" are really fragments by writing the appropriate letters in the blanks. Then circle S, V, or Both to indicate whether the fragments lack a subject, a verb, or both.

1. [A]Bill Gillen set the mile record in five-object joggling. [B]A sport involving running while juggling. [C]Gillen ran the mile in eight minutes, 28 seconds. [D]Another joggler, Albert Lucas, completed the Los Angeles marathon of 26.2 miles in just over four hours while juggling three balls all the way.

   Fragment _____ lacks a: S   V   Both

2. [A]The amazing Brazilian soccer player known as Pele scored 1,281 goals during his career. [B]He played from 1956 until his retirement in 1977. [C]Finished his career playing for the New York Cosmos of the North American Soccer League. [D]A French magazine named him "Athlete of the Century."

   Fragment _____ lacks a: S   V   Both

3. [A]The first table tennis games were played by English university students in 1879. [B]They hit a champagne cork over books stacked in the middle of a table. [C]Later, balls made of rubber and then celluloid replaced the cork. [D]With a net taking the place of the books.

   Fragment _____ lacks a: S   V   Both

4. [A]The Chinese language is made up almost entirely of one-syllable words. [B]There are only 405 syllables in Chinese. [C]The same word, therefore, may have several meanings. [D]The meaning depending on how the syllable is pronounced. [E]The word *wan* can mean "to bend," "to finish," "late," or "10,000."

   Fragment _____ lacks a: S   V   Both

5. [A]Learning to write in the Chinese language is very difficult. [B]With some 3,000 characters to be memorized for a basic vocabulary. [C]Elementary pupils in China spend half their time learning the language. [D]Typing in Chinese seems nearly impossible. [E]Typewriters having 2,200 keys.

   Fragment _____ lacks a: S   V   Both

   Fragment _____ lacks a: S   V   Both

Check the Answer Key before continuing.

Solution #1: Correcting Sentence Fragments

Each of the following groups of words breaks at least one of the three rules for complete sentences. Change these fragments into sentences by adding the necessary subjects or verbs.

1. Left the party at midnight.

   _____

   The subject is missing. *Who* left the party?

   (correction) <u>Cinderella</u> left the party at midnight.

2. The man in the blue cape.

_____

The verb is missing. *What* does the man (subject) *do?*

(correction) The man in the blue cape <u>can leap</u> tall buildings at a single bound.

3. On a tropical island.

_____

Both the subject and the verb are missing. *Who* does *what* on a tropical island?

(correction) <u>Robinson Crusoe</u> [subject] <u>lived</u> [verb] on a tropical island.

4. Snow White living with seven dwarfs.

_____

A complete verb is missing. Remember, an *-ing* word such as *living* cannot be the main verb of a sentence. Such verbs need helping verbs, such as *is, was,* and *has been.*

(correction) Snow White <u>was living</u> [or <u>lived</u>] with seven dwarfs.

✓

SPOTCHECK 2-3 *Add subjects or verbs or both to turn the following fragments into complete sentences.*

EXAMPLE: Reading a book.

The third-grader was reading a book.
_____

1. A small airplane.

_____

2. While eating lunch.

_____

3. After the movie.

_____

4. The dog barking at passing cars.

_____

5. A clerk in the shoe department.

_____

Compare your answers with those in the Answer Key.

✓

SPOTCHECK 2-4   _Add subjects or verbs or both to turn these fragments into complete sentences._

    EXAMPLE: Eating his lunch.

    Tom was eating his lunch._____

1. A red convertible.

_____

2. While driving home.

_____

3. Before the exam.

_____

4. The plumber fixing the sink.

_____

5. A cashier at the theatre.

_____

Compare your answers with those in the Answer Key.

Solution #2: Joining Sentence Parts

    Often a sentence fragment should really be part of the complete sentence in front of or behind it. Study these examples:

We set out for the fairgrounds. <u>Hoping to watch the fireworks.</u>

The underlined fragment can be corrected by making it part of the first sentence.

    (joined) We set out for the fairgrounds, hoping to watch the fireworks.

    Mr. Williams planned to do some fishing. <u>And enjoy the beauties of nature.</u>

    (joined) Mr. Williams planned to do some fishing and enjoy the beauties of nature.

    <u>Lurking in the bushes.</u> The cat eyed the birdbath.

    (joined) Lurking in the bushes, the cat eyed the birdbath.

SPOTCHECK 2-5   *Get rid of any sentence fragments in the following items by joining the fragments to neighbouring sentences. Change punctuation and capital letters as needed.*

1. In Egypt stands the Great Pyramid of the pharaoh Cheops. The largest stone structure in the world.

2. Covering 5 hectares of desert. It is as tall as a 40-storey building.

3. It is made up of about 2.5 million stone blocks. some weighing 70,000 kg each.

4. Hundreds of thousands of workers toiled for 20 years. To build a monument considered one of the wonders of the world.

5. The workers hauled the blocks upward with ropes made of reeds. And their own muscle power.

6. Fifty centuries after being built. The pyramid still inspires awe in the viewer.

Check the Answer Key before continuing.

SPOTCHECK 2-6   *The following paragraph contains seven sentence-fragment errors. Underline them. Then, in the space below, revise the paragraph. Correct all fragments by supplying needed subjects or verbs or by joining each fragment to a neighbouring sentence.*

[1]Helen Keller provides an inspiring example. [2]Of a person who overcame great physical handicaps. [3]She was made deaf and blind by illness. [4]Before the age of two. [5]With the help of a teacher, Anne Sullivan. [6]Helen learned to communicate by spelling out words on a person's hand. [7]She learned to speak by the time she was 16. [8]As a result of her own hard work and Miss Sullivan's patience. [9]Graduating from Radcliffe College in 1904 with honours. [10]She began working to improve conditions for the blind. [11]By writing books, lecturing, and appearing before legislative bodies. [12]Two movies tell of her life. [13]*The Helen Keller Story* and *The Miracle Worker*.

_____

_____

_____

_____

_____

_____

_____

_____

_____

_____

_____

_____

_____

Compare your answers with those in the Answer Key. Each sentence can be corrected in more than one way.

Quickcheck on Sentence Fragments

✓ A sentence must have a subject and a complete verb, and it must express a complete thought.

✓ You can often correct a fragment by joining it to a neighbouring sentence.

✓ Any fragments in your writing may stand out more clearly if you edit your paper by starting at the last sentence and reading toward the first.

◆ WRITING PROCESS

PREWRITING: NONSTOP WRITING

Most writers hate to face a blank piece of paper or a blank screen. Prewriting is a way to discover ideas to help fill that blankness. This chapter and the next three chapters suggest prewriting methods that will make writing easier for you. These prewriting techniques can be used in an assignment for your composition class or for any other writing you have to do.

One method of prewriting is called <u>nonstop writing</u>. In this method you put your pen to a piece of paper, begin writing about a topic, and keep writing without stopping for three minutes. If you cannot think of anything new to say about this topic, you can repeat your last word until something new occurs to you. The important rule is to keep on writing without stopping. Do not worry about punctuation, capitalization, or spelling.

Sometimes you don't know what you think about a topic until you put ideas down on paper and examine them. Nonstop writing gets you in touch with your thoughts. It gives you some initial ideas that you can examine and use as a starting point for your first draft. Reading your nonstop writing may help you generate a good topic sentence.

In this chapter you have been asked to write a narrative paragraph on one of these topics:

1. The time I tried to fix my car (or other object)

2. When a teacher embarrassed me

3. A memorable experience

4. The day I learned how to . . . (swim, drive, dance, etc.)

5. The time I learned an important lesson

6. A child's lesson

A STUDENT
DEMONSTRATION

Step 1

Duncan did not have any ideas for this assignment, so he tried some nonstop writing to get in touch with an idea. Duncan used the word *memorable* from the third suggested topic as a trigger for his nonstop writing. Here is what he wrote:

> memorable memorable memorable memories memories are hard to remember remember remember i always have a hard time remembering things i hate memorizing we always had to memorize poetry in school and recite it i used to race through my poem when it was my turn so i would get it out without forgetting any words i bet the teacher did not even know what i was saying because i was reciting so fast once a teacher forced the class to memorize the cremation of sam mcgee by robert w. service and i remember i was able to say it in thirty seconds at home but when it came time to recite it in class she made me say it slowly but i could only do it fast

Step 2

Duncan's nonstop writing put him in touch with a long-forgotten memory. After Duncan finished, he read over his nonstop writing and underlined the part that he felt could be used in a narration:

> <u>once a teacher forced the class to memorize the cremation of sam mcgee by robert w service and i remember i was able to say it in thirty seconds at home but when it came time to recite it in class she made me say it slowly but i could only do it fast</u>

Step 3

Next, Duncan divided this incident into events and put them in order:

1. Teacher had class memorize

2. Could say in 30 seconds at home

3. Said quickly in class

4. Teacher made say slowly

5. Could not do it

Step 4

Duncan was now ready to write the first draft of his narrative paragraph.

NOW YOU TRY IT

Try nonstop writing to discover ideas for writing a narrative paragraph. Try it for the description paragraph assigned in the next chapter and for the other writing assignments in this text.

Quickcheck on Nonstop Writing

✓ Begin with a trigger word (such as *accident* or *hospital*).

✓ Do not worry about spelling, punctuation, or capitalization.

✓ If you cannot think of anything to write, just repeat your last word.

✓ Write for three minutes without stopping.

✓ Underline any ideas that could be used in a first draft.

✓ Arrange these ideas in order.

✓ Start your first draft.

CHECKPOINT 2-1

In the blank spaces below, write C *if the word group is a complete sentence. Write* F *if it is a fragment.*

_____   1. Toronto's CN Tower, the world's tallest free-standing structure.

_____   2. Measuring 553 metres tall.

_____   3. It was completed on April 2, 1975.

_____	**4.**	By taking a high-speed elevator.
_____	**5.**	You can go to the top.
_____	**6.**	Where there is a revolving restaurant.
_____	**7.**	Offering magnificent views of the city.
_____	**8.**	The giant structure attracts many visitors.
_____	**9.**	Particularly as it is right next to the SkyDome.
_____	**10.**	At the base, there is a simulated space ride.

No answers are given for Checkpoint quizzes.

3

THE DESCRIPTION PARAGRAPH

◆ READING

DESCRIPTION PARAGRAPHS APPEAL TO OUR SENSES

PRECHECK

Everybody has to start school sometime. Rudy Wiebe, an award-winning Saskatchewan author, describes his rural life just before his first day at school, and also what his school teacher actually gave to him. This description of life in rural Saskatchewan during World War II gives the reader an idea of what it was like to grow up using, and *believing in,* one language, and then suddenly to be thrown into another.

Speaking Saskatchewan

—Rudy Wiebe

trussed wrapped

In summer the thick green poplar leaves clicked and flickered at 1 him, in winter the stiff spruce rustled with voices. The boy, barefoot in the heat or trussed up like a lumpy package against the fierce, silver cold, went alone to the bush where everything spoke to him: warm rocks, the flit of quick, small animals, a dart of birds, tree trunks, the great lights in the sky at night, burning air, ground, the squeaky snow: everything spoke as he breathed and became aware of it, its language clear as the water of his memory when he lay in the angle of the house rafters at night listening to the mosquitoes slowly find him under his blanket, though he had his eyes shut and only one ear uncovered. Everything spoke, and it spoke Low German.

Like his mother. She would call him long, long into the summer 2 evening when it seemed the sun burned all night down into the north, call high and slow as if she were already weeping and when he appeared beside her she would bend her wide powerful hands about his head and kiss him so hard his eyes rang.

"Why don't you answer, you?" she would speak against his hair. **3** "Why don't you ever answer when I call, it's so dark, why don't you ever say a word?"

nuzzled   snuggled

While he nuzzled his face into the damp apron at the fold of her **4** thigh, and soon her words would be over and he heard her skin and warm apron smelling of saskatoon jam and dishes and supper buns love him back.

His sister laughed at his solitary silence. "In school are twenty- **5** seven kids," she would say, "you'll have to talk, and English at that. You can't say anything Low German there, and if you don't answer English when she asks, the teacher will make you stand in the corner."

"R-r-r-right in front—of—people?" he would ask, fearfully. **6**

"Yeah, in front of every one of them, your face against the wall. So **7** you better start to talk, English too."

And she would try to teach him the English names for things. But **8** he did not listen to that. Rather, when he was alone he practised standing in the corners of walls. Their logs shifted and cracked, talking. Walls were very good, especially where they came together so warm in winter.

muskrat   beaver-like rodent

But outside was even better, and he followed a quiet trail of the **9** muskrat that had dented the snow with its tail between bullrushes sticking out of the slough ice, or waited for the coyote to turn and see him, its paw lifted and about to touch a drift, its jaw opening to its red tongue laughing with him. In summer he heard a mother bear talk to her cubs among the willows of the horse pasture, though he did not see them, but he found their sluffing paw prints in the spring snow and

sluffing   left, discarded

his father said something would have to be done if they came that close to the pig fence again. The boy knew his father refused to own a gun, but their nearest neighbor west gladly hunted everywhere to shoot, whatever he heard about, and so he folded his hands over the huge, wet paw prints and whispered in Low German, "Don't visit here any more. It's dangerous."

The school sat on the corner, just below the hill where the road **10** turned south along the creek to the church and the store. In the church every Sunday there were hands waiting for him. At the top of the balcony stairs that began in the corner behind where the men sat, up there among wooden benches, with the visiting sound of people talking like heavy rain under them, were hands that could find things inside him. Huge hands with heavy broad thumbs working against each other on his neck, pressing down, together, bending his small bones until through his gaping mouth they cawed:

"c - c - c - - CAT!" **11**

"Yes, yes, like that, try to say it again, 'cat.'" **12**

And he would, try; desperately, those marvelous hands holding **13** him as if everything on earth were in its proper place and all the brilliant sounds which he could never make when anyone listened coming out of him as easily as if he had pulled a door, open.

"Cat." 14

He never looked at the school, the tiny panes of its four huge win- 15 dows staring at him, just staring when they passed. The day before he had to go there every day like his sister, the planes came over for the first time.

Their horses were pulling the wagon up the hill as slowly, steadily 16 as they always did and it happened very fast, almost before he looked around. There had been a rumble from somewhere like thunder, far away, though the sky was clear sunlight and his father had just said in a week they could start bindering the oats, it was ripening so well, and his mother sat beside him broad and straight as always, her braided, waist-long hair coiled up for church under her hat, when suddenly the roaring planes were there as he turned, four of them, yellow-and-black, louder than anything he had ever heard. West over the school and the small grain fields and pastures and all the trees and hills to the far edge of the world. His father would not look around, holding the horses in carefully, muttering.

"Now it comes here too, that war training." 17

But the boy was looking at his mother. Perhaps his own face looked 18 like that next morning when the yellow planes roared over the school at recess, so low he saw huge glass eyes in a horrible leather head glare down at him before he screamed and ran, inside to the desk where his sister had said he must sit. When he opened his eyes the face of the teacher was there, her gentle face very close, smiling almost up-side-down at him between the iron legs of the desk beneath which he crouched. Her gentle voice, speaking.

"Come," she said, "come," and after a moment he scrambled to his 19 feet. He thought she was speaking Low German because he did not yet know that what that word meant was spoken the same way in English. "Come."

Not touching him, she led him between desks to a thin cupboard 20 against the wall opposite the windows and opened its narrow door. Books. He has never imagined so many books. There may be a million.

She is, of course, speaking to him in English and later, when he re- 21 members that moment again and again, he will never be able to explain how he can understand what she is saying. The open book in her hand shows him countless words: words, she tells him, he can now only see the shape of, but he will be able to hear them when he learns to read, and that the word "READ" in English is the same as the word "SPEAK," *raed,* in Low German and by reading all the people of the world will speak to him from books, he will hear them, when he reads he will be able to hear them, and then he will understand. He is staring at what he later knows are a few worn books on a few shelves, and then staring back at the few visible but as yet unintelligible words revealed by the book open in her hands, and slowly, slowly he understands that there are shelves and shelves of books in great stacks on many, many floors inside all the walls of the enormous libraries of the world where he will go and read: where the knowing she will now help him discover within himself will allow him to listen to human voices speaking from everywhere and every age, saying everything, things

bindering cutting

both dreadful and beautiful, and all that can be imagined between them; and that he will listen. He will listen to those voices speaking now for as long as he lives.

CHECKING MEANING AND STYLE

1. What language did the boy learn first? How did he associate that language with life around him?

2. What was the difference between his home life as a young child and his future school life? Why did this make him afraid?

3. From his description, what impression does the reader have of the place where the boy grew up?

4. What events were taking place while the boy was starting school? What gave him an opportunity to understand where his future lay?

CHECKING IDEAS

1. What are the descriptive passages that tell of the author's relationship with his family and with nature?

2. Is English your first language? Did you ever have difficulties with English, as a native or non-native speaker?

3. Can you remember what your first day of school was like?

4. What did the author feel about the connection between books, language, and his future life?

5. Would you agree with Wiebe's high value of reading?

◆ WRITING MODELS

THE DESCRIPTION PARAGRAPH

In "Speaking Saskatchewan," Rudy Wiebe starts with a description of the boy's life before school. The writing appeals to our senses with words and phrases such as "a dart of birds" and "the squeaky snow." Wiebe's depiction of his mother, father, and sister are all very vivid as a result of his descriptive powers. It is almost as if we were there with him in his Saskatchewan village. Look again at some of the colourful detail that in the following example has been condensed into a single paragraph:

Model Description Paragraph #1

Everything spoke, and it spoke Low German. Like his mother. She would call him long, long into the summer evening when it seemed the sun burned all night down into the north, call high and slow as if she were already weeping and when he appeared beside her she would bend her wide powerful hands about his head and kiss him so hard his eyes rang.

The *images* are so rich in this description that we feel we are there, with an understanding of the mother's love and the boy's desire to get away to explore. As the description is so powerful, we can almost hear the mother's cry and feel the boy's reluctance to be drawn.

Model Description Paragraph #2

Notice how the underlined sensory details enable us to share this experience.

Last week I arrived at work with a small head cold; by the time I left I felt like I had the Hong Kong flu. Usually I don't mind helping the workers on the construction site with their hammering and sawing. Because of my cold, however, the buzzing of the electric saw vibrated my head as if a fly were in my ear. The strong smell of damp wood cleared my sinuses at first, but later it only stuffed them up. The sawdust in my nostrils felt like an itch that I just couldn't scratch the right way. The hammering was no better. Since the rooms had no furniture, the pounding was amplified at least ten times. It was as though someone was using my head as a drum. By the time I got home, I was in no condition for school or work the next morning.

In addition to helping us see a place and feel an experience, description paragraphs can also make it possible for us to meet people.

Model Description Paragraph #3

Would you like to meet the person described in this paragraph?

Major Cartier was the most intimidating man I had ever met. He had a smile like an ax-murderer's; it screamed, "I'm psychotic!" Standing six-feet-five and weighing 240 pounds, he had a Mr. Universe build. His growling, snarling, voice earned him the nickname "The Bear," and his eagle eyes never missed a recruit's slightest misstep. To top it all, his mind could produce the right answer to a question faster than a mainframe computer.

1. Which senses are appealed to in this paragraph?

2. Which words and phrases bring Major Cartier to life?

◆ WRITING ASSIGNMENT

A DESCRIPTION PARAGRAPH

Two of the model description paragraphs were about a thing (the common cold) and a person (the major). When you describe people, places, and things, your sentences are often more effective if they appeal to the senses of sight, sound, touch, smell, and taste.

WRITE A DESCRIPTION PARAGRAPH

Write a paragraph using specific descriptive details on one of the following topics:

1. A room in your house or apartment

2. An unpleasant experience (Model #2)

3. A favourite object

4. A favourite recreation spot

5. A person whose looks you like or dislike (Model #3)

Your topic sentence should make clear what impression you want to create, as in the following examples:

1. Anyone who looks at my room knows at once that I enjoy sports. (This topic sentence would lead to a description that appeals to the sense of sight.)

2. Running my first marathon was a combination of agony and ecstasy. (Observe how this topic sentence would lead you to write about how it feels to run a first marathon.)

3. My grandfather's gold watch is a thing of beauty. (This topic sentence opens the paragraph for a description of how the gold watch looks, feels, and sounds.)

After you write your topic sentence, you will need to follow it with sentences containing specific descriptive details. Make notes for your first draft on the form below. (Your description may not involve all the senses.)

(Your own topic sentence) _____

_____

(Sight notes) _____

_____

(Sound notes) _____

_____

(Touch notes) _____

_____

(Smell notes) _____

_____

(Taste notes) _____

_____

Revise your first draft. Eliminate any sentence fragments by making sure that each sentence has a subject and a verb and expresses a complete thought.

◆ SENTENCE STRUCTURE

MISTAKING CLAUSE FRAGMENTS FOR SENTENCES

The Problem: Avoiding Clause Fragments Written as Sentences

The sentence fragments we looked at in the last chapter were made up of <u>phrases</u>. Phrases are groups of related words that do not contain both a subject and a verb. These are phrase fragments:

Covering 5 hectares of desert. (no subject, no complete verb)

Before the age of two. (no subject, no verb)

Now we are going to look at another kind of word group—the <u>clause</u>. A clause *does* contain a subject and verb. Here are some examples of clauses:

The <u>pyramid</u> [subject] <u>covered</u> [verb] 5 hectares of desert.

<u>She</u> [subject] <u>became</u> [verb] deaf and blind before the age of two.

If you think those clauses look a lot like sentences, you are right. They meet the three tests of the sentence: (1) Each has a subject, (2) each has a verb, and (3) each expresses a complete thought—it makes sense by itself.

So is a clause the same thing as a sentence? Not always. Look at these clauses:

Because <u>Cinderella</u> [subject] <u>left</u> [verb] the party.

While <u>Robinson Crusoe</u> [subject] <u>lived</u> [verb] on an island.

Each one is a clause because it has a subject and a verb. But neither one is a sentence because neither one expresses a complete thought. Each needs more words to finish the idea.

Because Cinderella left the party, <u>the prince was sad.</u>

While Robinson Crusoe lived on an island, <u>Mrs. Crusoe worked crossword puzzles at home.</u>

Without the added words, each is an example of our enemy the fragment.

So we now have two kinds of clauses. *Independent clauses* are complete in themselves and can stand alone as sentences. *Dependent clauses* depend on other words to complete their meaning.

IMPORTANT: Every sentence must contain at least one independent clause.

Test yourself on the following examples by marking the independent clauses Ind *and the dependent clauses* Dep.

_____ **1.** Alicia arrived early at work yesterday.

_____ **2.** Because Alicia arrived early at work yesterday.

_____   **3.** Mrs. Ng admired the roses.

_____   **4.** Although Mrs. Ng admired the roses.

_____   **5.** The Alexopouloses moved to Prince Edward Island.

_____   **6.** Until the Alexopouloses moved to Prince Edward Island.

All six are clauses because they have subjects and verbs. Examples 1, 3, and 5 are independent clauses. They are complete sentences and make sense by themselves. Examples 2, 4, and 6 are dependent clauses. They depend on other words to complete their meaning. They are sentence fragments.

What is it that turns the complete sentences into sentence fragments? It is just one word in each case: *because* in Example 2, *although* in Example 4, and *until* in Example 6. Since they turn independent clauses into dependent clauses, we will call such words dependent words.

Here is a longer list of dependent words. Study it carefully.

after	in order that	whenever
although	since	where
as	so that	wherever
as if	than	whether
because	that	which
before	though	whichever
even if	unless	while
even though	until	who
ever since	what	whom
how	whatever	whose
if	when	why

✓
SPOTCHECK 3-1   *Fill in the blanks with the dependent word that best completes the meaning of the sentence.*

1. Mr. and Mrs. Moya jumped from their chairs _____ their daughter received the prize.

2. _____ a balanced diet provides all the vitamins a person needs, many people take them in capsule form.

3. The accountant arrived late _____ he had forgotten to set his alarm clock for daylight saving time.

4. Early experiments with electric vehicles took place in Europe _____ an electric cart was built in 1887.

5. _____ his team loses, the coach locks himself in his office for several hours.

Compare your answers with those in the Answer Key.

✔️
SPOTCHECK 3-2

In the blank spaces, write C for a complete sentence and F for a fragment. Underline the dependent words in the fragments.

_____ **1.** Because Dave had sold more TV sets than anyone else at Smith's Department Store in January.

_____ **2.** Dave and his wife, Liz, won an expenses-paid vacation to Palm Springs.

_____ **3.** The temperature was balmy when they arrived.

_____ **4.** Even though it was snowing back home.

_____ **5.** Before they went out to dinner.

_____ **6.** They took a swim in the pool at their resort.

_____ **7.** Since many movie stars have homes in Palm Springs.

_____ **8.** Liz thought it would be fun to drive around and look at some of the houses.

_____ **9.** Later she suggested that they take a ride on the aerial tramway that climbs to an elevation of more than 8500 feet above Palm Springs.

_____ **10.** Although she knew that Dave didn't like heights.

Check the Answer Key before continuing.

Solution #1: Joining Fragments to Sentences

You can usually correct a <u>dependent-word fragment</u> by joining it to the sentence in front of it or behind it.

> When his computer stopped working [fragment]. Gordon was glad the warranty hadn't expired.

> **(corrected)** When his computer stopped working, Gordon was glad the warranty hadn't expired.

The fragment has been added to the sentence following it.

> Jim will gain weight. Unless he stops drinking so much beer [fragment].

(corrected) Jim will gain weight unless he stops drinking so much beer.

The fragment has been added to the sentence in front of it.

Notice that a comma separates the two clauses in the first example but not in the second. Here is the rule: Use a comma if the dependent-word clause comes first; do not use a comma if the independent clause comes first.

Another way to correct this kind of fragment is simply to get rid of the dependent word.

(fragment) Because Sean bought a Porsche.

(corrected) Sean bought a Porsche.

SPOTCHECK 3-3   ✓   *Make complete sentences by adding an independent clause before or after these dependent clauses. Underline the dependent words. Remember to use a comma when the dependent clause comes first.*

1. Although the wind was blowing _____

    _____ .

2. _____

    _____because it was Ahmed's birthday.

3. Whenever Kimberly entered the classroom _____

    _____ .

4. _____

    _____ as Curtis picked up the phone.

5. Since it was raining _____ .

Are you sure the words you added are independent clauses? Could they stand by themselves as complete sentences?

Compare your answers with those in the Answer Key.

Solution #2: Using *Who,*
Which, and *That* in Sentences

Sometimes a dependent word is the subject of the dependent clause. Words often used that way are *who, which,* and *that.*

subject   verb

Mr. Mohamed is a friend <u>who</u> <u>can be trusted</u>.

The subject of the dependent clause is the dependent word *who.* The verb is *can be trusted.* (The independent clause is *Mr. Munson is a friend.* Remember that every sentence must have at least one independent clause.)

Sometimes the dependent clause is in the middle of the sentence.

A friend <u>who can be trusted</u> is valuable.

The dependent clause, *who can be trusted,* interrupts the independent clause, *A friend is valuable.*
Sometimes the dependent word *that* is left out.

(correct) The officials assumed <u>that the queen would be present.</u>
(also correct) The officials assumed <u>the queen would be present.</u>

SPOTCHECK 3-4 ✓ *These sentences use* who, which, *and* that *to introduce dependent-word clauses. Underline the entire dependent clause.*

> **EXAMPLE:** Winnie, <u>who works harder than anyone else,</u> should be paid more.

1. April 30, which is the day taxes are due, should be a national holiday.
2. A specialist is a person who knows more and more about less and less.
3. "O Canada" has a French version that we sing.
4. Celine Dion stocked her show, which was scheduled to appear in many cities, with 130 speakers and 124 computerized lights.
5. A province that has many mountains is British Columbia.

Check the Answer Key before continuing.

Solution #3: Choosing Between *Who* and *Which* in a Sentence

Use *which,* not *who* or *whom,* to start a clause about animals or things.

> Sandra was feeding her horse, which [not *who*] had a sore leg.

Use *who,* not *which,* to start a clause about people.

> On the bus were the teachers who [not *which*] were attending the conference.

Whose may be used with people, animals, or things.

> All photos *whose* colors are fading should be protected from light.

DOUBLECHECK 3-1 ✓ *Underline any dependent clauses in these sentences, and write the dependent words in the blanks at the left. Write X if the sentence contains no dependent clause.*

_____ 1. Canada, which is the largest country in the Western Hemisphere, has a total of 9,970,610 square kilometres.

_____ 2. It stretches from Cape Spear, Newfoundland, to the Yukon–Alaska border, which is a distance of 5,514 kilometres.

_____ 3. There are four major physiographic regions.

_____ 4. The Canadian Shield, which is also known as the Precambrian Shield, is located in the central part of the continent.

_____ 5. In fact, the Shield, which is composed of ancient rock, covers over half of Canada.

_____ 6. Although the Shield's rock is ancient, the mountains of the Appalachian Region to the east are younger.

_____ 7. To the west of the Shield, everyone knows of the Prairies' distinctive flatness.

_____ 8. This area is known as the Interior Plains and stretches to the lowlands around the Great Lakes.

_____ 9. Of all the regions, the Western Cordillera developed most recently.

_____ 10. Where erosion has not yet worn away the sharp peaks, the highest mountains are found.

Check the Answer Key before continuing.

Quickcheck on Sentence Clauses and Fragments

✓ A *clause* contains a subject and a verb.

✓ If a clause expresses a complete thought by itself, it is an *independent* clause.

✓ If a clause depends on other words to complete its meaning, it is a *dependent* clause.

✓ Dependent clauses begin with *dependent words*, such as *although, because,* and *since.*

✓ The dependent words *who, which,* and *that* are often the subjects of dependent clauses. Do not use *who* to refer to animals or things; do not use *which* to refer to people.

✓ A dependent clause written as a sentence causes the error called a *sentence fragment.*

DOUBLECHECK 3-2   *Edit this paragraph to correct the two sentence fragments remaining in it. (Another fragment has been corrected as an example.) The fragments may be either phrases or clauses. Correct them by adding subjects and verbs or by joining the fragment to a neighbouring sentence.*

The term *martial arts* covers a variety of fighting methods based on ancient Asian combat skills. The martial arts are practised today for a number of reasons, including self-defense, physical fitness, and sports competition. Styles, techniques, and teaching methods vary. Even within a given branch of the martial arts, such as karate. Although adherence to ancient traditions is usually emphasized.

Compare your answers with those in the Answer Key.

DOUBLECHECK 3-3   *Edit this paragraph to correct the three sentence fragments in it.*

Although the exact origins are uncertain. The Asian styles of the martial arts seem to have come to China from India and Tibet. Where they were used by monks for exercise and protection against bandits. The arts flourished in Japan. Although Japan was among the last of the Asian nations to learn them. For a time, the practise of the martial arts was restricted to the Japanese warrior class, but the peasants practised in secret.

Compare your answers with those in the Answer Key.

DOUBLECHECK 3-4   *Edit this paragraph to correct the three sentence fragments in it.*

The martial arts can be divided into two categories. Those that use weapons and those that don't. In the weaponless methods, such as karate and kung fu, the contestant depends on kicks and on hand and arm blows. As well as on various holds, chokes, and twists, to subdue an opponent. In one of the branches using weapons, kendo, based on ancient Japanese sword fighting. Contestants today use bamboo swords cased in leather.

Compare your answers with those in the Answer Key.

✓
DOUBLECHECK 3-5   *Edit this paragraph to correct the two sentence fragments in it.*

T'ai chi is the most gentle of the martial arts. Slow, graceful movements that bear little resemblance to the original blows and blocks on which the movements are based. Used today for conditioning and flexibility. Some use it as a form of meditation.

Compare your answers with those in the Answer Key.

◆ WRITING PROCESS

PREWRITING: BRAINSTORMING

Another type of prewriting to use when you need ideas is <u>brainstorming</u>. As with any kind of prewriting, brainstorming can be used in an assignment for your composition class or for other types of writing and thinking you must do.

In brainstorming, you jot down whatever ideas about your subject pop into your mind. You do not worry about grammar, spelling, or sentence structure. You do not even worry about whether the ideas are good or not. Just list as quickly as possible all thoughts about a subject that occur to you without stopping to reflect or censoring your ideas. When you are finished brainstorming, go back and circle all the ideas that could be useful.

Brainstorming is especially useful for writing about a personal experience or a subject you know well. For a paper about a common experience, you might work with a group to brainstorm. Sharing ideas in a group can be helpful to all.

A STUDENT
DEMONSTRATION

Joe had to write a paragraph describing a person, place, or thing. He decided to use brainstorming to get in touch with his thoughts about his grandfather's gold watch. Here are the results of Joe's brainstorming:

Gold watch

antique   on chain   always wore   slender   once pawned

message on back   silent ticks   handsome   masculine

warm to touch   smooth   valuable   heirloom   my family

Now You Try It

Try brainstorming about a person, a place, an experience, or an object.

_____

_____

_____

_____

_____

_____

Quickcheck on Brainstorming

✔ Write down your topic word.

✔ Quickly list all of the words that come into your mind about your topic.

✔ Do not censor yourself or worry about spelling.

✔ Go back and circle all the worthwhile ideas.

A special kind of brainstorming is called *clustering*. This is how it works. First, choose a single word or phrase as the starting point. Put it in the centre of a blank page and circle it. Let your mind make connections with the topic word. Write your new ideas down, forming a web all around the central word. Put ideas near each other that seem related. When you are finished, decide on the cluster that most interests you and write about it.

A Student Demonstration

Here is how Joe clustered his thoughts about another topic, college life.

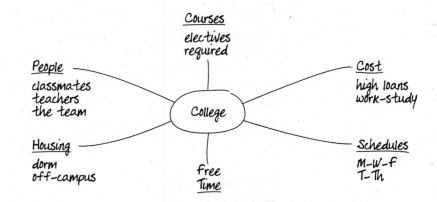

Now You Try It

With a partner, cluster your thoughts about your college's cafeteria. Use all your senses to describe it.

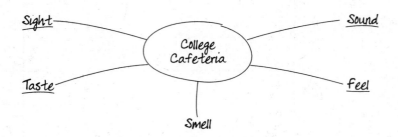

Quickcheck on Clustering

✓ Place your topic in the centre of the page.
✓ List ideas all around your topic.
✓ Connect the ideas in a web.
✓ Do not censor yourself or worry about spelling.
✓ Select the cluster that most interests you, and begin writing.

CHECKPOINT 3-1

At the end of the following paragraph, write the identification numbers of any sentence fragments. Then write the dependent words contained in the fragments. The fragments may be more obvious if you give the paragraph a second reading, starting with the last sentence.

¹Icebergs are huge chunks of ice floating in the ocean. ²They are made of frozen fresh water. ³That breaks off from glaciers. ⁴The icebergs in the North Atlantic come from Greenland. ⁵Which is an island almost entirely covered by a sheet of ice many metres thick. ⁶Because icebergs are made of fresh water, sailing ships used to replenish their drinking-water supply from pools formed on the ice. ⁷Icebergs are a danger to ships, of course. ⁸One of the worst sea disasters occurred in 1912. ⁹When the ocean liner *Titanic* sank after hitting an iceberg. ¹⁰While it was on its first transatlantic trip. ¹¹An estimated 1,517 people lost their lives. ¹²The danger to ships is less today. ¹³Because the Canadian Coast Guard keeps a lookout for icebergs.

No.	Dependent word
____	_____
____	_____
____	_____
____	_____
____	_____

No answers are given for Checkpoint quizzes.

THE PROCESS PARAGRAPH

◆ READING

PROCESS PARAGRAPHS TELL HOW SOMETHING COMES ABOUT

PRECHECK

Most people have heard the name Roots, even if they do not personally own any Roots clothing. The success of Roots is a story that spans three decades, and emphasizes successful marketing strategies. This article discusses the *process,* or stages, by which this success came about.

The Story of Roots

—*Michael Posner*

One could argue that the dawn of Roots was in the summer of '55, when two Americans, Don Green and Michael Budman, spent the summer at Camp Tamakwa, on Tea Lake, Algonquin Park. After that summer's experience with nature, the boys never looked back: Budman has spent the best part of thirty years in the park; Green twenty. Without the formative and enduring influence of Algonquin and its magnetic tug, it's fair to say that the friendship between Budman and Green would never have been sealed, and that they would never have settled in Toronto or gone into business together.

Without the camp experience, there would have been no Roots, the little counterculture shoe store that the entrepreneurial young Americans opened in August 1973, immediately and cleverly appropriating that most Canadian of logos—the beaver. Two decades later, as it closes in on $100 million in annual sales, Roots is a major success story—an international, 500-employee, vertically integrated, privately

formative influential

appropriating taking to use for one's own purposes

owned empire in progress. Today, with sales increasing annually, it has fifty-one stores in Canada, five in the U.S., two in Japan and more on the way; its wide product range has been tailored to the tastes of the rich and famous, who have been assiduously cultivated and used to promote Roots products.

assiduously with great concentration, effort

It all began in the late 60's when, after a summer as a Tamakwa 3 camp director, Budman bought a cottage on Smoke Lake and moved up to Toronto from Detroit. Green joined him there eventually, after first travelling with Budman from Quebec to Jamaica's Negril.

On their settling in Toronto, with a view to changing their "eco- 4 nomic reality," the boys investigated many products before being directed to a Michigan lifestyle store that was selling Earth Shoes, the improbably designed negative heel which laid claim to orthopaedic correctness by daring to suggest that this was precisely how God had intended humankind to walk, with our toes an inch above our heels.

improbably not in the usual or common way

Having decided to make their own version of this shoe, they 5 pooled their savings and then approached a manufacturer under B in the yellow pages, tiny Boa Shoes, owned by Jan Kowalewski, scion of seven generations of Polish shoemakers. He modified the Earth design and produced several styles: moccasin, desert boot, city and sport. Looking for a name organic enough to rival the competition, Green discovered the word "roots" in a textbook on trees. "Your feet are connected to the ground, like a tree is," he says. "Really, your feet are your roots."

scion descendant

On opening day in their rented store at Yonge and Davenport, 6 August 15, 1973, they sold seven pairs of shoes. The second Saturday, they sold thirty pairs, and after three weeks it had become an Event—with lineups down the block.

By year's end, Budman and Green had bought Kowalewski's 7 business and moved the operation into larger premises with new equipment. They went from making thirty pairs of shoes a day to 2,000 within a year. Within eighteen months, there were Roots shoe stores across the continent.

In their marketing, they stressed Kowalewski's made-in-Canada 8 craftmanship, and ran sepia-toned advertisements featuring Jan and sons in work aprons, implying each Roots shoe had been lovingly handmade. With that native American genius for marketing, the Roots boys have turned what might have been just another retail chain into a legitimate cultural icon. It says something about the crisis of identity in contemporary society, the desperate longing to belong to something, that Budman and Green have been able to persuade millions of North Americans that wearing the Roots logo confers instant membership in a not-so-private club—their club, Team Roots.

sepia-toned dark brown

icon item significant to a culture

Even more remarkably, they have somehow managed to trans- 9 plant the ideology of conservation onto its very antithesis—the act of consumption—making the purchase of a Roots sweatshirt synonymous with selfless, ecological virtue and oneness with Nature. They've packaged the wilderness and sold Canadians back their

antithesis direct opposite

authentic genuine, real

own myths. A marketing ploy? You bet—but one rooted in their authentic and unmistakable love for Algonquin Park.

By 1976, even though the negative heel was going the way of the 10 bell bottom pant, Budman and Green were churning out rubber-soled versions of other shoe styles, as well as a new line of leather jackets and handbags. After the birth of Green's first child, Roots launched the baby and kids' line, with immediate success.

accumulation collection

But the real accumulation of gold was literally spun from cot- 11 ton—the sweatshirt. Between '85 and '87, the country seemed overcome by fleece frenzy. "It started very small," an associate recalls. "A few sweatshirts in a basket in a corner, more for staff than anything else. And it evolved. The numbers became unbelievable. We couldn't give enough floor space, time, effort to it. I remember a Boxing Day at the Eaton Centre store, bringing product out from the back and being almost killed by customers."

By 1990, Roots was not alone in experiencing sweat fatigue, the 12 entire retail sector was spinning into a black hole. Ironically the recession may be one of the best things to have happened to Roots, a much needed wake up call. "Their work habits had become pretty slack," says one former Roots employee. That changed, literally overnight.

Rima Greenberg, an employee of the company, credits the com- 13 pany's survival to the durability of the Roots name, the flexibility of factory ownership and the push to expand the wholesale division, which sells leather jackets, sweatshirts, etc., to sports clubs, movie crews and corporations and now accounts for a third of all revenues.

"We've learned it over and over," says Green. "Your results in 14 business are directly proportionate to the time you give it. It's not a complicated formula." Indeed, for the Roots boys it has been a most successful one.

CHECKING MEANING AND STYLE

1. Why does Michael Posner see the beginning of Roots in Budman and Green's stay in Algonquin Park?

2. How was the Earth Shoe intricately linked to the beginning of Roots?

3. What events prompted Roots to diversify and expand?

4. How have the Roots stores managed to survive the recessions Canada has been through?

CHECKING IDEAS

1. What does Posner see as remarkable about the use of the beaver as the Roots logo?

2. What are the features of a "vertically integrated" management style?

3. What does this article illustrate about entrepreneurial success in North America?

4. Do you choose your clothes with brand names in mind? Are there any brand names that have particular meaning for you?

◆ WRITING MODELS

THE PROCESS PARAGRAPH

To describe a process is to tell, step by step, how something is developed: how to teach a dog to roll over, how to make a good chili, how Canada became a confederation. Most of "The Story of Roots" is an example of process writing. The article discusses the steps by which Budman and Green developed an extremely successful retail chain. These were the major stages:

1. In 1973, Budman and Green began selling their version of Earth Shoes at Yonge and Davenport.

2. By the middle of 1975, they had a chain of stores across Canada.

3. By 1976, they had branched into new lines of shoes; they had also begun selling handbags and jackets.

4. In 1985, their Roots sweatshirt stormed the market.

5. In the 1990s, restructuring saved Roots from the recession.

The amount of detail the author adds depends on whether the writing is a paragraph, an essay, or a book.

The following is a process paragraph based on these significant steps in the reading selection.

Model Process Paragraph #1

The underlined topic sentence states what process is being examined.

The development of the Roots retail success began in 1973. By 1975, Budman and Green were selling a type of Earth Shoe in Roots stores across Canada. In 1976 they began to manufacture other leather goods like handbags and jackets, as well as making other shoe styles. Their fame and financial success were cemented in 1985, when they began to sell the famous Roots sweatshirts. In the early 1990s, they restructured for the recession years. Nowadays the Roots beaver logo is seen everywhere.

Read the following process paragraph, and then answer the questions below it.

Model Process Paragraph #2

Notice how the first sentence establishes the topic of the paragraph.

Levi Strauss arrived at the riveted blue jeans so popular today through a series of major developments. First, he made a pair of pants from canvas for a California Gold Rush miner who wanted sturdy trousers. Other miners put in requests. When an order for more canvas was not filled, he made pants from "denim," a tough brown cloth made in Nimes, France. Almost from the beginning, he had his cloth dyed the distinctive indigo that gives blue jeans their name. Later, he adopted riveted pockets after a miner complained that the pockets weren't strong enough to hold ore samples.

1. What did Strauss do first?

2. What did Strauss do when he could not get more canvas?

3. What colour did Strauss dye the denim?

4. Why did he rivet the pockets to the pants?

The above four questions identify the steps Levi Strauss went through in the process of developing his famous blue jeans.

Study the organization of the following step-by-step description of how to judge a car in a used-car lot.

Model Process Paragraph #3

Observe the underlined transition words that help keep track of steps.

If you're thinking about buying a used car from a dealer, *Consumer Reports* magazine says you can learn a good deal about a car by examining it carefully in the lot. First, look for leaks. Oil spots under the car or greenish-white stains on the radiator could mean trouble. Next, examine the body. Fresh welds, fresh paint on a car under three years old, panels that don't match the rest of the car—all could mean the car has been in an accident. Look for rust on the door edges and trunk floor; lift the floor covering to check the metal underneath. Now, inspect the tires. Uneven wear suggests an accident or an alignment problem. To check the suspension, grab the top of each front wheel and push and pull; it shouldn't move or clunk. Finally, go over the interior. Look for stains from water leaks; sniff for the musty odour of mildew. Check the safety belts, seat adjustments, and other interior hardware. Test the wipers, radio, air conditioner, and other accessories. If you're still interested, take the car for a test drive.

◆ W RITING A SSIGNMENT

A P ROCESS P ARAGRAPH

The topic sentence of a process paragraph usually says something about the process, such as that it is easy, fun, or worthwhile. Here are three examples:

> Changing the wallpaper in your kitchen is not an easy task, but the job can be simplified if you follow these steps.
>
> A bill follows a complex path in Parliament before it becomes a law.
>
> A major-league ballplayer probably has been playing the game at least since he was six.

Transition words or phrases, such as those underlined in Model Process Paragraph #3, can be helpful in making the steps of a process clear. However, do not overdo them; use transition words only when they help. Here are some more examples:

to start with	the first step	second
the next step	after that	the last step

WRITE A PROCESS
PARAGRAPH

Write about a process that can be described in one paragraph. Write on one of these subjects:

1. How to plan a wedding
2. How to spend a pleasant Sunday with a child
3. How to do something around the house
4. How to do something in sports
5. How to become a citizen of Canada
6. How to make something (Model #2)
7. How to buy something (Model #3)

To get started on your process paragraph, do the exercises below. If your mind is blank, use the prewriting techniques discussed earlier (nonstop writing and brainstorming).

1. Write a topic sentence for your process paragraph.

    _____

    _____

2. What is the first step?

    _____

    With what transition word or phrase will you start?

    _____

3. What is the second step?

    _____

    What will be your next transition word or phrase?

    _____

4. What is the third step?

    _____

    What will be your next transition word or phrase?

    _____

5. What is the fourth step?

    _____

    What will be your final transition word or phrase?

    _____

Before you write your process paragraph, be sure that all steps in the process are included and that each step is clear. You may need more than four steps.

◆ SENTENCE STRUCTURE

RUN-TOGETHER SENTENCES

The Problem: Avoiding Run-Together Sentences

This paragraph is hard to read:

> Raymond was supposed to meet Jennifer in the library at 3 o'clock he got there 15 minutes early he sat down to read a copy of *Maclean's* magazine, it was so interesting that he didn't look up again until someone tapped him on the shoulder it was Jennifer, Raymond looked at his watch it was 4:30 "hi," she said.

Of course it's hard to read. That's because the reader expects to see a <u>capital letter</u> at the beginning of each sentence and a <u>period</u> at the end. Without these guides, the reader quickly gets lost.

The paragraph is full of <u>run-together sentences</u>, which result when two or more sentences are written as if they were one.

Sometimes there is no punctuation used to separate the sentences, resulting in a <u>fused sentence</u> or <u>run-on</u>.

> It was snowing the road to the cabin was blocked.

Sometimes a comma is used, causing a <u>comma splice</u>.

> It was snowing, the road to the cabin was blocked.

A sentence, you will remember, has a subject and a verb and expresses a complete thought. Both *It was snowing* and *The road to the cabin was blocked* qualify separately as sentences. A comma cannot separate them.

Solution #1: Use a Period and a Capital Letter

Run-together sentences can be corrected in five different ways. The first is to use a period and a capital letter to make two sentences.

> It was snowing. The road to the cabin was blocked.

SPOTCHECK 4-1

Correct these run-together sentences by adding a period and a capital letter between the two independent clauses.

> **EXAMPLE:** England is smaller than Manitoba. Its people founded one of the world's largest empires.

1. Most of England's colonies became independent after World War II its empire has all but vanished.

2. Traditions are important to the English they hold the royal family in affection.

3. Elizabeth II became queen in 1952 she has been a popular monarch.

Check the Answer Key before continuing.

Solution #2: Use a Comma and a Connecting Word

Use a comma and one of the following <u>connecting words</u> (coordinating conjunctions):

and but or for nor yet so

(It's a good idea to memorize this short list.)

It was snowing, <u>and</u> the road to the cabin was blocked.

Note that there is an independent clause (a sentence) on each side of the connector, *and*.

SPOTCHECK 4-2

Correct these run-together sentences by adding a comma and a connecting word between the two independent clauses.

yet
EXAMPLE: England is smaller than Manitoba, ∧ its people founded one of the world's largest empires.

1. Most of England's colonies became independent after World War II its empire has all but vanished.

2. Traditions are important to the English they hold the royal family in affection.

3. Elizabeth II became queen in 1952 she has been a popular monarch.

4. Canada has had close ties with England many of the earliest settlers came from that country.

5. Canadian visitors to England will probably spend much of their time in London they may enjoy touring the beautiful countryside instead. It depends on their interests.

Compare your answers with those in the Answer Key.

SPOTCHECK 4-3

Use the connecting words shown to write sentences containing two independent clauses. Use a comma after the first clause.

EXAMPLE: (yet) Timothy has a good job, <u>yet</u> he is always borrowing money.

1. (and) _____

_____

2. (but) _____

_____

3. (or) _____

_____

4. (so) _____

_____

Compare your answers with those in the Answer Key.

Solution #3: Make One Clause Dependent

Make one of the clauses dependent by using a <u>dependent word</u> such as *because, since, while,* or *unless.* (You may want to review the list of dependent words on page 44.)

<u>Because</u> it was snowing, the road to the cabin was blocked.

✔️

SPOTCHECK 4-4

Correct the following run-together sentences by changing one of the independent clauses into a dependent clause by using a dependent word. Be sure that the punctuation and capitalization are correct.

Although

EXAMPLE: ∧   Carlos had a full-time job, he got good grades.

because

EXAMPLE: Carlos got good grades   ∧   he studied hard.

1. Mother gets home early we will have a good dinner.

2. The bulldozer knocked down the trees the neighbours watched in dismay.

3. She was already ten minutes late Yolanda decided not to go to class.

4. We always have a good time we go camping.

5. The electricity went out Terry lit some candles.

Compare your answers with those in the Answer Key.

✔️

SPOTCHECK 4-5

Use the dependent words shown to write sentences containing one independent clause and one dependent clause. (Put a comma after the dependent clause if it begins the sentence.)

EXAMPLE: (while) The sun went down <u>while</u> we were fishing.

1. (before) _____

_____

2. (unless) _____

_____

3. (although) _____

_____

Compare your answers with those in the Answer Key.

Solution #4: Use a Semicolon

Use a <u>semicolon</u>. This mark suggests a closer relation between the two clauses than a period would.

It was snowing; the road to the cabin was blocked.

(Be sure you always have independent clauses on *both sides* of the semicolon.)

SPOTCHECK 4-6

Correct these run-together sentences with a semicolon.

EXAMPLE: Wilson got into his car; it wouldn't start.

1. Canadians have great faith in education they believe it is the solution to most problems.

2. Education can help people "get ahead" it produces citizens who can make intelligent decisions when they vote.

3. Many parents read to their small children those children are likely to enjoy reading as adults.

Check the Answer Key before continuing.

Solution #5: Use a Semicolon and a Transitional Word

Use a semicolon and a <u>transitional word</u> (conjunctive adverb) or <u>phrase</u> that reflects the change (transition) from the first part of the sentence to the second.

It was snowing; therefore, the road to the cabin was blocked.

(A period may be used instead of a semicolon. In that case, be sure to capitalize the next word. A comma is usually placed after the transitional word when the word comes at the beginning of the clause.)

Following are some more examples of transitional words. You will notice that they have about the same meaning as the more common connecting words (*and, but,* etc.) The transitional words make your writing seem somewhat more formal, which may or may not be desirable.

Transitional words similar in meaning to *and:*

furthermore   moreover   also   besides   in addition

Transitional words similar in meaning to *but:*

however   instead   nevertheless   on the other hand

Transitional words similar in meaning to *so:*

therefore   consequently   thus   as a result

Other transitional words:

still	for example	next
meanwhile	in fact	then
even so	first	finally
otherwise	second	

SPOTCHECK 4-7   *Use a semicolon and a transitional word to correct these run-together sentences. Put a comma after the transitional word.*

however,

EXAMPLE: Wilson got into his car; ∧   it wouldn't start.

1. Canadians have great faith in education they believe it is the solution to most problems.

2. Education can help people "get ahead" it produces citizens who can make intelligent decisions when they vote.

3. Many parents read to their small children those children are likely to enjoy reading as adults.

4. People tend to think of education as something that takes place in schools we learn in many ways outside of school.

5. Most experiences are "educational" television teaches us more than we realize.

Compare your answers with those in the Answer Key.

SPOTCHECK 4-8   *Use a semicolon and the transitional words shown to write sentences containing two independent clauses. (Put a comma after the transitional word.)*

EXAMPLE: (nevertheless) Today is Mohamed's birthday; <u>nevertheless</u>, he plans to work until eight o'clock.

1. (furthermore)   _____

_____

2. (otherwise)   _____

_____

3. (however)   _____

_____

4. (for example)   _____

_____

Compare your answers with those in the Answer Key.

DOUBLECHECK 4-1

Each of the following sentences contains two clauses. Draw one line under the subject and two lines under the verb in each clause. In the blanks at the left, write RTS *for a run-together sentence or* C *for a correctly punctuated sentence.*

_____C_____   **EXAMPLE:** We take cars for granted, but they haven't always been around.

_____   **1.** The automobile was introduced in North America at the end of the nineteenth century; it brought many changes.

_____   **2.** Farmers could easily drive to the city, and city dwellers could go to the country for recreation.

_____   **3.** Highways and motorways made long-distance travel easy, motels were built along the roads.

_____   **4.** When families owned cars, they could move to the new suburbs to live.

_____   **5.** Cars made shopping centres practical; moreover, drive-in movies, drive-in restaurants, and even drive-in banks became common.

Check the Answer Key before continuing.

DOUBLECHECK 4-2

Each of the following sentences contains two clauses. Draw one line under the subject and two lines under the verb in each clause. In the blanks at the left, write RTS *for a run-together sentence or* C *for one that is correct.*

_____   1. If you are a typical North American, you eat about 50 litres of popcorn a year.

_____   2. The Indians brought popcorn to the first Thanksgiving in 1621, the Pilgrims apparently liked it.

_____   3. Popcorn is a good snack since one litre of dry-popped popcorn contains only 100 calories.

_____   4. Even if you add cooking oil and salt, popcorn compares favourably with potato chips or corn chips.

_____   5. Oil-popped popcorn has one-third the calories of potato chips, it has one-fourth the fat of potato chips.

Check the Answer Key before continuing.

✓

DOUBLECHECK 4-3   *Add connecting words, dependent words, and transitional words to complete these paragraphs.*

Bathing suits did not make an appearance until the middle of the 1800s _____ recreational bathing was not popular before then; _____, at that time doctors began to prescribe the "waters" for a variety of ailments. Europeans flocked to the streams, the lakes, and the ocean, _____ they sought relief from "nerves" or other disorders. Standards of modesty were different in those days, _____ bathing suits covered more of the body than they do today. Women wore knee-length skirts in the water; _____, they wore bloomers and black stockings under the skirts. _____ a wet bathing suit could weigh as much as the bather, the accent was on *bathing,* not swimming.

_____ she wanted greater privacy, a woman could use a "bathing machine" at the ocean. Attendants would wheel her and the portable dressing room into shallow waters. _____ she had changed into a loose head-to-toe gown, she would step down a ramp into the surf _____ the attendants shooed away any interested males.

A Danish immigrant to the United States named Carl Jantzen revolutionized swim wear in 1915 _____ he invented a knitting machine that yielded a stretchy fabric. The fabric resulted in a body-clinging fit; _____, swimsuits still had sleeves and reached to the knees. Swimsuits became more revealing in the 1930s _____ narrow straps and backless models paved the way for the two-piece suit.

It wasn't until 1946 that the bikini made its appearance. World War II had recently ended, _____ the United States was testing an atom bomb in the Pacific. A French designer was about to introduce a skimpy swimsuit model, _____ he didn't have a catchy name. _____, the atomic blast at Bikini Atoll on July 1, 1946, gave him the name for the "explosive" suit he displayed to the world four days later.

Compare your answers with those in the Answer Key.

DOUBLECHECK 4-4 ✔️

Correct each run-together sentence in three ways: (1) with a connecting word, (2) with a dependent word, and (3) with a semicolon and a transitional word or phrase. Use the correct punctuation.

> **EXAMPLE:** Most people waste a large part of their lives, they spend five years standing in line.
>
> **EX 1.** . . . their lives, for they spend . . .
>
> **EX 2.** . . . their lives because they spend . . .
>
> **EX 3.** . . . their lives; for example, they spend . . .

    A. Mrs Frisbee has been with the company five years, she will get a raise.

A1. _____

A2. _____

A3. _____

B. Ruth is a hard worker, she will not get a raise.

B1. _____

B2. _____

B3. _____

Compare your answers with those in the Answer Key.

Quickcheck on Run-Together Sentences

✓ You can correct a run-together sentence in five different ways:

   1. Use a period and a capital letter.
   2. Use a comma and a connecting word (*and, but,* etc.).
   3. Use a dependent word (*although, because,* etc.).
   4. Use a semicolon by itself.
   5. Use a semicolon and a transitional word (*however, therefore,* etc.) with a comma after it.

✓ A comma cannot be used alone to separate two independent clauses. A semicolon or period is required.

✓ A semicolon must have an independent clause (sentence) on each side of it. You can test your use of a semicolon by asking if you could use a period instead. If not, the semicolon is wrong.

✓ Be sure you understand the differences between the connecting words (*and, but,* etc.), the transitional words (*however, therefore,* etc.), and the dependent words (*since, although, because,* etc.). Study the punctuation that goes with each type.

◆ WRITING PROCESS

PREWRITING: ASKING "HOW?" AND "WHY?"

Often you can find details to support your topic sentence by asking "How?" and "Why?" Let's say you are looking at this topic sentence about a particular kind of high school:

> The high school I attended was beginning to seem more like a prison than an institution of learning.

Like most topic sentences, it is rather general. You need specific details to make the rest of the paragraph interesting and convincing.

Ask yourself *how* it seemed like a prison. Then jot down whatever ideas come to mind. Remember, you are brainstorming, so don't worry about whether the ideas are good. You can get rid of the bad ones later.

high fences kept students on campus at lunchtime

guards checked students for weapons

armed guards patrolled hallways

principal checked lockers for drugs and weapons

buildings were getting old and run-down

student gangs

graffiti on walls

Now ask *why* the school became like a prison.

students bring knives and guns

drugs being sold

students beaten and robbed

misbehaviour in class

vandalism

faculty threatened or injured by students

students left after signing in

neighbourhood businesses complained

These ideas should provide enough details for a paragraph. In fact, there should be enough for two—one based on "how" and one on "why." Limit yourself to the "how" items. After crossing out some and rearranging and merging others, you might write a paragraph like this one:

"HOW?" PARAGRAPH

> The high school I attended was beginning to seem more like a prison than an institution of learning. In the morning, we were greeted by armed guards who checked our book bags and jacket pockets for knives and guns. Later the guards patrolled the hallways to make sure everyone was in class. From time to time, the principal and her aides would inspect all the lockers for guns and drugs. One time they even brought in a German shepherd trained to sniff out concealed drugs. The campus was surrounded by a high metal fence, and the gates were guarded during noon recess to keep students in and nonstudents out. At the end of four years, I wasn't sure if I was being graduated or paroled.

On the other hand, you might have decided to use the second list to discuss "why" your high school became like a prison. That decision might have resulted in a different topic sentence, and a paragraph like this one:

"WHY?" PARAGRAPH

> I didn't like the way my high school came to resemble a prison, but I understood some of the reasons the guards were hired and the campus was

"closed." Marijuana and crack were routinely dealt and smoked—inside and outside the building and on the streets around the school. Some students brought weapons to intimidate others, and some brought them to defend themselves. During class hours it sometimes seemed that there were more students in the hallways than in the classrooms. In class the teachers tried to keep people reasonably quiet, hoping to avoid injury to the students or themselves, but not always succeeding. At noon, some of the neighbourhood businesses locked their doors to prevent shoplifting. Things were quieter after the guards were hired, but I was glad to graduate and leave.

Even if you make your "how" and "why" lists more detailed than those in the example, you will probably think of new details as you write the paragraph. Include them, of course, if they help support the topic sentence. Sometimes, only one of the questions will work. If, for example, the boss asks for a memo on *why* you should get a raise, you are going to let the boss worry about *how* to pay for it.

In our two sample paragraphs, all the other sentences are more *specific* than the topic sentences that open the paragraphs. It is important to realize, however, that an entire paragraph (or a full-scale essay) could easily be written just about the day the drug-sniffing dogs visited or just about rowdy behaviour in the classroom.

Now You Try It

Ask "How?" or "Why?" to get specific details to develop each general statement.

EXAMPLE: Spring is my favourite season.

a. The flowers and fruit trees are in blossom. _____

b. Baseball season opens. _____

c. I can wear lightweight clothes. _____

1. Susan spends too much money on clothes.

a. _____

b. _____

c. _____

2. Yesterday was one of the worst days in my life.

a. _____

b. _____

c. _____

3. A dictionary is a useful reference work.

a. _____

b. _____

c. _____

✓

CHECKPOINT 4-1   *In the blank to the left of each paragraph, write the letter of the run-together sentence in that paragraph.*

_____   1.   ᴬAutomobiles were introduced in the 1890s. ᴮAt first, they seemed very strange, in fact, they were displayed in circuses. ᶜBefore cars, most long-distance travel was done in horse-drawn carriages, which explains why the first autos were called "horseless carriages."

_____   2.   ᴬThe first vehicles that could move themselves were built as early as the eighteenth century; however, they were powered by steam, not gasoline. ᴮA steam carriage in England in the 1830s reached a speed of 25 kilometres an hour, and some of the vehicles carried as many as 22 passengers. ᶜThe success of steam-powered road vehicles worried the railway people, they got laws passed limiting the use of steam carriages.

_____   3.   ᴬCars powered by electric batteries were the most popular. ᴮThey were cleaner and quieter than those powered by steam or gasoline, but they had major drawbacks, they couldn't go fast, and their batteries had to be recharged every 80 kilometres. ᶜGasoline-powered cars gradually replaced steam and electric cars.

_____   4.   ᴬAlthough the gasoline-powered car originated in Europe with such men as Gottlieb Daimler and Karl Benz, the first successful North American car of that type is usually credited to two brothers, Charles and Frank Duryea. ᴮThat car was built in 1894, in 1895 the Duryeas started the first company to manufacture gasoline-powered cars. ᶜMen such as Henry Ford and Ransom Eli Olds soon were also making cars.

_____   5.   ᴬIn the United States, the young car industry was helped in 1901 by the discovery of huge oil fields in Texas, in addition, mass production methods were introduced to make cars cheaper. ᴮOne no longer had to be rich to afford a car. ᶜNot surprisingly, cars became a popular means of transportation.

_____ 6. [A]The Olds Motor Works in Detroit had the first auto assembly line. [B]Parts for the cars were made at a variety of machine shops; they were then brought to a central factory to be assembled into cars. [C]This made the work go faster, production jumped from 425 cars in 1901 to 5,000 cars in 1903.

_____ 7. [A]Henry Ford wanted to make a car that almost everyone could afford, to do that he introduced the moving assembly line. [B]A conveyor belt moved the frame of the car through the plant while workers on each side of the belt added parts brought to them on other conveyor belts. [C]This method cut the time needed to assemble a car from 12½ hours to 1½ hours.

_____ 8. [A]By cutting assembly time, Ford was able to cut costs. [B]The famous Model T Ford dropped in price from $850 to less than $400, making it cheaper than any other car. [C]More than 15 million Model Ts were sold between 1908 and 1927, half the cars sold in America in that period were Fords.

No answers are given for Checkpoint quizzes.

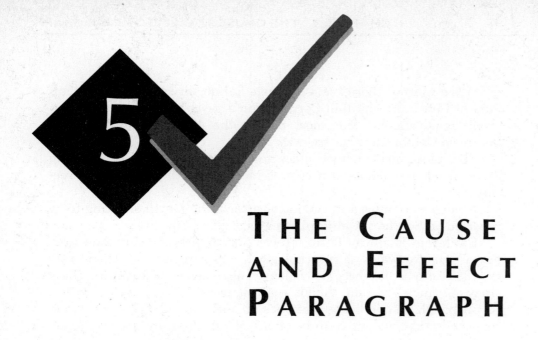

THE CAUSE
AND EFFECT
PARAGRAPH

◆ READING

ANALYZING CAUSE AND EFFECT

PRECHECK

Speeding bullets had joined speeding cars on the Southern California freeways when the following story appeared in the *Los Angeles Times*. The author of this article analyzes the problems that *cause* drivers to become frustrated and the *effect* their anger has on other motorists. Ontario's 401 is the busiest highway in North America: could this happen here?

Road Warriors of the Freeways

—Lonn Johnston

Los Angeles—Barreling along the freeway at about a mile a 1 minute, Harold Harvey Hawks pulled out a 12-gauge shotgun and fired. Later, he told police that he just meant to scare the driver of a van who had flashed his bright headlights, thrown a can and cut him off.

On June 30, Hawks received the maximum term of 17 years to life 2 for the shot he fired that killed a passenger in the van—Patricia Dwyer, an off-duty Corona policewoman whose husband was driving.

"Two hotheads met on the freeway and neither one of them would 3 give in," summed up jury forewoman Joyce Beck, after jurors found Hawks guilty of second-degree murder.

It was the first in a recent spate of Southern California freeway 4 shootings—a new kind of urban warfare that California Highway Patrol officials and others fear may be a trend.

urban found in cities

"It's a war out there," said Dr. Ange LoBue, director for medical af- 5 fairs at College Hospital in Cerritos and a psychiatrist specializing in stress management. "For most people, the most stressful place in Southern California is the freeway."

The latest incident took place early yesterday when a tailgating 6 driver fired three shots at a woman motorist on the Hollywood Freeway.

No one was injured in the latest attack, the fourth shooting to be 7 reported on Southern California freeways since June 20.

California Highway Patrol officer Matt Clark of Santa Ana com- 8 pares the freeways to psychological experiments in which rats crowded into a box become violently aggressive. "People are going crazy out there," he said. "And it's getting worse."

consensus agreement

Although no one keeps statistics on such things, there is a broad 9 consensus that violent confrontations on the freeway are rising, according to state CHP spokesman Kent Milton. The reasons, say those who study driver aggression, are as complicated as a rush-hour commute:

inhibitions feelings that control behaviour

• Cars offer anonymity, a feeling of power and the chance to escape, 10 lowering inhibitions to aggressiveness. "It's the private bubble that brings out Mr. Hyde," said Raymond W. Novaco, a professor at the University of California at Irvine who studies freeway driver stress and anger.

• Traffic congestion is worsening because freeway construction has 11 not kept pace with population growth. Rush hour has become creep hour. As driver frustrations and blood pressures rise, Novaco said, "there is a highly significant decrease in tolerance."

condones accepts or allows

• American society increasingly condones violence, said Arnold 12 Goldstein, director of the Center for Research on Aggression at Syracuse University in New York.

escalate increase

In advertising and television, for example, we see "great levels of 13 displayed violence but fewer and fewer restraints," he said. "So now if someone cuts you off on the freeway, instead of yelling or an obscene gesture, the violence of the response may escalate to actual physical injury. In some cases with a gun."

CHECKING MEANING AND STYLE

1. This article discusses the effects of freeway violence as well as the causes of that violence. Where do the paragraphs dealing with the effects of violence end and those dealing with the causes begin?

2. Can you explain the sentence "[Cars are] the private bubble that brings out Mr. Hyde"? (Paragraph 10)

3. What three things do cars provide that encourage violence? (Paragraph 10)

4. What two things condition Americans to accept violence? (Paragraphs 12 and 13)

CHECKING IDEAS

1. You probably haven't seen any shootings, but have you seen other kinds of aggressive or hostile driving behaviour that could cause injury or death? What were they?

2. What highway behaviour or conditions irritate you most?

3. Do you agree that cars can "bring out the worst" in people? How do you feel while driving in congested traffic?

4. What do you think drivers might do to ease their tensions when traffic gets heavy?

5. This article was prompted by the situation on freeways in Southern California. Are there similarities to that situation here in Canada? Give reasons for your opinion.

◆ WRITING MODELS

THE CAUSE AND EFFECT PARAGRAPH

What causes some people to shoot at other motorists on the Southern California freeways? That is the question reporter Lonn Johnston sets out to answer in his newspaper story.

Johnston first presents the effects or results of freeway violence: specific cases of death or injury. But most of his article deals with what causes this crazy behaviour. Here is a breakdown of the effects and causes he names:

Effects:

1. Reckless, hostile driving

2. Shooting at other drivers

Causes:

1. Cars give sense of power

2. Cars protect identity

3. Cars give a chance to escape

4. Congested traffic creates anger

5. TV suggests that violence is okay

These effects and their causes could have been discussed in just one paragraph:

Model Cause and Effect Paragraph #1

The topic sentence states that this paragraph will explain causes.

Experts say reckless and hostile freeway driving—even to the point of shooting at other motorists—has several causes. Cars give us a sense of power. At the same time, they protect our identity and give us a chance to escape after we have been rude or hostile. Moreover, as we creep along in congested traffic, our blood pressure rises, and we are quick to get angry when someone cuts in front of us. Finally, the television programs and advertising we see often suggest that violent behaviour is acceptable.

Study the two model paragraphs that follow, noting the causes and effects that are discussed in each one.

Model Cause and Effect Paragraph #2

In this example, the effect is mentioned first; then, two causes are described.

> Two reasons why many students drop out of college are that they hang around with the wrong crowd, or they have to go to work to support their family. If they associate with students who go to school just to socialize, they are likely to neglect their studies and possibly fail their courses. Their friends may encourage them to cut classes to "hang out." If they fall behind in their classes, they may drop out altogether. Other students drop out because they are the only ones to support the family. They may have done well in school, but now they need to work full-time.

1. What effect is discussed in this paragraph?

2. What two causes are mentioned for this effect?

This paragraph might have been improved if the writer had given all his attention to just one of the two reasons. Then he could have given more details about that one reason, making the paragraph more interesting and worthwhile, as in Model Paragraph #3. Do not try to cover too much ground in a single paragraph.

Model Cause and Effect Paragraph #3

Here the topic sentence—the first sentence—leads into a discussion of causes.

> My friend Ali had to drop out of college to support his family. Ali's father has been unemployed since the local steel mill shut down. His mother quit her job as a nurse years ago because of back trouble. His two brothers are still in elementary school, and his sister is in high school. Even though Ali had been working from 4 p.m. to midnight at a filling station and his father receives unemployment insurance, the family was having trouble making house payments. So Ali added a 2 to 6 a.m. job stocking shelves at a supermarket. He tried to continue his classes, too. However, when he found that he was coming to classes unprepared and often dozing off, he decided to postpone his college education until the family finances were in better shape.

1. What is the main effect discussed in this paragraph?

2. What caused other members of Ali's family not to contribute more to its support?

3. What seems to be the final factor that caused Ali to take a second job?

4. What two factors finally caused Ali to drop out of school?

◆ WRITING ASSIGNMENT

A CAUSE AND EFFECT PARAGRAPH

Your college instructors may call on you to analyze a subject in terms of cause and effect: What caused World War I? What are the causes of the high divorce rate in Canada? What were the effects of the invention of electric lights? How does television viewing affect students' grades?

When writing a cause and effect paragraph, you analyze either the causes or the effects of something. You do not analyze both the causes and the effects at the same time.

Start with a topic sentence that may look similar to one of these:

The slow pace is the main reason I enjoy baseball. (cause)

A major cause of teen drug use is loneliness.

My life has been miserable since I met Lucy. (effect)

Obtaining my high school diploma had a positive effect on my life.

This is a good time to look at the difference between the words *affect* and *effect*. *Affect* is an action verb meaning "influence."

The medicine <u>affected</u> Brad's driving ability.

Effect is a noun meaning "result."

Did the pill have an <u>effect</u> on Brad's driving?

WRITE A CAUSE AND EFFECT PARAGRAPH

Write a cause and effect paragraph. Choose your subject from the two lists following. The six suggested subjects are dependent-clause fragments. Be sure your topic sentence is a true sentence, not a fragment.

CAUSE

Subjects Emphasizing *Cause*

1. Why I bought the kind of car (bicycle, motorcycle) I did

2. Why I chose to attend this college

3. Why I am a Liberal (vegetarian, jogger, etc.)

EXAMPLE FOR TOPIC 2

I. Topic sentence about the effect

I chose to attend this college in order to save money.

Observe how all four reasons are part of the same *cause*.

Explanation about the cause

A. Night classes, so could work days

B. Community college tuition is less

C. Could live at home and save on expenses

D. Nearby, so save on transportation costs

Subjects emphasizing *cause* could use this outline:

FOR YOUR OWN NOTES

II.　Topic sentence about the effect

_____

_____

Explanation of the cause

A. _____

B. _____

C. _____

D. _____

EFFECT

Subjects Emphasizing *Effect*

1.　How my life has changed since I quit smoking (started drinking, joined a church, etc.)

2.　How driving affects my emotions and behaviour

3.　How friends improve (spoil) my life

EXAMPLE FOR TOPIC I

I.　Topic sentence about the cause

My life has changed since I quit smoking. _____

Observe how all four reasons are part of the same *effect.*

Explanation about the effect

A.　Have more money to spend on food _____

B.　Food tastes better now _____

C.　Put food in mouth instead of cigarette _____

D.　Have put on a few pounds _____

Subjects emphasizing *effect* could use this outline:

FOR YOUR OWN NOTES

II.　Topic sentence about the cause

_____

_____

Explanation about the effect

A. _____

B. _____

C. _____

D. _____

Develop your topic sentence by writing at least half a dozen sentences of explanation or examples. When revising, watch out for fragments and run-together sentences.

◆ SENTENCE STRUCTURE

USING VERBS CORRECTLY

The Problem: Using the Right Verb Forms

Verbs change their form to show changes in time. Most verbs are *regular:* that is, they show past time in a consistent way, by adding *-ed* or *-d* to the present-time form.

Present Time	Past Time
jump	jumped
dance	danced
hope	hoped

But that isn't true of all verbs. Look at the verbs in these past-time sentences:

Angela <u>knowed</u> the words to all the Top 40 songs.

Ms. Greene <u>losed</u> her wedding ring in the potato salad.

Obviously, adding *-ed* or *-d* to *know* or *lose* just results in embarrassing errors because they are *irregular* verbs. Their past-time forms are made in irregular or inconsistent ways. Those sentences should have been written as follows:

Angela <u>knew</u> the words to all the Top 40 songs.

Ms. Greene <u>lost</u> her wedding ring in the potato salad.

Solution #1: Memorize the Irregular Verbs

To avoid mistakes with irregular verbs, memorize the past-time form and the past participle for each one. The past participle is the form used with the helping verbs *has, have,* and *had.*

Present time	Today Violet <u>sings</u>.
Past time	Yesterday Violet <u>sang</u>.
Past participle	Violet <u>has sung</u> all week long.

Unfortunately, the list of irregular verbs is rather long (the following list is not complete).

Present	Past	Past Participle (used with the helping verbs has, have, had)
arise(s)*	arise	arisen
become(s)	became	become
begin(s)	began	begun
bite(s)	bit	bitten
blow(s)	blew	blown
break(s)	broke	broken
bring(s)	brought	brought
buy(s)	bought	bought
catch(es)	caught	caught
choose(s)	chose	chosen
come(s)	came	come
do (does)	did	done
draw(s)	drew	drawn
drink(s)	drank	drunk
drive(s)	drove	driven
eat(s)	ate	eaten
fall(s)	fell	fallen
feed(s)	fed	fed
feel(s)	felt	felt
fight(s)	fought	fought
find(s)	found	found
fly (flies)	flew	flown
forget(s)	forgot	forgotten
get(s)	got	got or gotten
give(s)	gave	given
go (goes)	went	gone
grow(s)	grew	grown
hurt(s)	hurt	hurt
keep(s)	kept	kept
know(s)	knew	known
lay(s) [to place]	laid	laid
lead(s)	led	led
leave(s)	left	left
let(s)	let	let
lie(s) [to recline]	lay	lain

*Present-time verbs add an -s or -es if the subject is he, she, or it.

Present	Past	Past Participle (used with the helping verbs has, have, had)
lose(s)	lost	lost
make(s)	made	made
meet(s)	met	met
pay(s)	paid	paid
rise(s)	rose	risen
ride(s)	rode	ridden
ring(s)	rang	rung
run(s)	ran	run
say(s)	said	said
see(s)	saw	seen
send(s)	sent	sent
shoot(s)	shot	shot
shut(s)	shut	shut
sing(s)	sang	sung
slide(s)	slid	slid
sit(s)	sat	sat
speak(s)	spoke	spoken
spend(s)	spent	spent
steal(s)	stole	stolen
swim(s)	swam	swum
take(s)	took	taken
teach(es)	taught	taught
tell(s)	told	told
think(s)	thought	thought
throw(s)	threw	thrown
wear(s)	wore	worn
win(s)	won	won
write(s)	wrote	written

To see if any of the irregular verbs are a problem for you, cover the "past" and "past participle" columns and test yourself. Make up sample sentences for the present, past, and past participle forms. The sentences don't have to make a lot of sense to serve your purpose. For example:

Today I <u>write</u> a letter. Yesterday I <u>wrote</u> a letter. I <u>have written</u> two letters.

Today Mike <u>throws</u> the ball. Yesterday Mike <u>threw</u> the ball. He <u>has thrown</u> the ball all week.

Solution #2: Practise the Irregular Verbs

Put a check beside any verbs you had trouble with; then practise them again and again until the correct forms seem natural. Errors in verbs show up in both your speaking and your writing, so time spent on these problems will be time well invested.

Present-time verbs are used not only to express an action that is going on right now but also to express an action that continues from the past into the present and future. Examples:

Loretta <u>sings</u> in the choir at First Baptist Church.

A dissatisfied car buyer <u>tells</u> his troubles to an average of 22 people.

✓ SPOTCHECK 5-1

Use all three forms of the verbs in italics—present, past, and past participle (in that order). Remember that the present-time verb ends in -s if the subject is he, she, *or* it. *The past participle is always used with one of the following helping verbs:* has, have, *or* had.

> **EXAMPLE:** Six-year-old Billy likes to *draw*. He <u>draws</u> whenever he gets a chance. He <u>drew</u> a Corvette for his dad's birthday. He has <u>drawn</u> since he was two years old.

1. Baby birds quickly learn to *fly*. They _____ within days of being hatched. A baby robin _____ for the first time this morning in my yard. By October it will have _____ to a warmer location.

2. Some people *eat* more than is good for them. For example, Tom usually _____ between meals. He _____ two dough-nuts this morning during coffee break at work. By bedtime, he has usually _____ a candy bar or two.

3. It is really discouraging to *forget* what one has learned in class. I _____ the forms of irregular verbs if I don't review them frequently. In a test yesterday I _____ the past participles of *forget* and *swim*. I'm afraid I have also _____ the difference between *affect* and *effect*.

4. Jacqueline likes to *go* dancing. She _____ almost every Saturday night. Last week she _____ to a club called the Top Hat. She didn't like the band; she says she has _____ there for the last time.

5. It is easy to *hurt* oneself skiing. Curtis and Jake usually _____ themselves at least once each season. Curtis _____ his ankle at Horseshoe Valley last weekend. Jake has _____ his arm three times in two winters.

Check the Answer Key before continuing.

✓ SPOTCHECK 5-2

Underline the correct verb form in parentheses.

1. Sandra (buy/bought) a new motorcycle yesterday.

2. She had (gave/given) the purchase a good deal of thought.

3. Finally, she (threw/throwed) aside all her doubts.

4. The salesman at the cycle shop (tell/told) her she should buy a helmet, too.

5. He mentioned statistics that the Canadian Automobile Association had (brung/brought) out on motorcycle safety.

Check the Answer Key before continuing.

✓
SPOTCHECK 5-3   *Write the correct form of the verb given in parentheses.*

1. (teach) Mr. Tam has _____ at Acadia University for 15 years.
2. (sing) Louis and Besonda have _____ together on a local television program.
3. (fly) Charles Lindbergh _____ alone across the Atlantic Ocean in 1927.
4. (eat) Cathy had _____ two bags of potato chips while watching a horror movie on TV.
5. (drink) Meanwhile, Farida had _____ a six-pack of root beer.

Check the Answer Key before continuing.

✓
SPOTCHECK 5-4   *Write sentences using the verb forms in parentheses. Use helping verbs where needed.*

1. (seen) _____

_____

2. (became) _____

_____

3. (rang) _____

_____

4. (known) _____

_____

5. (driven) _____

_____

Compare your answers with those in the Answer Key.

Solution #3: Watch for
Participles Used as
Adjectives

Sometimes the past participle is used not as a verb but as an *adjective*, a word that describes a noun or pronoun. In those cases it comes after a linking verb or before a noun.

The runner was <u>exhausted</u>. (after the linking verb *was*)

The <u>stolen</u> car was recovered. (before the noun *car*)

☑

SPOTCHECK 5-5   *Underline past participles used as adjectives.*

1. Carmen looked excited when the news came.
2. A frightened rabbit hurried across the road.
3. Two grown men were swinging in the playground.
4. The speaker seemed annoyed at the interruption.
5. Donald thought the clerk was prejudiced.

Check the Answer Key before continuing.

Solution #4: Watch for
These Three Irregular Verbs

Three irregular verbs that sometimes cause trouble are *be, have,* and *do*. Be sure you are familiar with the forms of each.

Present Time (be)		*Past Time* (be)	
Singular	**Plural**	**Singular**	**Plural**
I am	we are	I was	we were
you are	you are	you were	you were
he (she, it) is	they are	he (she, it) was	they were

Present Time (have)		*Past Time* (have)	
Singular	**Plural**	**Singular**	**Plural**
I have	we have	I had	we had
you have	you have	you had	you had
he (she, it) has	they have	he (she, it) had	they had

Present Time (do)		*Past Time* (do)	
Singular	**Plural**	**Singular**	**Plural**
I do	we do	I did	we did
you do	you do	you did	you did
he (she, it) does	they do	he (she, it) did	they did

SPOTCHECK 5-6   *Underline the standard verb form in parentheses.*

1. Graduation (be/is/are) a happy occasion.

2. Yesterday Winnie (have/has/had) a surprise visit from an old high school classmate.

3. Country music (have/has) gained many new fans in recent years.

4. Kelvin usually (does/do) the 100 metres in around ten seconds.

5. Yesterday he (did/done) it in over 11 seconds.

Check the Answer Key before continuing.

Solution #5: Watch for *-s* and *-ed* Endings

The *-s* and *-ed* endings of regular verbs sometimes get dropped (or added) when they shouldn't be.

No: John <u>hope</u> to get a job at the foundry.
Yes: John <u>hoped</u> (or <u>hopes</u>) to get a job at the foundry.
No: Cindy always <u>play</u> the piano at our parties.
Yes: Cindy always <u>plays</u> the piano at our parties.
No: Today the boys <u>says</u> they will share the toys.
Yes: Today the boys <u>say</u> they will share the toys.

Following are the standard forms for a typical regular verb. If any of them don't "sound right," they are worth practising until they do.

Present Time		*Past Time*	
Singular	**Plural**	**Singular**	**Plural**
I work	we work	I worked	we worked
you work	you work	you worked	you worked
he (she, it) works	they work	he (she, it) worked	they worked

Notice that the past-time forms are all the same and that the only change in the present-time forms is the *-s* added in the singular (*"he or she works"*).

SPOTCHECK 5-7   *Underline the correct verb form in parentheses.*

1. Marlene's three-year-old daughter (know/knows) the alphabet by heart.

2. Wasn't Raymond (suppose/supposed) to paint the garage over the weekend?

3. The instructor (ask/asked) the class to write 500 words on one of the four topics.

4. Lucy (say/says) she won't be home for dinner.

5. Carlos and Cynthia (run/runs) six kilometres every day.

Check the Answer Key before continuing.

SPOTCHECK 5-8 ✓ *Edit the paragraph that follows to change all the underlined subjects and verbs from the plural to the singular, as in the first sentence.*

<u>**Sam walks**</u>   **he needs**
~~Sam and Joe walk~~ over to the library because ~~they need~~ some information to write a psychology class paper on hypnotism. <u>They ask</u> a librarian for help. <u>They are</u> told that the *Readers' Guide to Periodical Literature* lists articles from about 200 magazines. <u>They look</u> under "hypnotism" and <u>see</u> the titles of many articles on the subject. <u>They decide</u> to request the April 1982 issue of *Essence* because <u>they are</u> attracted to an article called "Hypnosis: Put Your Mind Power to Work."

Check the Answer Key before continuing.

DOUBLECHECK 5-1 ✓ *In the blanks at the left of each sentence, write the correct form of the verbs in parentheses. Use* past-time verbs *in the first five sentences. Then switch to* present-time verbs *in the last five sentences.*

_____   1. Emily Carr (be) the name of a British Columbian painter and author who is now recognized as a great Canadian painter.

_____   2. She (live) in a strict, disciplined atmosphere in Victoria in the 1890s.

_____   3. In 1891, after her parents' death, she (go) to study at the California School of Design in San Francisco.

_____   4. When she (return) two years later, she set up art classes for children in Victoria.

_____   5. The trip to England that she (take) in 1902 resulted in an illness that lasted until 1904.

Use present-time verbs *for the next five sentences.*

_____ **6.** She then (go) to France where her art develops under the influence of post-impressionism.

_____ **7.** She (begin) to paint the Indian sites she had begun to record in 1908.

_____ **8.** After several years, she (produce) a tremendous record of vanishing native villages, houses, and totem poles.

_____ **9.** She (meet) the Group of Seven on a trip to Eastern Canada that revitalizes her art.

_____ **10.** After this time, her art work (receive) the recognition it still enjoys today.

Check the Answer Key before continuing.

◆ WRITING PROCESS

PREWRITING: AUDIENCE

We have discussed prewriting methods for getting in touch with your ideas through nonstop writing, brainstorming, and questioning. The ideas in your paper are very important, of course, but another point to consider is the *audience* you are writing for.

We all have different ways of speaking, depending on whom we are speaking to. We talk differently to a child than to an older person and to a close friend than to a boss.

NOW YOU TRY IT

Imagine that you were unable to go to work today and you called in to report this. Demonstrate how your audience would influence your approach.

You (talking to a co-worker over the phone): _____

_____

_____

_____

You (talking to your boss over the phone): _____

_____

_____

_____

✓
CHECKPOINT 5-1

In the blank at the left of each sentence, write the correct form of the verb in parentheses.

_____ 1. The manufacturer says this breakfast cereal has been (shoot) from cannons.

_____ 2. You could see that Muriel had (lie) in the sun too long while at the beach.

_____ 3. Luis said the movie had already (begin) when he and Martina arrived.

_____ 4. The car (run) onto the shoulder of the road before tipping over.

_____ 5. Have all the students (bring) their books to class?

_____ 6. I wonder where all the cookies (go) that I bought yesterday.

_____ 7. Timmie said he had no idea where they had (go).

_____ 8. If Lynn had (know) that Paris was a town in Ontario, she would have had a perfect score on the test.

_____ 9. She knew it last week, but by test time she had (forget).

_____ 10. The estimated value of the average housewife's labour has (rise) to $40,000 a year.

No answers are given for Checkpoint quizzes.

6

THE EXAMPLE PARAGRAPH

◆ READING

USING EXAMPLES TO EMPHASIZE A POINT

PRECHECK

Do you believe in ghosts? Many people have a favourite ghost story, often passed down from generation to generation. For Tom Wood, a doctor in London, Ontario, people's tales were not enough to convince him that ghosts existed. To emphasize his disbelief, he gives examples of the many ghost stories he had heard, but had refused to believe until a personal experience convinced him about ghosts.

When the Talk Turns to Old Haunts

—Tom Wood

I was at a dinner party last week, and the woman sitting next to me said, "I don't believe in ghosts." 1

"I didn't used to either," I told her, "but I had to change my mind." 2

My wife is an Anglican minister, and I often have to make polite conversation with people I don't know. To get some kind of talk going I inquire about the origin of their surnames. People usually like to talk about their names (especially if they are uncommon), but sometimes this ploy doesn't work. In that case I ask whether they've ever seen a ghost. 3

I grew up hearing ghost stories—my mother's family were Irish people by the name of Shaw—but I was always sceptical about the anecdotes they told. My grandfather, for example, said that one morning when he was shaving he saw his sister Sarah behind him in the mirror, but that when he turned round to greet her she wasn't there. 4

ploy tactic in a conversation or game

Shaw, George Bernard Irish playwright, gifted speaker

sceptical doubting of others' beliefs

Then, when he went down to breakfast, the telephone rang; it was my cousin Birdie calling to say that Aunt Sarah had just died.

So at these gatherings I've attended as clergy spouse, I've heard a lot of good ghost stories, and I always had the suspicion they weren't true. Even so, some of them were so interesting that I remembered them in order to tell them later to my wife. 5

icon   an image or symbol representing a saint or item of cultural importance

For example, a Presbyterian minister's wife told me she had lived in a haunted manse. She used to keep a Russian icon on the sideboard in their dining room, leaning against the wall, and every time she came back into the room the icon would be lying on the floor under the sideboard, face down. She never actually saw a ghost, but another woman who had lived there said she used to see a tall old man with white hair walking through that room on dark winter afternoons. 6

exorcised   got rid of evil spirits by religious means

A university professor told me she'd bought a century farmhouse that she had to have exorcised. The real-estate agent said it was haunted, but the woman hadn't told her daughter, even though the ghost was supposed to appear in the daughter's room. One day, the daughter mentioned that she'd seen a tall boy in the closet, but the woman still didn't do anything, until a few days later she overheard her daughter in her room saying, "I promised you I wouldn't bother you, but when I'm trying to study, you've got to leave me alone." 7

skittish   lively, difficult to manage

The woman called in the priest to exorcise the house, and the tall boy wasn't seen again. But after that the horses in the barn were skittish, and the lights in the carriage shed flashed on and off unexpectedly for a week. 8

A church warden lived in an elegant old house near St. Mary's, Ontario, that 100 years earlier had been a country inn. For many years, at about 11 o'clock on Saturday evening before Christmas, his family used to hear horse's hooves stamping in the snow outside and sleigh bells ringing and people laughing and having a good time. The people would start shouting, "Goodbye, goodbye," "Merry Christmas" and "Happy New Year." Then the ghostly party would fade away. 9

I used to think such stories were invented, but a few years ago I began to think there was some truth in them. I changed my mind because of something that happened to my wife. 10

My father-in-law was a gentle man, and he and my wife were very close. He had two unusual habits whenever he was deeply moved: he cleared his throat repeatedly and he had to leave to urinate. 11

aneurysm   a sac in a dilated blood vessel

He died suddenly of a ruptured abdominal aneurysm, and after the funeral my wife became very depressed. We went away to Florida, and one night we conceived a baby, our last. My father-in-law had enjoyed his grandchildren, and throughout the pregnancy we often commented that we were sorry he'd never know this child. 12

The baby was born four days before Christmas; it was a little boy. Because it had been an uncomplicated delivery, and he was our fifth child, and because the holiday was so close, our doctor let my wife and the baby come home the same day. I had stopped working when my wife went into labour, and I stayed at home for a week. That year we had the happiest, closest Christmas we've ever had. At 6 o'clock on Boxing Day morning, my wife woke suddenly with the feeling that there was someone in the house. She was surprised that she didn't feel 13 afraid. She walked through the house and found no sign of anyone; then the baby began to cry. She picked him up and fed him, and had the feeling that someone was watching them all the time. When she'd finished the feeding and put the baby back in the bassinet, she heard someone clearing his throat in the hall outside, and the toilet downstairs flushed. She walked through the house again and everyone was asleep in bed.

bassinet cradle

When I woke up at 8 o'clock my wife was so happy. "Pa knows all 14 about the baby," she said. "This morning he was back."

CHECKING MEANING AND STYLE

1. What is the main idea in Paragraph 3?

2. Why did Tom Wood hear so many ghost stories when he was growing up?

3. Describe one of the examples of a ghost story that he gives.

4. Paragraph 12 is an example of description, process, narration, or cause and effect?

5. Do these examples of ghost stories have anything in common?

6. What was it that made the author's wife so content in the end? Why was she so sure that the ghost was her father?

CHECKING IDEAS

1. Why did Wood remember other people's ghost stories even though he was so sceptical?

2. What do you think made Wood believe his wife's story?

3. Do you think you need to see a ghost to believe in one?

◆ WRITING MODELS

THE EXAMPLE PARAGRAPH

In "When the Talk Turns to Old Haunts," Tom Wood gives us many interesting examples of ghost stories from the personal experience of his family and friends. These examples make an engaging introduction to his wife's experience which makes him finally change his mind about ghosts.

Here is an example paragraph based on the reading:

Model Example Paragraph #1

The topic sentence introduces the subject of ghosts.

Many people are skeptical about ghosts, but many people have a ghost story to tell. Tom Wood had heard many good ghost stories from his relatives; later, he listened to stories from guests he tried to converse with at dinner parties. For example, a Presbyterian minister's wife told him about the moving icon, and a church warden described the voices she used to hear outside at Christmas time. Finally, because of his wife's personal experience, Wood changed his mind about ghosts.

In the first paragraphs, Wood uses many examples of stories that he has heard about ghosts from others' real-life experiences. However, he could have made up ghost stories to illustrate that he did not believe in ghosts; such examples would be *hypothetical* ones, not real-life ones. Hypothetical examples are effective only if they are believable. For instance, Wood could not have used absurd, highly unbelievable examples and still proved his point about his *personal* disbelief in ghost stories.

In the following paragraph, a woman discusses parents in general by using her own parents as real-life examples:

Model Example Paragraph #2

Observe the opening topic sentence.

Even though it may sometimes be difficult, parents should give their teenage children considerable privacy. When my parents realized it was embarrassing for me to talk to boyfriends on the phone in the kitchen, they had a phone installed in my bedroom. If I was in my room with the door closed, they always knocked and asked if it was all right to come in. Of course I can't know for sure, but I'm confident they never searched my room for drugs or whatever else it is parents are often suspicious about. They respected my privacy, so I always tried to behave in a way that justified their trust.

1. How many examples about her parents does the writer give?

2. In each example, what did her parents do?

The next paragraph, which takes a different view of privacy, uses hypothetical parents or "parents in general" as examples.

Model Example Paragraph #3

Observe the opening topic sentence.

With more teenagers getting into serious drug trouble these days, parents need to keep a close watch on their children, even if it means "invading" their privacy now and then. Parents should listen in on their children's phone conversations and be sufficiently acquainted with slang to know that Johnny's remark about "snow" might not be about a ski trip. When Mom puts clean clothes in the kids' dresser drawers, she should keep an eye out for suspicious bags or surprising wads of money. Dad might call the attendance office at school now and then just to be sure that's where Susie is spending her days. Parents may not like playing the role of narcotics agents, but that may save their children from the real narcs later on.

1. What names does the writer give to the four members of this hypothetical family?

2. Why do you suppose the writer chose to use these names?

3. How many examples about these parents does the writer give?

4. In each example, what are the parents doing?

◆ WRITING ASSIGNMENT

AN EXAMPLE PARAGRAPH

When you write an example paragraph, you have a couple of decisions to make. You have just seen a demonstration of the difference between using a true example from your own life and a hypothetical example that you made up. Another choice you have to make is whether you will give one extended example or several short examples.

John had decided to write an example paragraph about the way some teachers can bring out the worst in students. He was going to base his example on his own sixth-grade teacher, Mr. Clark. John had several true examples in mind:

1. Mr. Clark would assign homework but never collect or grade it, so no one did it.

2. Mr. Clark never started class until everyone was ready, so students never got ready.

3. Mr. Clark would laugh at students' mistakes, so they never volunteered to answer questions.

John liked all of these true examples about his former teacher, but he decided that his paragraph would have more power if he just used one of these examples and fully developed it. Here is what John finally wrote:

> Some teachers bring out the worst in their students. I remember my sixth-grade teacher, Mr. Clark. Every day at the end of math class he would assign us a page of practise problems. The first night just about everyone did them, but the next day he did not collect the homework or grade it. The second time he assigned homework, fewer people bothered doing it. By the end of the week, no one was doing the math homework. Then came our first midterm test in math. Everyone had a horrible time on the test because we had never practised the problems he had demonstrated on the board each day. I still blame my poor background in math on Mr. Clark's careless attitude.

Write an Example Paragraph   *Write a unified paragraph on one of the following numbered subjects. Use either real-life or hypothetical examples to support the topic sentence.*

1. Women (Men) can be hard to understand.

2. Some teachers bring out the best (worst) in a student. (see example above)

3. Mothers who work outside the home usually have busy lives.

4. Small children can be a real joy (headache) to their parents.

5. People who use drugs are inviting trouble.

6. Parents should (should not) respect privacy. (Models #2 and #3)

Will you use several examples to write about one subject, or will you use only one example but develop it fully? Use the planning form below to make some notes about what you might include in your example paragraph.

(Topic sentence) _____

_____

_____

(First example) _____

_____

_____

(Second example) _____

_____

_____

(Third example) _____

_____

_____

Does one of these examples seem considerably more interesting than the others? Would your paragraph be better with all three examples or with just the most interesting one fully developed? Decide on the best way to organize your example paragraph.

In revising your first draft, be sure to correct any sentence fragments, run-together sentences, or faulty verb forms.

◆ SENTENCE STRUCTURE

MAKING SUBJECTS AND VERBS AGREE IN A SENTENCE

The Problem: Making Subjects and Verbs Agree in a Sentence

Subjects and verbs must agree. That means that singular (one-item) subjects need singular verbs and plural (more-than-one-item) subjects need plural verbs.

Usually we don't have problems with subject–verb agreement:

Mary <u>attends</u> college. (subject and verb both singular)

The Olson <u>boys</u> <u>attend</u> college. (subject and verb plural)

A complication to keep in mind: A plural subject usually ends in *-s* (*boys*), while a singular verb often ends in *-s* (*attends*).

Here are some other situations to consider.

Subjects joined by *and* are usually plural.

Solution #1: Subjects Joined by *And*

<u>Latanya</u> and <u>Baroum</u> <u>have</u> [not *has*] <u>announced</u> their engagement.

<u>Swimming</u> and <u>walking</u> <u>are</u> [not *is*] good exercise.

SPOTCHECK 6-1   *Underline the correct verb in parentheses.*

1. Anagrams and Scrabble (is/are) word games.

2. Mr. and Mrs. Choy always (plays/play) bridge when they get a chance.

3. Four cats and one dog (runs/run) down the street.

Check the Answer Key before continuing.

Solution #2: Subjects Joined by *Either . . . or* or *Neither . . . nor*

When subjects are joined by *either . . . or* or *neither . . . nor*, the verb agrees with the nearer subject:

Either <u>Jim</u> or his <u>parents</u> <u>are meeting</u> the plane. (The plural verb *are meeting* agrees with the nearer subject, *parents*.)

Neither the <u>Kims</u> nor their <u>daughter</u> <u>has</u> reservations. (The singular verb *has* agrees with the nearer subject, *daughter*.)

Or rewrite the sentence:

The Kims don't have reservations. Neither does their daughter.

SPOTCHECK 6-2   *Underline the correct verb in parentheses.*

1. Either Terrie or Jonathan (plans/plan) to bring the games to tonight's party.

2. Of course, neither Naomi nor Richard (expects/expect) to attend the party because of final exams coming up.

3. Neither Joey nor his parents (enjoys/enjoy) word games.

Check the Answer Key before continuing.

Solution #3: Beware of Words That Separate Subject and Verb

Words that come between the subject and verb may cause confusion. Phrases that begin with *in addition to, along with,* or *as well as* do not affect the number of the verb.

<u>Phil</u>, along with several friends, <u>is attending</u> Caribana.

The apple <u>pie</u>, in addition to two dozen cookies, <u>was eaten</u> by the squirrels.

REMEMBER: A word in a prepositional phrase is never the subject of the verb. To help pinpoint the subject, you might cross out the prepositional phrases, as in these examples:

The <u>stamps</u> ~~in the desk drawer~~ <u><u>belong</u></u> ~~to Harold~~.

Only <u>one</u> ~~of the books~~ <u><u>is</u></u> overdue.

Some of the common prepositions are *of, in, into, for, on, at, by, to, from, with, above, below, through, during, among, before,* and *after.* The noun or pronoun that comes after the preposition completes the prepositional phrase.

SPOTCHECK 6-3

Draw one line under the subject and two lines under the correct verb in parentheses. Cross out any prepositional phrases if that will help you locate the subject.

1. One of Canada's best-known writers (is/are) Margaret Atwood.

2. The cause of the computer's problems (is/are) static electricity.

3. A banana, along with whole grains, (adds/add) important nutritional value at breakfast.

4. Several workers in the front office (is/are) getting raises.

5. The woman wearing the hat and carrying the roses (thinks/think) she is a princess.

Check the Answer Key before continuing.

Solution #4: Sometimes the Subject Follows the Verb

Sometimes the subject comes after the verb instead of in front of it. Remember that the word *there* is never the subject.

          verb   **subject**

~~Inside the boxes~~ <u>was</u> a <u>collection</u> ~~of old magazines~~.

     verb   **subject**

There <u>are</u> not many <u>clues</u> ~~in the case at this time~~.

SPOTCHECK 6-4

Draw one line under the subject and two lines under the correct verb in parentheses.

1. At the edge of the trees (is/are) an old abandoned house.

2. There (is/are) also the remains of two rusty cars.

3. Across the street (is/are) the tombstones of the local cemetery.

4. There (is/are) a scary quality about the whole area.

5. Inside my stomach (is/are) some nervous feelings.

Check the Answer Key before continuing.

Solution #5: Indefinite Pronouns Are Always Singular

Words called <u>indefinite pronouns</u> are almost always singular, even though some of them seem to be plural. Here are some examples:

each   either   neither   everyone   everybody   someone

somebody   anybody   nobody   something   everything

When one of those words is the subject, the verb must of course be singular.

<u>Everybody</u> <u>has</u> [not *have*] to bring a hot dish or a salad to the party.

<u>Everything</u> the committee planned <u>is</u> [not *are*] taking place on schedule.

However, *both, few,* and *several* always take a plural verb.

<u>Both</u> of the vases <u>are</u> to be auctioned.

(compare) <u>Neither</u> of the vases <u>is</u> to be auctioned.

✅
SPOTCHECK 6-5

Draw one line under the subject and two lines under the correct verb in parentheses. You may want to cross out prepositional phrases to make the subject more obvious.

1. One of our neighbours (owns/own) a complete set of the novels of Charles Dickens.

2. Both of the family bicycles (has/have) flat tires.

3. Everyone in the cast of the school play (was/were) invited to a party.

4. Each of the pies (tastes/taste) delicious.

5. Nobody among Scott's friends (is/are) going to lend him money.

Check the Answer Key before continuing.

Solution #6: Beware of *Who, Which, That*

When *who, which,* or *that* is used as the subject of a dependent clause, its verb may be singular or plural. It is singular if the word the pronoun stands for is singular; it is plural if the word it stands for is plural.

Whistler is a resort area <u>that</u> <u>is</u> very popular. (The verb is singular because *that* stands for a word that is singular, *area*.)

Whistler is one of those resort areas <u>that</u> <u>are</u> very popular. (The verb is plural because *that* stands for a word that is plural, *areas*.)

✅
SPOTCHECK 6-6

Underline the correct verb in parentheses.

1. The vice-president of the company is a woman who (has/have) a master's degree in business administration.

2. Winnipeg has residents who (doesn't/don't) mind the winter cold.

3. Motorists who (drives/drive) Highway 401 know the meaning of boredom.

4. The leader of the expedition into the Himalayas is one of those people who (loves/love) adventure.

5. David's Camaro, which (costs/cost) him $90 a month just for insurance, will have to be sold.

Check the Answer Key before continuing.

Solution #7: Group Nouns Are Usually Singular

Group nouns look plural but are usually singular. Here are some examples of group nouns:

family   team   class   committee   audience   band

flock   herd   group   department store   gas company

They usually require singular verbs:

The Dupree family <u>has</u> a cabin on Lake Simcoe. (The family is one unit or group.)

This year's class <u>was</u> the largest in ten years. (The class is a single unit.)

But sometimes when we use group nouns we are thinking of individual members of the group acting separately. We are thinking "they" rather than "it." Then we need a plural verb.

The Dupree family <u>have</u> interesting jobs. (Individual members have separate jobs.)

This year's class <u>are</u> getting good job offers. (*Class* refers to individual members.)

✅
SPOTCHECK 6-7   *Draw one line under the correct verb in parentheses.*

1. The audience always (gives/give) a standing ovation after the orchestra plays.

2. The government class (plans/plan) a field trip to the courthouse tomorrow.

3. The Army (is/are) holding manoeuvres near the river.

Check the Answer Key before continuing.

Solution #8: Beware of Singular Nouns Ending in -s

Some nouns end in *-s* and look plural but take a singular verb: *politics, news, measles, mathematics, physics, economics,* etc.

The <u>news</u> from home <u>was</u> encouraging.

Dave said <u>physics</u> <u>is</u> his most difficult course.

✅
SPOTCHECK 6-8   *Draw one line under the correct verb in parentheses.*

1. Politics (seems/seem) like an attractive field to Harry.

2. The news about her mother (has/have) brightened Sylvia's day.

3. Mathematics (is/are) difficult for some people.

Check the Answer Key before continuing.

DOUBLECHECK 6-1   *Draw one line under the correct verb in parentheses.*

1. Everyone in the boats (knows/know) how to swim.
2. There (was/were) a beautiful rainbow after the storm.
3. Luis is one of those guys who (is/are) reliable when the going gets rough.
4. Among the crowd at the theatre (was/were) Mr. and Ms. Greenberg.
5. The average Canadian household (watches/watch) TV for about seven hours a day.
6. Neither the Mighty Ducks nor the Calgary Flames (is/are) going to win the Stanley Cup this year.
7. Centennial College, which (was/were) founded in 1967, was the first community college in Ontario.
8. The dishes in the sink (needs/need) to be washed before dinner time.
9. Where (is/are) the ribbons for wrapping these presents?
10. Everybody in the back row (has/have) to move to the front row.

Check the Answer Key before continuing.

DOUBLECHECK 6-2   *Some of the underlined verbs do not agree with their subjects. In the blanks, write the subject of the verb and the correct verb. If the verb is correct, write C.*

1. There <u>is</u> many people these days who are taking aerobic exercise classes or building muscles with weight training.

   subject _____   verb _____

2. Which of the two kinds of exercise do you think <u>has</u> more health benefits?

   subject _____   verb _____

3. The answer to that question <u>lie</u> in understanding the terms *aerobic* and *anaerobic*.

   subject _____   verb _____

4. The first of the terms <u>mean</u> "with oxygen," while *anaerobic* means "without oxygen."

   subject _____   verb _____

5. One of the sports that <u>stimulates</u> beneficial activity of the heart and lungs is aerobic.

    subject _____   verb _____

6. Activities like brisk walking, running, cycling, and swimming <u>are</u> healthfully aerobic.

    subject _____   verb _____

7. They make the body work hard and <u>increases</u> the demand for oxygen.

    subject _____   verb _____

8. Lifting weights, on the other hand, <u>is</u> anaerobic—building muscles but not strengthening the heart and lungs.

    subject _____   verb _____

9. Either walking or swimming <u>produce</u> good aerobic results without the risk of injury that is a drawback in running.

    subject _____   verb _____

10. Aerobic exercise, <u>says</u> medical experts, can increase endurance, lower blood pressure, and reduce stress.

    subject _____   verb _____

Check the Answer Key before continuing.

Quickcheck on Subject–Verb Agreement

✓ Singular subjects take singular verbs; plural subjects take plural verbs.

✓ Subjects joined by *and* are plural.

✓ When two subjects are joined by *either . . . or* or *neither . . . nor,* the verb agrees with the nearer subject.

✓ Don't mistake the object of a preposition for the subject of the verb.

✓ The subject usually comes before the verb, but sometimes it comes after.

✓ *There* is never the subject of the sentence.

✓ Indefinite pronouns such as *each, either,* and *everybody* are always singular.

✓ When used as subjects, *who, which,* and *that* agree with the words they stand for.

✓ Group nouns such as *committee, audience,* and *team* are usually singular.

◆ WRITING PROCESS

WRITING

Doing some prewriting—nonstop writing, brainstorming, or asking "How?" and "Why?"—will make it easier for you to write the first draft of your paper. Having identified your audience will make your writing more effective. If you are writing the assignment outside of class, here are some more steps that can contribute to a good result.

• Before starting on your first draft, you might find it helpful to lay your notes aside for a while and just think about the ideas you discovered during prewriting, maybe while taking a walk. Or perhaps you could talk over the ideas with a friend or family member or enter them into a tape recorder. Your ideas will start to come into focus and organize themselves during this "simmering" period.

• When you are ready to write the first draft, go to a quiet place where you can concentrate. Do not let the blank piece of paper (or computer screen) scare you. You have already given this project a lot of thought. You *are* ready to write.

• Remember that whatever you write, it is just the first draft. You can always change it.

• In this first draft, you are the creator. Later you can become the editor, making your original words better.

CHECKPOINT 6-1

In the blanks at the left, write the subject and the correct verb form for each sentence.

(s) _____ **1.** The provincial parks in summer (is/are) crowded with campers.

(v) _____

(s) _____ **2.** Of all her courses, biology and chemistry (is/are) Rosanne's favorites.

(v) _____

(s) _____ **3.** There (is/are) no trees in Iceland.

(v) _____

(s) _____ **4.** The election committee (is/are) going to meet Tuesday evening.

(v) _____

(s) _____ **5.** The neighbours have one of those dogs that (barks/bark) night and day.

(v) _____

(s) _____ **6.** Flitting about among the many blossoms in the garden (was/were) two hummingbirds.

(v) _____

(s) _____ **7.** Either Mr. Jong or Ms. Daniels (is/are) driving the scouts to the museum.

(v) _____

(s) _____ **8.** Neither of the parents (was/were) eager to make the trip.

(v) _____

(s) _____ **9.** The waterfalls in Niagara (is/are) usually at their best in the springtime.

(v) _____

(s) _____ **10.** Neither the players nor the coach (is/are) ready for the National tournament.

(v) _____

(s) _____ **11.** There (is/are) many advantages in knowing how to speak standard English.

(v) _____

(s) _____ **12.** The audience (was/were) less rowdy than the theatre manager had expected.

(v) _____

No answers are given for Checkpoint quizzes.

THE DEFINITION
PARAGRAPH

◆ READING

DEFINITIONS OF WORDS

Many essays are written to clarify and explain definitions of words or phrases in current use—"Generation X" or "the information highway," for example.

In this essay, columnist Michele Landsberg defines "the beauty myth" that writer Naomi Wolf claims preserves male dominance.

Beauty Myth Preserves Male Dominance

—*Michele Landsberg*

Ever wonder why you can't convince your teenage daughter that 1
she's perfectly lovely as she is? That her thighs aren't too fat, her bottom too big, her breasts too small, her hair too flat, her nose too pointed?

"Aaw Mum, you just say that because you're my mum." 2

According to Naomi Wolf's strongly argued book, *The Beauty Myth,* 3
just published by Random House, that teenager is in the grip of a North American obsession. The beauty myth, spread through our culture by millions of images of ideal feminine beauty, is a belief system designed "to keep male dominance intact."

"Our families can't inoculate us," Wolf told me in an interview. 4
"There's a disease in the air."

The disease is women's physical self-loathing. "We are in the midst 5
of a violent backlash to feminism that uses images of female beauty as a political weapon against women's advancement," she writes.

dominance   control of power

self-loathing   strong dislike of oneself

105

obsession persistent idea that won't go away

gender roles function of males, females in society

adamant firm, insistent

mutilation injury, wound

It's no wonder that young women are not carrying on the feminist 6 fight; they're "weakened and paralyzed by their obsession with appearance and half of them are living on the same semi-starvation caloric intakes as prisoners in World War II Japanese prison camps."

"The beauty myth isn't a conscious conspiracy," said Wolf. "It doesn't have to be. Societies invent necessary fictions, and both men and women in our society are stunned and panicky about the rapidity of change in gender roles. An obsession with beauty keeps women divided and distracted." 7

When Wolf read from her book at the Women's Book Store in 8 Toronto last week, an overflow crowd stayed to talk excitedly for four hours. "It was like a consciousness-raising session," she laughed.

She may have hit a nerve. Her argument is all the more persuasive since she herself is 27 years old, brilliant, slender, blue-eyed and beautiful. A Yale graduate and a Rhodes scholar, the San Francisco-born Wolf is adamant that "it's a lie that there are winners in the beauty game. Beautiful women may be heaped with rewards they didn't earn, but they are divided from other women, who are trained to hate and envy them, and can never be sure they are valued or loved for themselves." 9

The beauty myth is big business. The diet industry rakes in $32 10 billion a year; cosmetics, $20 billion; cosmetic surgery, the fastest growing medical specialty, is already worth $300 million annually, according to her book.

Wolf's book has caused a firestorm of controversy in Britain (it 11 won't be published in the United States till next spring) where it has leaped on to the bestseller lists. Reviewers have compared her work to Germaine Greer's or Kate Millett's.

What's certain is that she draws together the current evidence in a 12 powerful way. Even skeptical readers will find it hard to wave aside her blood-curdling chapter on the violence of the beauty business. Stomach-stapling, jaw-wiring, intestinal bypasses, liposuction, chemical skin peeling, facelifts, breast alterations—how different are these painful tortures, really, from Chinese foot-binding and the genital mutilation practised on millions of African women?

All are painful, dangerous and done in the near-religious belief 13 that they will enhance the woman's sexual value. "Breast surgery very often leads to loss of all sensation in the nipples, yet the ecstatic women report that they are more sexually fulfilled. Amazing, isn't it? We are trained to identify with the male erotic response to the female body."

The most menacing of Wolf's findings are those relating to work. 14 All through the '70s, as women surged back into the labor force, U.S. and British courts were piling up judicial decisions that a woman's beauty was a "bona fide qualification" for many kinds of work, from television anchor to senior manager. The Catch 22: sex harassment cases are frequently thrown out because the woman's beauty "caused" the harassment.

Wolf's book left me newly appalled by the deadening anxieties imposed on today's young women. They ought to be the most free, vibrant 15 and hopeful young women ever. Instead, 60 per cent of U.S. female students suffer from eating disorders.

I won't soon forget Wolf's vision of those privileged young women, 16 dulled and apathetic, moving like death camp zombies across the grassy quadrangle—followers of the cult of hunger in the midst of intellectual and material plenty.

trajectory path of a moving item

Besides, Wolf points out, the rigid scale on which women's worth is 17 judged reverses the usual trajectory of success: once her youthful beauty fades, the woman's worth declines as the man's stature, income and security rise.

Wolf argues that there's nothing natural about our artificial norms 18 of female beauty—or about our reversal of the natural order, in which male animals compete with their beauty to attract the fertile female. In any case, "beauty" is a standard that changes with the times.

anorexic unable to eat for fear of becoming fat

"My age group is the first to grow up as the anorexic–pornographic 19 generation. The images of soft porn are everywhere in advertising; they inescapably define the ideal woman for us."

CHECKING MEANING AND STYLE

1. What occasion was this article written for?

2. For whom do you think Michele Landsberg is writing?

3. How is "the beauty myth" defined in this article? Where does it come from?

4. Why is the word "myth" used?

5. What is the result of this "beauty myth," according to Naomi Wolf?

CHECKING IDEAS

1. Do you agree that there is a "beauty myth"?

2. What does Wolf mean by "[it] isn't a conscious conspiracy"?

3. Look at the list of practices in the beauty business. Many people might add piercing and tattooing. What do you think of the efforts people go to to change their looks?

4. Do you agree with Wolf that there is a difference in attitudes about men and women as they get older?

5. Is this "beauty myth" purely a female problem, or do you think men have something similar to contend with?

◆ WRITING MODELS

THE DEFINITION PARAGRAPH

Not everybody would understand what was meant by "the beauty myth" if it weren't defined clearly. In "Beauty Myth Preserves Male Dominance," Michele Landsberg helps make Naomi Wolf's definition clear to everyone. Here is a definition paragraph based on the selection.

Model Definition Paragraph #1

The opening sentence states what is being defined.

The words "beauty myth" define an obsession that is gripping teenagers in North America. It is spread through our culture by millions of images of ideal feminine beauty and is designed "to keep male dominance intact." It isn't a conscious conspiracy, says Naomi Wolf; it is a fiction invented by society that keeps women divided and distracted. The beauty myth reverses the natural order of the animal species where the males usually compete with their beauty in order to attract the females. In our society, the beauty myth makes females go to all sorts of lengths—from dieting to surgery—in order to attract males. Instead of letting women be free and vibrant, the beauty myth keeps women dull and apathetic.

In the following paragraph, the writer defines the term *bad habit* by giving specific details about how a bad habit changed his life.

Model Definition Paragraph #2

Observe how the paragraph begins with a topic sentence.

Smoking was a bad habit that threatened my health, irritated others, cost too much, and weakened my marriage. Every pack carried a warning that smoking was damaging to my health. At work and in restaurants, people complained if I lit up, making me feel like a criminal. My wife, who doesn't smoke, pointed out that we could go out to dinner once in a while with the money saved if I didn't smoke. She also complained that my foul-smelling clothes and breath didn't exactly excite her. Quitting wasn't easy after ten years at two packs a day, but I'm glad I finally did it.

1. What term is the author defining?
2. What activity is the writer focusing on to define *bad habit?*
3. Name four specific details that made the habit bad.

The next paragraph demonstrates how a person can be used as an example to demonstrate specific details about a word the writer wants to define.

Model Definition Paragraph #3

Observe how the paragraph begins with a topic sentence.

My friend Anthony practically defines the word "ambition." He wants to be a lawyer. He takes a full course load at a community college, attending classes from 8 a.m. to noon five days a week. He works 40 hours a week for a janitorial service, cleaning office buildings at night. On weekends, he catches up on his sleep and his school homework—when he isn't doing yard work for others. Tony says he can become a lawyer in six or seven years and cash in with a high-paying job with a big law firm—if he lives that long.

1. What word is being defined?

2. What example does the writer use to define *ambition?*

3. What three specific details show how ambitious Anthony is?

◆ Writing Assignment

A Definition Paragraph

The dictionary definition of a word is called its <u>denotation</u>. The emotional meanings that attach themselves to a word are its <u>connotations</u>. The following words all denote *policeman*. Do they have favourable or unfavourable connotations? Are some neutral—neither favourable nor unfavourable?

   officer   peace officer   cop   pig

Good (or bad) examples of the use of connotations often appear in political language. For example, troops trying to overthrow a foreign government are called "freedom fighters" if we want them to win; otherwise, they are "rebels" or "terrorists." Advertising also provides many examples of language used to sway our emotions. Consider the cigarette brand Marlboro. This English name was originally meant to suggest elegance and sophistication. Because of advertising, what are its connotations today? What are the connotations of these perfumes: Obsession, Passion, Scoundrel? Or Kool cigarettes?

We need to be alert to the connotative value of words for two reasons. One is to make our own writing clear, precise, and, yes, persuasive. Another is to detect efforts by others to influence our opinions through emotional language or "loaded" words.

SPOTCHECK 7-1 *In the following comparisons, describe yourself by using words with favourable connotations and describe the other person with words that have similar denotations but negative connotations.*

   EXAMPLE: I am hard-working. You are <u>a workaholic</u>.

1. I am slender. You are _____.

2. I am lively. You are _____.

3. I am punctual. You are _____.

4. I am _____. You are old.

5. I am _____. You are childish.

6. I am _____. You are lucky.

7. My clothes are colourful. Yours are _____.

8. I am firm in my beliefs. You are _____.

Compare your answers with those in the Answer Key.

✓

SPOTCHECK 7-2

After each sentence are several words with similar denotations but different connotations. Fill in each blank with the word that is most appropriate.

1. Claudette says she will never forget the love of her _____.
   female parent   old lady   mother   mommy

2. The Patels have built a charming _____ at the lake.
   cottage   shanty   shack

3. Mr. Turco criticizes his son-in-law as a mere _____.
   lawyer   attorney   ambulance chaser

4. Grandmother boasted that little Sammy got good grades because
   he was so _____.
   bookish   studious   nerdish

5. The driver said in court that he had been only a little tipsy, but
   the police officer testified that he had been _____.
   pickled   boiled   stewed   intoxicated

Check the Answer Key before continuing.

WRITE A DEFINITION
PARAGRAPH

Write a paragraph in which you define one of the following terms. Do not try to imitate a dictionary definition. Instead, you may want to use examples to make the meaning clear. Or you might tell a story (narrative) that illustrates the word's meaning. For that, you could start with a topic sentence along the lines of "I learned the meaning of fear the night our house caught fire" or "My Aunt Brenda is a good example of a person with common sense."

common sense | friendship
forgiveness | a good neighbour
ambition (Model #3) | a bad habit (Model #2)
macho | "cool"

Start with a topic sentence that includes the term you plan to define and that identifies the specific person or event that will be used to define the term:

_____

_____

_____

After you write your first draft of the definition paragraph, revise the paragraph; give special attention to fragments, run-together sentences, verb forms, and subject–verb agreement.

◆ SENTENCE STRUCTURE

SELECTING THE RIGHT PRONOUN

The Problem: How to Select the Right Pronoun

Pronouns are words used to take the place of nouns. If we did not have pronouns, our writing might read something like this:

> The man asked the woman if the woman knew what time it was. The woman told the man the time was ten o'clock. The man thanked the woman.

With pronouns, we can avoid the annoying repetition of nouns:

> The man asked the woman if *she* knew what time it was. *She* told *him* that *it* was ten o'clock. *He* thanked *her*.

The pronouns *she, her, he, him,* and *it* take the place of the nouns *woman, man,* and *time* to make the writing smoother.

Solution #1: Knowing the Subject and Object Forms of Pronouns

Most pronouns change their form, or *case*, depending on whether they are used as the subject or the object of a sentence. In the example just given, we noticed that *she* and *her* both refer to *woman*.

Here are the subject and object forms of the personal pronouns, both singular and plural:

Singular		Plural	
Subject	Object	Subject	Object
I	me	we	us
you	you	you	you
he	him	they	them
she	her	they	them
it	it	they	them

SPOTCHECK 7-3

Enter the appropriate pronoun forms in the blanks.

Subject	Object		Subject	Object
1. he	_____	5.	I	_____
2. _____	them	6.	_____	us
3. it	_____	7.	you	_____
4. _____	her	8.	_____	him

Check the Answer Key before continuing.

Solution #2: Knowing About Subject, Direct Object, Indirect Object, and Object of a Preposition Forms of Pronouns

Use the <u>subject form</u> when the pronoun is the subject of the sentence.

<u>I</u> will deliver the message.
<u>They</u> travelled in Europe.

Notice that subject form pronouns usually come *before* the verb. Use the <u>object form</u> in these situations:

1. When the pronoun is acted upon by the verb (is the <u>direct object</u>).

   verb object
   The boss praised *her*.

   verb object
   The biology test confused *me*.

2. When the pronoun is the <u>indirect object</u> of the verb. (To find an indirect object, ask *for whom* or *to whom* something is done.)

   The doctor gave *us* blood tests.

   To whom were the tests given? To *us*. *Us* is the indirect object of the verb *gave*. (*Tests* is the direct object.)

   Martin has done *me* many favours.

For whom were the favours done? For *me. Me* is the indirect object of the verb *has done.* (*Favours* is the direct object.)

Notice that direct object pronouns and indirect object pronouns usually come after the verb.

3. When the pronoun follows (is the object of) a preposition.

The letter was addressed <u>to</u> *her.*

The ball rolled <u>between</u> *us.*

SPOTCHECK 7-4 *Indicate whether the underlined pronoun is the subject (S), direct object (DO), indirect object (IO), or object of a preposition (OP).*

_____ **1.** The store sent <u>her</u> a refund for the returned blouse.

_____ **2.** <u>They</u> ate their lunch in the park.

_____ **3.** When will you mail <u>them</u> the cheque?

_____ **4.** The farmer walked with <u>us</u> to the gate.

_____ **5.** Whoever hears <u>him</u> in a concert is lucky.

_____ **6.** On our way to work, <u>we</u> stopped at Harvey's.

_____ **7.** The clerk gave <u>us</u> a big smile.

_____ **8.** The spotlight struck <u>her</u> in the eyes.

Check the Answer Key before continuing.

SPOTCHECK 7-5 *Substitute a pronoun for the underlined words. Say whether the pronoun is the subject, direct object, indirect object, or object of a preposition. Write your answers in the blanks.*

      EXAMPLE: The government sent <u>Mr. Nelson</u> a big income tax refund.

         <u> him </u>   <u> indirect object </u>

1. <u>The Nelsons</u> built a swimming pool in their backyard.

    <u>   </u>   <u>   </u>

2. Workers finished <u>the pool</u> in four weeks.

    <u>   </u>   <u>   </u>

3. The crew boss gave <u>Mr. Nelson</u> a pair of fins.

_____   _____

4. Mr. Nelson gave the fins to <u>his son</u>.

_____   _____

5. The son uses <u>the fins</u> amost every day.

_____   _____

Check the Answer Key before continuing.

Solution #3: Knowing About Pronouns in Compound Subjects and Objects

Usually we don't have much trouble using the correct pronoun form. For example, we're not likely to say or write, "*Me* saw *she* at the movies."

But there are a few times when pronoun errors are likely to appear. One of them is when there is more than one subject or object. Which pronoun is correct in the following sentences?

1. Between you and (I/me), Jason should have got the job.

The object form *me* is needed as the object of the preposition *between.*

2. The family sent Mark and (he/him) thank-you letters.

Him is the indirect object of the verb *sent.*

3. The Zhangs and (we/us) deserve credit for the job.

We is part of the subject, along with *The Zhangs.*

4. The audience applauded the violinist and (she/her).

Her is the object of the verb *applauded,* along with *violinist.*

Tip for Pronoun in Compound Subject

If you had trouble with any of those, here is a tip that should clear up your problem: When the pronoun is accompanied by another word in a compound subject or object, *cross out the other word.* Your ear will then probably tell you the correct form.

The audience applauded ~~the violinist and~~ (she/her).

Of course, the audience applauded *her.* In the same way, your ear would tell you that the family sent *him* a letter (Sentence 2).

NOTE: It is considered a courtesy to refer to the other person first in such uses as "Mildred and I went . . ." or ". . . sent to my husband and me."

SPOTCHECK 7-6

Underline the correct pronoun after crossing out any accompanying words that might cause confusion.

EXAMPLE: The package was addressed to ~~Anthony and~~ (I/<u>me</u>).

1. Sam and (I/me) don't have dates for tomorrow night's dance.

2. The teacher gave Dwight and (he/him) a scolding for arriving late.

3. (We/Us) NDPers have to stick together.

4. The stampeding elephants frightened (we/us) tourists.

5. The dishwashing duties are shared by my wife and (I/me).

6. The police officer gave the other hikers and (we/us) tickets for jay-walking.

7. The LaFlairs and (she/her) will vacation together.

8. The convention featured a debate between the senator and (he/him).
(Note that the crossout method doesn't work with the preposition *between*.)

Check the Answer Key before continuing.

Solution #4: Knowing About Pronouns in Comparisons

Problems in choosing the right pronoun can also appear in comparisons. Which pronoun is right in the following comparison?

Alfredo studies harder than (I/me).

At least in somewhat formal writing, *I* would be preferred. Why? Because *I* is the subject of the implied verb *study*. Look at the following comparisons in which the verb is implied but not stated:

We go to the movies more often than *they* [do *or* go].
Calvin is not as interested in jazz as *I* [am].

Comparison sentences usually contain the word *than* or *as*.

SPOTCHECK 7-7   *Underline the formally correct pronouns.*

1. Margaret earns more money than (I/me).

2. Richard doesn't waste as much time as (I/me).

3. They go shopping more than (we/us) [do].

4. Michele is not as interested in football as (he/him) [is].

Check the Answer Key before continuing.

Solution #5: Knowing About Who and Whom

Many people feel a little uncomfortable when they have to choose between the pronouns *who* and *whom*. Keep in mind that *who* is the subject form and *whom* is the object form.

Mr. Lee saw the thief *who* had robbed his market the night before. (*Who* is the subject of the verb *had robbed*.)

It was Irene *whom* the class elected. (*Whom* is the object of the verb *elected*.)

To *whom* was the package addressed? (*Whom* is the object of the preposition *to*.)

Whom is not much used in conversation or in informal writing. It seems too fancy or pretentious. For instance, many people would prefer to say "Who was the package addressed to?"—avoiding the formally correct *whom.* You will have to decide when the formal approach is better. If in doubt, use *who,* but remember *whom* can never be the subject of a verb.

SPOTCHECK 7-8   *Underline the formally correct pronouns.*

1. (Who/Whom) did you see at the mall?
2. Chantelle is the friend (who/whom) is always ready to help out.
3. John saw the child (who/whom) was missing.
4. To (who/whom) should I address this letter?

Check the Answer Key before continuing.

Solution #6: Knowing About -self Pronouns

Careful writers do not use *-self* pronouns such as *myself* and *themselves* in place of regular pronouns (*me, them,* etc.).

The Premier awarded medals to Sergeant Foster and *me* [not *myself*].
Nancy and *you* [not *yourself*] will arrange the centrepiece.

The *-self* words have two uses: to provide emphasis and to reflect an action back to its performer.

The Premier *himself* presented the medals to us. (emphasis)
Nancy stuck *herself* with a pin while arranging the flowers. (reflects action back to performer)

NOTE: Avoid using *hisself* for the standard *himself.* Also avoid using *ourself* for *ourselves.* Use *themselves* rather than *themself* or *theirselves.*

SPOTCHECK 7-9   *Underline the formally correct pronouns.*

1. Frank addressed the letter to (himself/hisself).
2. The first prize was shared by Sharon and (me/myself).
3. They can do the job (themselves/theirselves).
4. Paul and (you/yourself) are invited.

Check the Answer Key before continuing.

DOUBLECHECK 7-1   *Underline the correct pronouns.*

1. (We/Us) club members will provide transportation.
2. Just between you and (I/me), the boss is incompetent.
3. Antoine weighs less than (I/me) since going on a diet.

4. It was William Lyon Mackenzie King (who/whom) said, "Not necessarily conscription, but conscription if necessary."

5. Ahmed wrote the poem for (hisself/himself), not for Judith.

6. The Halls are the couple (who/whom) we met on vacation.

7. The sophomores will have to decorate the gym (theirselves/themselves).

8. My wife and (I/myself) attended the awards dinner.

9. An argument broke out between Mr. Eng and (she/her) over the mayor's policies.

10. Sell the car to the person (who/whom) offers the most cash.

11. I hope that you and (they/them) can resolve your problems.

12. The choir director sent the altos and (we/us) our parts for Tuesday's rehearsal.

13. Either the Swedes or (we/us) Canadians will host the next Olympics.

14. Ms. Galvez is the person (who/whom) I believe will run for MPP.

15. (I and the auditor/The auditor and I) will inspect the firm's books.

16. (We/Us) young drivers have to pay high car insurance premiums.

17. Although those of (we/us) drivers between 16 and 24 make up only 20 percent of licensed drivers, we are involved in 42 percent of alcohol-related traffic deaths.

18. Experts say that traffic accidents are the biggest killer for people (who/whom) are between the ages of 15 and 19.

Check the Answer Key before continuing.

DOUBLECHECK 7-2   *Write sentences using the words in parentheses.*

1. (herself) _____

_____

2. (whom) _____

_____

3. (me) _____

_____

4. (themselves) _____

_____

5. (who) _____

_____

6. (Patrick and she) _____

_____

7. (Kimberly and me) _____

_____

Compare your answers with those in the Answer Key.

◆ WRITING PROCESS

REVISING: ELIMINATING WORDINESS

Revision literally means to "re-envision," to "see again." If time permits, revise your writing only after you have laid your first draft aside for a while and given yourself a break from the writing process. By putting your work on the "back burner," you can return to it later with a fresh viewpoint, ready to see your work again and improve it.

There are several approaches to polishing a paper. One is to make sure that every word counts—that is, to eliminate wordiness.

Following are some tips for making your writing more concise.

1. Do not pad your writing with unnecessary words.

   (wordy) Due to the fact that her essay had been written with a pencil, Kayla was asked to write it once more, this time with a pen.

   (concise) Kayla was asked to rewrite her essay using a pen instead of a pencil.

2. Notice how one word can take the place of several.

   due to the fact that (because)

   during the time that (while)

   at the present time (now)

   in the near future (soon)

   hold a meeting (meet)

3. Get rid of unneeded words.

   After ~~the~~ class ended, we went to the cafeteria.

   The package was square ~~in shape~~.

Rich got home at 3 a.m. ~~in the morning~~.

4. Do not waste space with such expressions as "it seems to me" and "in my opinion."

~~In my humble opinion~~, (T)he mayor should be thrown out of office.

5. Sentences that begin *It is, It was, There is,* or *There are* are often wordy.

(wordy) There is a need for more widgets in Department B.
(concise) Department B needs more widgets.
(wordy) It is clear that Canada has great country music.
(concise) Canada has great country music.

SPOTCHECK 7-10   *Revise the following sentences to eliminate wordiness.*

1. On account of being talented and a good musician, Sheila was chosen to play in the concert.

_____

_____

2. Agnes' dress was bright blue in colour.

_____

_____

3. Late in the month of June, heavy rain fell on the city and made everything wet.

_____

_____

4. Because of the fact that he is a pacifist, Eric opposes war.

_____

_____

5. As far as tomorrow night's game is concerned, it seems to me our team should win.

_____

_____

6. There are many occasions when we need good advice.

_____

_____

Compare your answers with those in the Answer Key.

CHECKPOINT 7-1

Write the formally correct pronouns in the spaces at the left.

_____ 1. Except for you and (I/me/myself), no one seems to know what is going on.

_____ 2. Alex is the kind of person (who/whom) is friendly with everyone.

_____ 3. To (who/whom) should the telegram be delivered?

_____ 4. Henri is more industrious than (he/him).

_____ 5. The coach should have stopped the fight (himself/hisself).

_____ 6. He is the man (who/whom) we saw on the train.

_____ 7. Many people enjoyed the skit put on by Pat and (I/me/myself).

_____ 8. The roses were meant for Mrs. Holloway and (you/yourself).

_____ 9. I will never be able to play the piano as well as (he/him).

_____ 10. There was great friendship between Suresh and (we/us).

_____ 11. Bruce was excited when the company president sent (he/him) an answer to his letter.

_____ 12. Is Shania Twain the singer (who/whom) we heard last season?

_____ 13. On Tom's team, it's every man for (himself/hisself/theirselves).

_____ **14.** Ruth can run a kilometre a lot faster than (I/me).

_____ **15.** The palm reader said that Harry and (I/me) will be millionaires before we're 30.

No answers are given for Checkpoint quizzes.

8

THE COMPARISON PARAGRAPH

◆ READING

PARAGRAPHS COMPARING SIMILARITIES (AND CONTRASTING DIFFERENCES)

PRECHECK

When did you last watch women playing competitive sports on TV? Laura Robinson, a former member of Canada's national cycling team, writes that today there is far less coverage of women in sports than men; yet, she argues, when compared to men's way of playing, women's use of skill deserves more attention.

Feminine Finesse Versus Brute Force

—Laura Robinson

More and more women are becoming decision makers, and sometimes women make decisions that men don't like. 1

For example, to the dismay of football fans and sports writers, Gloria Bishop, head of programming for CBC Radio, has decided not to broadcast the Vanier Cup this year. 2

Critics of the move have argued that the university championship game, to be played Saturday at Toronto's SkyDome, is a Canadian tradition. Perhaps so, but it is a male tradition. Women have an equally rich sporting history, but society—including the media—makes no equivalent effort to honor women athletes. 3

equivalent equal

Traditions are kept alive by those best served by the myths that surround them. So, it is a mystery to most women why men get so excited when other men smash into one another, forming a pile of bodies with an oddly shaped ball at the bottom. Then they disentangle them- 4

Freud   founder of
psychoanalysis

hybrid   mixture

perpetuate   continue

toehold   starting position

selves, get up, pat each other on the bottom and proceed to do it all over again. If only Freud could have watched football.

But Freud would have had to travel to North America to see a 5
game. The rest of the world cares little for our hybrid of soccer and rugby. Football serves the frontier myth of men tackling their rivals head on, claiming territory a yard at a time. It was a male myth, and the women of yesterday who stood by the sides of their men are today's cheerleaders, who bob up and down and scream support for stadium heroes.

The Vanier Cup, first awarded in 1964, helps to perpetuate this 6
myth, but there are many women's sports with a similarly lengthy tradition that receive no media fanfare. Why doesn't women's sport captivate male sport writers and fans? It used to.

Does the idea of women squaring off against one another for the 7
sisterly sake of the game somehow lessen male sport? Women's sport is full of strong, talented athletes. They weren't defending territory, but rather challenging the tradition that gave them only a domestic toehold.

This remains true today. Canadians dominate international 8
women's hockey, and Dave McMaster, who coaches the University of Toronto Lady Blues and the national squad, defends both teams' style of play—skill over brute force.

"We play a thinking woman's game of hockey. The opponents know 9
we're there to get the puck. We are there psychologically and physically. We don't have to tell them by hitting them."

The tradition of excellence in women's sport runs deep. There has 10
been a women's tennis cup at University of Toronto since 1903, and communities across the country supported many other sports for women in highly organized and competitive leagues from the early 1900s to the 1950s.

In 1930, the Sunnyside Ladies Football League played "under the 11
floodlights" in Toronto for the Daily Star Trophy, and people lined up by the hundreds on the surrounding streets to see the games. Four years later, sports writer Alexandrine Gibb, whose column was entitled "No Man's Land of Sport," wrote that "there is still no softball or baseball league in women's or men's divisions which amassed gate receipts to equal Sunnyside."

Also in the thirties, Canadian women's hockey teams toured the 12
United States and played to packed arenas. The legendary Edmonton Grads basketball team played 522 games between 1915 and 1940, winning 502 of them. They also won the Underwood Challenge Trophy in international basketball 17 years in a row. At the time, women's basketball was just an exhibition sport at the Olympics, but the Grads won every game they played there.

Since the Second World War, media coverage of women's sport has 13
declined. The CBC could use the newly freed air time to try to make up for the past 40 years and cover the sport heroines who have been ignored.

Half the CBC is "owned" by women taxpayers, so giving equal air 14
time to women athletes would be most sporting. Newspapers and private TV stations might want to examine this option as well.

CHECKING MEANING AND STYLE

1. How does Laura Robinson introduce her topic?

2. What is her opinion of men's football?

3. What is the myth that the Vanier Cup helps to perpetuate?

4. What do women bring to sports?

5. What does Robinson mean by her reference to "newly freed air time"? What is the significance of "newly"?

CHECKING IDEAS

1. What is the main purpose of Robinson's comparison of men and women's sports?

2. Do you watch women's team sports?

3. Do you think there is a difference in how men and women play sports?

4. Would you agree that more air time needs to be given to women's sports?

5. What is the main point of Robinson's comparison between men and women in sports?

◆ WRITING MODELS

THE COMPARISON PARAGRAPH

There are two basic ways of organizing a comparison of two items. One is the block method. In this approach, all the details about one of the items are presented, followed by all the details about the second item. The point-by-point method goes back and forth between the two items, discussing one point of similarity at a time.

This will be clearer if we take Laura Robinson's topic and outline how we might write about men and women in sports using first the point-by-point method and then the block method.

Point-by-Point Method

Point 1: Difference in reaction to men's football
- Men get excited when other men smash into each other
- Women find it hard to understand why men get so excited by football

Point 2: Men and women's sports have equally long histories
- Vanier Cup has been receiving media attention since 1964
- Long-standing women's competitions do not get same attention

Point 3: Difference in styles of play
- Men use brute force
- Women use skill

Block Method

Block A: Men

    1. Reaction to men's football

    2. Long history of their sports

    3. Style of play

Block B: Women

    1. Reaction to men's football

    2. Long history of their sports

    3. Style of play

Which method should you use, point-by-point or block? Use the method that helps you present your ideas and information in the clearest, most interesting way. It is up to you.

Here is how "A Much More Thinking Game" might have been written in a single paragraph, using first the point-by-point method and then the block method.

Model Comparison Paragraph #1

There is far more media coverage of men's sports than of women's. Women cannot understand why men get excited when they watch other men smash into each other when they play football. Although the Vanier Cup has been receiving attention since 1964, many long-standing women's sports do not get the same attention. Where men use brute force in games like football, women use skill. There should be equal air time for these women's sports.

Model Comparison Paragraph #2

There is far more media coverage of men's sports than of women's. Men get excited when they watch other men smash into each other when they play football. The Vanier Cup has been receiving media coverage since 1964. Men use brute force to win these games. Women, on the other hand, cannot understand why men get so excited by men's football. They, too, have long-standing traditions in sport. They get less media attention, even though they use skill to win their games. There should be equal air time for these women's sports.

Study the paragraph below and determine whether it is organized by the point-by-point method or the block method.

Model Comparison Paragraph #3

One would never guess by looking at us that Carla and I are sisters. Carla is tall and slender: five-feet-seven and 120 pounds. I am five-two and 130 pounds. Carla has blonde hair, which she cuts and perms in the latest style. My hair is dark and straight and reaches to the middle of my back; if I want to be fancy, I make braids or add a ribbon. Carla has blue eyes and fair skin, while my eyes are brown and my skin has a perpetual tan. To complete the differences, Carla likes to wear tailored suits during the day and slinky dresses when she goes out evenings. I'm content to wear jeans on most occasions, but I will put on my best sandals and peasant skirt to attend a friend's wedding. Yes, we are sisters. Carla takes after our mother, while I am more like our dad—Carl.

1. Is this paragraph organized using the point-by-point method or the block method?

2. Name five areas in which the writer compares Carla and herself.

3. Using the block method, outline the information given about Carla and the writer.

◆ WRITING ASSIGNMENT

A COMPARISON PARAGRAPH

In everyday life, you continually make comparisons: between your car and your friend's car, between high school and college, between Rosa's new hairdo and her old one, between Brand X toothpaste and Brand Y, between becoming a beach bum and becoming a nuclear physicist.

In college, exams and term papers often ask that you "compare and contrast" two poems, two characters in a play, two economic policies. (*Comparison* emphasizes the ways in which things are similar; *contrast* emphasizes differences. However, *comparison* can cover both similarities and differences.)

WRITE A COMPARISON
PARAGRAPH

Write one paragraph of comparison using the point-by-point method or one paragraph using the block method. Write on one of these topics.

1. Two movie stars or two musicians

2. College classes and high school classes

3. You and a family member (Model #3)

4. Two houses or neighbourhoods you have lived in

5. Two styles of dress

Some recommendations:

• Start with a topic sentence that makes clear the point of your comparison. Examples:

Life became more exciting when I moved from the farm to the city.

The differences in styles of dress are obvious at punk rock and heavy metal concerts.

- Ask "How?" and "Why?" to get details to support your topic sentence.

1. What two people, places, or things are you comparing?

_____

2. List at least three different ways you will compare these two.

_____

_____

_____

3. Will you organize your paragraph by the point-by-point method or by the block method?

_____

4. Write a topic sentence that makes clear the point of your comparison.

_____

_____

After you have completed the first draft of your comparison paragraph, examine the material with an eye especially for sentence construction and for verb and pronoun forms.

◆ SENTENCE STRUCTURE

PRONOUN AGREEMENT AND CLEAR REFERENCE

The Problem: How to Achieve Pronoun Agreement and Clear Reference

The word a pronoun refers to is called its <u>antecedent</u>. In this sentence, *Marta* is the antecedent of the pronoun *she:*

> <u>Marta</u> was given a scholarship because <u>she</u> is a talented violinist.

A pronoun must *agree* in number with its antecedent; that is, both must be singular or both plural.

> The <u>robin</u> has left <u>its</u> nest.

> The <u>robins</u> have left <u>their</u> nest.

It's easy to see that the singular pronoun *its* agrees with the singular antecedent *robin,* and the plural pronoun *their* agrees with the plural antecedent *robins.* But you probably won't be surprised to learn that things are not always that simple.

Each of the men brought (his/their) own tools.

You may have been tempted to choose *their*, but *his* is right. The singular pronoun *his* agrees with the singular subject *each*. (*Men* is the object of the preposition *of* and not the sentence subject.)

These *indefinite pronouns* are always singular:

one	someone	each
anyone	everybody	either
everyone	nobody	neither

The indefinite pronouns *both, several,* and *few* are always plural.

SPOTCHECK 8-1   *Underline the correct pronouns. It may help to cross out prepositional phrases first.*

1. Each of the television sets was missing (its/their) antenna.

2. Both of the orchestras have (its/their) good points.

3. Neither Christopher nor Ross could find (his/their) textbook.

4. Someone left (her/their) purse on the counter.

5. Everybody who goes into carpentry will find (his/their) situation challenging.

Check the Answer Key before continuing.

Solution #1: Avoid Sex Bias

You may not have liked the answer given for Sentence 5 in Spotcheck 8-1. You might have asked yourself why *everybody* should take the masculine pronoun *his* when the word could refer just as easily to women as to men. In the past, indefinite antecedents (neither masculine nor feminine) have worked that way. But many people today believe that that method gives a sexist bias to the language. Unfortunately, there is no easy way around the problem.

The most common "solution" is to use the plural pronoun *their*, which is neither masculine nor feminine. Thus we would have: "Everybody should pay their taxes." But this combination of plural pronoun and singular antecedent is ungrammatical and, at least in writing, should be avoided.

A somewhat better possibility is to say *his or her* in such situations, but this solution can be awkward if the words must be repeated very often.

> **(awkward)** Each applicant should bring *his or her* résumé to the office and be prepared to discuss *his or her* work experience with *his or her* interviewer.

A better approach is to make the antecedent plural when possible. This permits use of the gender-free pronoun *they*.

(revised) All <u>applicants</u> should bring *their* résumés to the office and be prepared to discuss *their* work experience with *their* interviewers.

Other ways of wording a sentence sometimes can be used.

(awkward) Did everyone remember to bring <u>his or her</u> sweater?

(better) Did everyone remember to bring <u>a</u> sweater?

(biased) Everyone should pay <u>his</u> taxes by April 30.

(better) Taxes should be paid by April 30.

SPOTCHECK 8-2

Rewrite the following sentences to avoid sex bias and pronoun disagreement.

1. Everybody at the picnic brought his own lunch.

   _____

2. Each of the drivers had to show their license.

   _____

3. If a person takes a shower instead of a bath, he uses only about half as much hot water.

   _____

   _____

4. A fan who brings his ticket stub from the rained-out game will get in free.

   _____

   _____

Compare your answers with those in the Answer Key.

Solution #2: Use Singular Pronouns with Group Nouns

Group nouns—such as *team, committee,* and *flock*—refer to more than one person or thing but are usually regarded as referring to a single unit. They therefore take singular pronouns.

The <u>committee</u> will hold <u>its</u> [not *their*] next meeting Tuesday.

The <u>gas company</u> promised to lower <u>its</u> rates before winter.

SPOTCHECK 8-3

Underline the correct pronoun in parentheses.

1. The Sparks family will take (its/their) vacation in Prince Edward Island this summer.

2. A neighbourhood street gang lost (its/their) leader in a shootout with police.

3. After deliberating for three days, the jury finally delivered (its/their) verdict.

4. The skiing team announced that (it/they) will enter the Winter Olympics.

5. This fall, the Barenaked Ladies rock band is on (its/their) third tour of England.

Check the Answer Key before continuing.

DOUBLECHECK 8-1   *Put a check mark in front of the better sentence in each of the following pairs.*

_____   **1a.** One of the companies gave its employees turkeys at Christmas.

_____   **1b.** One of the companies gave their employees turkeys at Christmas.

_____   **2a.** Anyone who sings well should put his name on the list.

_____   **2b.** Those who sing well should put their names on the list.

_____   **3a.** Neither France nor Germany would change their policy.

_____   **3b.** Neither France nor Germany would change its policy.

_____   **4a.** Not everyone will admit it when he has made a mistake.

_____   **4b.** Some people won't admit it when they have made a mistake.

_____   **5a.** The Girl Guides of Saskatchewan will hold their annual convention in Saskatoon.

_____   **5b.** The Girl Guides of Saskatchewan will hold its annual convention in Saskatoon.

_____   **6a.** A fool and his money are soon parted.

_____   **6b.** Fools and their money are soon parted.

_____   **7a.** Everybody brought a "We're No. 1" banner to the football game.

_____ **7b.** Everybody brought his "We're No. 1" banner to the football game.

_____ **8a.** The Bay will hold their "White Sale" on Monday.

_____ **8b.** The Bay will hold its "White Sale" on Monday.

_____ **9a.** People who buy Speedo cars should have their heads examined.

_____ **9b.** A person who buys a Speedo car should have his head examined.

_____ **10a.** One of those lipsticks cost more than they're worth.

_____ **10b.** One of those lipsticks costs more than it's worth.

Check the Answer Key before continuing.

Solution #3: Make Pronoun References Clear

Pronouns such as _he_ and _they_ have no meaning in themselves. They get their identity from the words they refer to, their antecedents. This connection must always be clear. Consider this sentence:

Chris told his father <u>he</u> needed a haircut.

Who needs a haircut, Chris or his father? The pronoun _he_ does not have a clear antecedent. Assuming it is the father who needs a haircut, the problem could be solved this way:

Chris told his father, "You need a haircut."

In the next example, is it Matthew or Eric who is in college?

(unclear) Matthew phoned Eric once a week when he was in college.
(clear) When Eric was in college, Matthew phoned him once a week.

✓

SPOTCHECK 8-4

Rewrite the following sentences to make the pronoun references clear.

1. As the umpire and the coach argued, <u>his</u> voice got louder and louder.

_____

_____

2. Frank told the instructor that <u>he</u> had a poor understanding of the subject.

_____

_____

3. When Ms. Stemley saw Ms. Wright, <u>she</u> gave her a big smile.

_____

_____

4. The truck hit the police car, but <u>it</u> wasn't damaged.

_____

_____

5. The hail was followed by a high wind; <u>it</u> caused extensive damage.

_____

_____

Compare your answers with those in the Answer Key.

Solution #4: Avoid Vague Pronoun References

A pronoun should refer clearly to a specific word or group of words. The pronouns *it*, *this*, *that*, and *which* sometimes appear without clear antecedents.

> **(weak)** Mr. Armajani gave his wife a dozen roses. <u>This</u> pleased her. (*This* has no specific antecedent.)
>
> **(revised)** Mr. Armajani gave his wife a dozen roses. The gift pleased her.
>
> **(weak)** Sharon had always wanted to go into law, so she was excited when she finally achieved <u>it</u>. (*It* has no antecedent.)
>
> **(revised)** Sharon had always wanted to go into law, so she was excited when she finally got her law degree.

Avoid the vague use of the pronouns *you*, *they*, and *it*. Be specific about the subject of the sentence.

> **(weak)** When <u>you</u> take an English course, <u>you</u> should revise your papers carefully.
>
> **(revised)** Students who take English courses should revise their papers carefully.
>
> **(weak)** <u>They</u> say a storm is on the way.
>
> **(revised)** The weather bureau says a storm is on the way.
>
> **(weak)** In the newspaper, <u>it</u> says the Don Valley Parkway will be closed for repairs.

(revised) The newspaper says the Don Valley Parkway will be closed for repairs.

SPOTCHECK 8-5   *Revise the following sentences to avoid weak pronoun references.*

1. Clint did weight training for a year before <u>it</u> became noticeable.

_____

_____

2. Jeffrey wants to be a rodeo rider, but he has never attended <u>one</u>.

_____

_____

3. When <u>you</u> drive on a highway, <u>you</u> have to stay alert.

_____

4. <u>They</u> always listen to the one who complains the loudest.

_____

_____

5. I did not respond to her invitation, <u>which</u> was impolite.

_____

_____

Compare your answers with those in the Answer Key.

DOUBLECHECK 8-2   *Rewrite these sentences to correct weaknesses in pronoun agreement or reference.*

1. When visiting Paris, you should see the Louvre museum.

_____

2. If a car needs premium gasoline, don't buy it.

_____

3. According to this magazine, it says the polar ice cap is melting.

_____

4. When suffering dizzy spells, you should see a doctor.

_____

5. On the radio, they said rainy weather is expected.

_____

6. The Jayanathans did not meet their neighbours until they invited them to a PTA meeting.

_____

_____

7. The committee finally made their recommendation at 1 a.m.

_____

8. Neither of the golfers lost their ball in the rough on the final round.

_____

_____

9. Emile told Winston he was certain to win the race.

_____

10. Not everyone knows his way around the Trans-Canada Highway.

_____

Compare your answers with those in the Answer Key.

◆ WRITING PROCESS

REVISING: ADJECTIVES AND ADVERBS

Adjectives and adverbs are words that modify or describe other words. When you revise your first draft, use adjectives and adverbs to add colour and precision to your writing.

ADJECTIVES Adjectives describe nouns or pronouns, as in these examples:

The campers watched the <u>beautiful</u> sunset. (*Beautiful* describes the noun *sunset.*)

She was <u>optimistic.</u> (*Optimistic* describes the pronoun *she.*)

With most adjectives, add *-er* when comparing two things; add *-est* when comparing three or more things.

Sheila is <u>taller</u> than Pat.

Sheila is the <u>tallest</u> member of the team.

Longer adjectives become awkward when *-er* or *-est* is added to them.

(awkward) The teacher is <u>intelligenter</u> than the banker.

With long adjectives, use *more* or *most* in front of the adjective instead of adding *-er* or *-est* at the end.

The teacher is more intelligent than the banker.

The plumber is the <u>most intelligent</u> person in town.

Never use *-er* and *more* together; never use *-est* and *most* together.

(wrong) My dog is <u>more smarter</u> than your dog.

(wrong) That is the <u>most dumbest</u> thing I've ever seen.

Some adjectives are irregular; that is, they are compared in a different way from the ways just discussed. Be sure to memorize the forms of these adjectives:

good	better	best
bad	worse	worst
many	more	most
little	less	least

A spelling tip: Adjectives ending in *y* change the *y* to *i* before *-er* or *-est*.

happy   happier   happiest   easy   easier   easiest

SPOTCHECK 8-6

In the blanks, write the correct form of the adjectives shown in parentheses.

1. (faded) Robert's jeans are _____ than Pete's.

2. (bad) *Last Action Hero* was the _____ movie Natalie had ever seen.

3. (happy) Who is _____, Stacie or Carrie?

4. (many) The SkyDome holds _____ people than Olympic Stadium.

5. (intelligent) Of the three sisters, Chandra is the _____.

Check the Answer Key before continuing.

ADVERBS

<u>Adverbs</u> describe verbs. They usually end in *-ly*.

The gas station attendant walked <u>slowly</u> to the pump. (*Slowly* is an adverb describing the verb *walked*.)

John <u>gladly</u> gave his bus seat to the old man. (*Gladly* describes the verb *gave*.)

Don't make the mistake of using an adjective instead of an adverb following a verb.

> Thomas spoke ~~angry~~ angrily to the dog's owner.
>
> The child ran ~~quick~~ quickly to her mother.

In writing, don't leave off the *-ly* in *really* and *easily*.

> Grant was ~~real~~ really angry when Debra filed for a divorce.
>
> Terry can make an apple pie ~~easy~~ easily.

Mistakes are often made with the words *well* and *good*. *Well* is an adverb; it describes verbs. *Good* is an adjective; it describes nouns and pronouns.

> Morgan is a good tennis player. (*Good* is an adjective modifying the noun *player*.)
>
> Morgan played well in the tournament. (*Well* is an adverb modifying the verb *played*.)

Use *well* when referring to health.

> Stephen left the campus early because he didn't feel well.

SPOTCHECK 8-7 *Underline the correct word in parentheses.*

1. Kevin (quick/quickly) picked up the phone.
2. Annie won the 100-metre dash (easy/easily).
3. The child gazed (envious/enviously) at the candy display.
4. It is (good/well) that Yuko had the spare tire inspected.
5. The basketball team played (good/well) in the conference finals.

Check the Answer Key before continuing.

The error called a double negative occurs when the adverb *not* is used with another negative word. (*Not* is often disguised in such contractions as *can't, won't, hasn't,* and *couldn't.*)

> **(wrong)** Jessica didn't have no time to go dancing.
>
> **(right)** Jessica didn't have any time to go dancing.
>
> **(right)** Jessica had no time to go dancing.

The words *hardly* and *scarcely* are negative and shouldn't be used with *not*.

> **(wrong)** The millionaire didn't pay hardly any taxes.
>
> **(right)** The millionaire paid hardly any taxes.

✓

SPOTCHECK 8-8   *Edit the following sentences to get rid of double negatives.*

EXAMPLE: Guylaine doesn't like ~~no one~~ ^{anyone} in the group.

1. Amy didn't take none of Susan's advice.
2. The soccer team doesn't have scarcely enough money for uniforms.
3. Frank doesn't contribute nothing to charity.
4. The Gregorys don't know no one in Halifax.
5. Since the accident, Mr. Chan can't hardly walk.

Compare your answers with those in the Answer Key.

✓

CHECKPOINT 8-I   *In the blanks, write **weak** for sentences with faulty pronoun agreement or reference, including sex bias. Write **ok** for sentences without such problems.*

_____   1. Ruth called her mother before she left for work.

_____   2. You see a lot of violence on television.

_____   3. The phone company gave its employees a holiday bonus.

_____   4. Rowena buys cotton blouses because it is cooler than synthetic fabrics.

_____   5. Anyone planning to travel abroad should order his passport well in advance.

_____   6. Philip wanted to be a chemist, but he changed his mind after getting a "C–" in it.

_____   7. Neither of the brothers mows his own lawn.

_____   8. Sarah refused the gift, which surprised Richard.

_____   9. They say that the world's population is growing too quickly.

_____   10. Each of the actresses owed her success to hard work and talent.

——————— **11.** Everyone who forgets their book will have to go home and get it.

——————— **12.** The counsellors who are on duty will give their advice to students who ask for it.

——————— **13.** A dog usually barks when they see a cat.

——————— **14.** Anyone who missed the exam should see their instructor about making it up.

——————— **15.** You need a lot of money to spend your vacation in New York City.

No answers are given for Checkpoint quizzes.

9

THE OPINION PARAGRAPH

◆ READING

PRECHECK

EXPRESSING AN OPINION

In this article on dating, Jane Merivale argues that being 20 and looking for a date is not an easy matter these days. The author would not want to be in that situation.

Twenty Again? Thanks, but No Thanks

—Jane Merivale

Next year will mark the 30th anniversary of the first municipally-funded birth control clinic in Toronto. The Pill became the preferred method of birth control for thousands of women and engendered a new lifestyle. No longer living with the fear of unwanted pregnancies because of the new birth control technology, many women in the West took control of their reproductive lives. They found a new freedom, a new way of exploring friendships, dating people, having sexual relationships. This was indeed liberating. When I reflect on those times, and compare them with today, I am glad I am not twenty and looking for a date. In this age, I wonder where on earth I would find one!

At work: This used to be an obvious answer. Not any more. The workplace has come to be a minefield of sexual harassment charges. Guidelines are passed around offices, memos are written defining "acceptable" behaviour, explaining types of sexual harassment and reminding staff of their rights. Finding a date is no longer an easy matter of chatting someone up at the water cooler. If the person approached feels that the compliment on her dress, for example, is in

precarious insecure
innocuous harmless

some way sinister, or sexual, she can report the offender. He would be in a very precarious position and could lose his job, however innocuous the compliment was intended to be. Touching a colleague in affection, sympathy or even in jest is no longer permissible. Look what happened to Michael Douglas in *Disclosure* to see the consequences of that!

So, no more dating in the office, but what about on a university or a college campus? Thousands of relationships have been formed between professors and students, as well as students. I recall at my small town university the mingling which often led to marrying and how much this mixing was taken for granted. But not any more. Date-rape has become such an obsession that no one would make someone's acquaintance and assume a date. This situation in the world of academia has had the effect of preventing many women from forming close relationships with colleagues and staff. For both men and women, anti-harassment laws have made it extremely difficult to form relationships. 3

burgeoned increased

Singles' bars, community clubs, sports centres have all burgeoned in recent years. At first, these were considered alternative meeting grounds. Nowadays, however, the safeness of picking up a stranger is highly questionable. Apart from the fear of sexually transmitted diseases, increasingly we understand in our society that even the most 'normal' person can actually be a horrendous monster. When Karla Holmolka, at 17, met Paul Bernardo, she thought she had met Prince Charming. No one needs to be reminded of the ending of her story. 4

dicey dangerous, tricky

It may still be a safe bet to be introduced to someone by a mutual friend. There's always an awkwardness, however, when Charlie is invited to dinner because Rita is coming, and they're both single. Blind dates are dicey. It may be the start of a fabulous partnership; on the other hand, it could be a social disaster for everyone. 5

anonymously without a name

That is perhaps why one hears of so many more people answering personal ads, enroling in computer date lines, and seeking friendships on the latest of the hot lines: the Internet. There, on the Internet, two people can talk to each other safely, facelessly, indeed even anonymously for months before they ever need even conceive of meeting. Before a meeting, they can exchange phone calls, or photographs, and respond to each other according to their reactions to the voice, or the picture. Talk shows are presenting viewers with couples who have 'made it' through the Internet, and who are now dating in real life, *even marrying*. 6

Marriage is not dead yet. I feel sorry, however, that people have to be confined to electronic channels in order to meet others. The present concern with anti-harassment and date-rape, though necessary, is responsible for changing the nature of relationships. I am certainly glad I am not 20 and trying to find a man. 7

CHECKING MEANING AND STYLE

1. What prompted this article about dating?

2. What does the author compare the work place to?

3. What audience does this article address?

4. What is the problem with an introduction by a friend?

5. What is the new method that people are using to meet partners?

CHECKING IDEAS

1. Would you agree that there is a current "obsession" with date rape and sexual harassment?

2. Where is it possible to meet new people, in your opinion?

3. Have the new harassment laws altered the way people behave towards each other?

4. What are other impediments to forming relationships from casual acquaintances?

◆ WRITING MODELS

THE OPINION PARAGRAPH

Model Opinion Paragraph #1

Here is how the article might look if it were condensed in a single paragraph:

Notice that the opinion is clearly stated in the opening sentence.

> The anniversary of the Pill prompts a reflection on how easy it *used to be* to find a partner: to meet someone, fall in love, and get married. These days, however, dating has become a difficult task. Before getting married, don't you have to fall in love? And before falling in love, don't you have to meet someone, somehow? This process has become less than simple, given the current obsession with date-rape and sexual harassment. The workplace used to be the best place to find a mate, but it has become a minefield. So has the university campus, which was another logical place to meet a mate. Of course people do still manage somehow to fall in love and get married, sometimes with computer help. But still, I would hate to be 20 and waiting for a date.

Here is how a paragraph stating the opposite opinion might look:

Model Opinion Paragraph #2

Observe how the opening sentence clearly states the opinion.

> Romantic-style marriages are back, which is great because meeting someone and falling in love are easier than ever. This process has become much simpler as a result of the new date-rape and sexual harassment laws. People in the workplace and on campuses are much more careful in the way that they treat each other. This makes it easier to feel safe with people, to get to know them, and to become friends. It is wonderful to be 20 and looking forward to finding a date.

◆ WRITING ASSIGNMENT

AN OPINION PARAGRAPH

We usually like to give our opinions on a variety of topics—the new model Turbozoom car, the Flames' chances of winning the Stanley Cup, lowering the drinking age, or abortion. Other people are more likely to listen to our opinions if we state them clearly and in a reasonable way.

OPINIONS AND FACTS

One way to state an opinion effectively is to back it up with some supporting facts. Opinions can be argued endlessly, but facts are statements that can be checked to see if they are true. Consider the following examples:

(opinion) Duke Ellington was the greatest American composer of the twentieth century.

(fact) Ellington's compositions include "Warm Valley," "Mood Indigo," and many concert suites.

(opinion) Canadian women have easier lives than men.

(fact) Canadian women outlive men by several years.

Practise distinguishing between opinions and facts in the following exercise.

SPOTCHECK 9-1

In the blanks, write fact *or* opinion.

_____ 1. Roger Bannister of England was the first person to run a mile race in under four minutes.

_____ 2. Singer Dean Martin was born Dino Paul Crocetti.

_____ 3. *The Diviners* is a greater novel than *The Stone Angel*.

_____ 4. Eating yogurt every day is good for people.

_____ 5. Newfoundland's salmon is not as tasty as British Columbia's.

_____ 6. Samuel Maclure (1860–1929), was a West Coast architect.

_____ 7. German car designers are the best in the business.

_____   **8.** The earth is about 150 million kilometres from the sun.

Check the Answer Key before continuing.

WRITE AN OPINION PARAGRAPH

Write an opinion paragraph on one of these topics:

1. Ordinary citizens should (not) be allowed to carry guns.

2. (Name of team) is the most exciting team in (football, basketball, baseball).

3. The most shocking music group today is (name of group).

4. (Movie, television program, book) is great family entertainment.

5. Liberals (Conservatives) usually meet the country's needs best.

Start your paragraph with a clearly stated opinion. Ask "Why?" to get specific points to support your opinion.

(Topic sentence) _____

_____

_____

(Supporting point) _____

_____

_____

(Supporting point) _____

_____

_____

(Supporting point) _____

_____

_____

(Supporting point) _____

_____

_____

After you write the first draft of your opinion paragraph, check your paper for errors in sentence construction, verbs, subject–verb agreement, and pronouns. Look especially for the kinds of errors marked on recent papers.

◆ SENTENCE PUNCTUATION

PART I: USING COMMAS IN SENTENCES

The Problem: Knowing When to Use Commas

We might be forgiven for turning to our TV sets if we ran into much writing like this:

> Having forgotten to let out her dog the faithful Poochie Isabel had to turn around at Medicine Hat Alberta and drive back home a trip of two hours.

That sentence makes a good deal more sense with the addition of a few commas:

> Having forgotten to let out her dog, the faithful Poochie, Isabel had to turn around at Medicine Hat, Alberta, and drive back home, a trip of two hours.

Unfortunately, commas are the punctuation marks most likely to cause despair among inexperienced writers. Here are five occasions for using them:

Solution #1: Use Commas Before Connecting Words

Use commas before the connecting words *and, but, or, for, nor, yet,* and *so* when they join two complete thoughts or independent clauses. You may want to return to the section on clauses (Chapter 3) for a quick review.

> The job is boring, but the pay is good.
> Mike liked the movie, so he told Fran to see it.

Be sure you are joining two independent clauses. In the following sentence, no comma is needed:

> Mike liked the movie and told Fran to see it. (single clause with one subject and two verbs)

SPOTCHECK 9-2

Use a comma and one of the connectors and, but, or, for, nor, yet, *or* so *between independent clauses.*

> **EXAMPLE:** The book is valuable, but you may borrow it.

1. Dinner isn't ready _____ you can take a nap first.

2. Rick is always late _____ he never has an excuse

3. You should get a raise _____ you deserve one.

4. That boy will apologize _____ I will tell his parents.

5. Cats are nice pets _____ they claw the furniture.

Compare your answers with those in the Answer Key.

SPOTCHECK 9-3 *Write three sentences, each using one of the connectors* and, but, *or* so *between independent clauses.*

1. _____

_____

2. _____

_____

3. _____

_____

Compare your answers with those in the Answer Key.

Solution #2: Use Commas After Introductory Expressions

Use commas after introductory expressions—words that lead up to the main part of the sentence (the independent clause).

> After a long and snowy winter, we were eager for spring to come. (introductory prepositional phrase)

> Because the dog was limping, Arnold took it to the vet. (introductory dependent clause)

The comma is often omitted if the introductory expression is short.

> On Friday [no comma] the entire office staff played a game of softball in Stanley Park.

But commas are used after such opening words as *well, yes,* and *no.*

> Yes, I returned the book to the library on time.

SPOTCHECK 9-4 *Put commas after introductory words.*

1. Grown in California and Oregon nectarines resemble peaches without fuzz.

2. To drink the juice of a coconut puncture a hole in the shell.

3. Known in the Mediterranean area as "the poor man's fruit" figs contain calcium, phosphorus, and iron.

4. No breadfruit is not used to make bread, but in the South Seas the wood of the plant is used to make canoes.

Check the Answer Key before continuing.

**Solution #3: Use Commas to
Separate Items in a Series**

Use commas to separate items in a series. A series is a list of *three or more* items.

The hairdresser took out his comb, brush, and scissors. (Some writers omit the comma before *and*.)

The truck driver jumped into the cab, turned on the ignition, and pressed her boot against the accelerator.

The instructor opened the book and started to read. (No comma—two items do not make a series.)

✓

SPOTCHECK 9-5

Put commas between items in series.

1. The Chinese eat kumquats fresh preserve them or make them into jams.

2. Most papayas in Canada come from Florida Texas Hawaii Mexico or Puerto Rico.

Write two sentences using commas to separate items in a series.

3. _____

    _____

4. _____

    _____

Compare your answers with those in the Answer Key.

**Solution #4: Use Commas to
Set Off Interrupting Words**

Use commas to set off words that interrupt the sentence if those words are not essential to the main idea. This rule will be clearer after you study these examples:

Marie, who completed all the work, will pass the course.
Any student who completed the work will pass the course.

In the first example, the main idea, *Marie will pass the course,* makes sense without the interrupting words *who completed all the work.* Since the extra words add nonessential information, they are set off by commas.

In the second example, the main clause, *Any student will pass the course,* is clearly nonsense. The interrupting words are essential to complete its meaning. Therefore, the interrupter is not set off by commas.

Here are some more examples of essential and nonessential interrupters.

> (**nonessential**) <u>William Leong</u>, who has been elected four times, <u>will run for mayor again this year</u>.

The interrupter *who has been elected four times* adds interesting but nonessential information. It is set off by commas.

> (**essential**) <u>A man</u> who has been elected four times <u>will run for mayor again this year</u>.

The main (underlined) clause does not make sense without the help of the interrupter. The interrupter is *not* set off by commas.

> (**nonessential**) <u>We read a poem</u>, "I Died for Beauty," <u>in English class</u>.
>
> (**essential**) <u>We read the poem</u> "I Died for Beauty" <u>in English class</u>.

Use commas to set off expressions such as *on the other hand* and *it seems to me* that interrupt the sentence.

> Kelvin, of course, has no intention of asking Jill to marry him.
>
> Columbus, according to some historians, was not the first European to dis cover America.

SPOTCHECK 9-6   *Add commas to set off nonessential elements and interrupting expressions.*

1. Bill's Diner which looks like it survived a tornado is a favourite student hangout.

2. My history teacher Mr. Jefferson has written a book on the Charlottetown Referendum.

3. The mating call of the Mediterranean fruit fly according to experts has the same frequency as the musical note F-sharp.

4. A goat that seems to be eating a tin can is probably just enjoying the glue on the can's label.

5. Pound cake which is one of my favourite desserts got its name from the pound of butter used in making it.

6. That fact of course won't keep me from enjoying pound cake—and putting on pounds.

7. Money is a bad master it has been said but a good servant.

8. Billy Bishop who failed RMC became Canada's ace pilot in 1917.

Check the Answer Key before continuing.

Solution #5: Use Commas in Place-Names, Addresses, and Dates

Use commas to separate geographical names and items in addresses and dates.

> Ming lived in Taipei, Taiwan, before coming to Canada.

Susan was born on Tuesday, September 15, 1966, in Calgary.

The letter was addressed to 91 Wilfrid Laurier Avenue, Quebec, Quebec.

NOTE: Use Postal Code abbreviations (ON, AB, QC, and so on) only in addresses at the tops of letters.

Write a sentence in which you give the month, date, and year of an event significant to you and the city and province (or country) where it happened. Be careful with the commas.

_____

_____

SPOTCHECK 9-7   *Add commas where needed.*

1. The highest temperature ever recorded in Canada was 45°C recorded July 5 1937 at Midale and Yellowgrass Saskatchewan.

2. The lowest temperature ever recorded in Canada was −63°C at Snag Yukon Territory, on February 3 1947.

3. The package was mailed to Mr. Robert Wong 213 West Pender Vancouver British Columbia.

4. Her son was born in Lethbridge Alberta on January 4 1962.

DOUBLECHECK 9-1   *Add commas where needed.*

1. Herbert Marshall McLuhan usually known as Marshall McLuhan was a world-renowned communication theorist.

2. He was born in Edmonton on July 21 1911 and died in Toronto on December 31 1980.

3. Because of his studies on the effects of the media he became famous in the 1960s.

4. He received a Ph.D. from Cambridge in 1943 and he was a professor at the University of Toronto where he became famous for his thoughts on the media.

5. A deeply literate man he formulated theories about modern culture.

6. His ideas were highly significant but he was misunderstood by a lot of people because of his revolutionary theories.

7. He made a distinction between "hot" and "cool" media where television for example conveys less information but requires more intensive listening.

8. When McLuhan published *Understanding Media* in 1964 he became famous worldwide.

9. In 1967 *The Medium Is the Message* was published and it soon became popular interntionally.

10. He founded the Centre for Culture and Technology at the University of Toronto and the McLuhan Teleglobe Canada Award was created in 1983 in his memory.

11. This award is very popular today because it carries a cash value of $50,000.

12. McLuhan asked us to change not only the way we considered information but also how we perceived knowledge.

Check the Answer Key before continuing.

DOUBLECHECK 9-2

Add commas where appropriate in this paragraph.

[1]According to archeologists men shaved their faces as far back as 20,000 years ago. [2]Drawings on caves show both bearded and beardless men and graves have contained the flints and shells that were the first razors. [3]As soon as humans learned to work with iron and bronze razors were hammered out of these materials. [4]Ancient Egyptians who sought status shaved their faces. [5]Greek soldiers shaved regularly because a beard was a handicap in hand-to-hand fighting. [6]In the New World Indian men used tweezers made from clams to pull out their beards one hair at a time.

Check the Answer Key before continuing.

Solution #6: Do Not Overuse Commas

The final rule is this: Don't use a comma unless you know why you're using it. If in doubt, leave it out.

Take care not to use commas where they are not needed. Here are some of the spots where unnecessary commas are most likely to appear:

• Before a connector (*and, but, or, for, nor, yet, so*) that does <u>not</u> join two independent clauses:

(no comma) Marianne could read French‚ but couldn't speak it. (one independent clause with two verbs)

(correct) Marianne could read French but couldn't speak it.

(correct) Marianne could read French‚ but she couldn't speak it. (two independent clauses joined by *but*)

• Between a subject and its verb, especially if the complete subject (italicized in the following examples) is long:

(no comma) *Fools and their money*‚ are soon parted.

(no comma) *A knife, some string, and some matches*‚ are useful on a camping trip.

• Between a verb and its object:

(wrong) The supervisor said, that she would be back at three.

(compare) The supervisor said, "I will be back at three."

(wrong) The snow plow has finished, clearing our driveway.

- Before the first or after the last item in a series:

(no comma) We could get along without, pollution, poverty, and war.

(no comma) She found a brush, comb, and mirror, on the dresser.

(no comma) The sunset was a beautiful, breathtaking, inspiring, sight.

SPOTCHECK 9-8   *Circle unnecessary commas.*

1. Throughout Canada, almost anyone, can buy a pack of cigarettes these days.

2. Confronted with the evidence, Susan admitted, that she had broken the vase.

3. Ferd's new car is, economical, dependable, and quite handsome.

4. Making the dean's honour list, was Terry's goal for the semester, but he knew he would have trouble with math.

5. Yuko, who hated baseball, decided to attend the Expos game with her family.

6. Under the cushion, Debra found, two quarters, a dime, and three pennies.

7. The camp counsellor, Alice Koyama, rowed out to the island in a canoe, and built a fire on the beach.

8. Next semester I will have to take algebra, history, and, English.

Check the Answer Key before continuing.

◆ WRITING PROCESS

REVISING: CHOOSING THE RIGHT WORD

In "Twenty Again? Thanks, but No Thanks" the author uses an informal, conversational style. She uses colloquialisms such as "dicey," as well as exclamation marks, question marks and short sentences which all make this essay very informal.

You might write informally in this way to a friend, but there are many occasions when this style would not be appropriate. You would not write a job application letter in this informal style, nor a report to your boss, or a college term paper on the Group of Seven. You would handle those subjects in a more formal style.

A good writing style, then, is *appropriate*—for its readers and its subject.

Here are some specific points to keep in mind:

SLANG words and expressions are acceptable in only the most informal writing. Words such as *groovy* quickly go out of fashion and mark their users as the opposite of "cool." They are also usually vague and unclear.

CLICHÉS or trite expressions were originally colourful and full of life but now are worn out from overuse. Avoid expressions that pop into your mind fully formed: *neat as a pin, sadder but wiser, last but not least.*

JARGON is the specialized language of a particular group or occupation, such as football players, computer programmers, or doctors. The following memo contains jargon (in italics) that a group of business consultants found objectionable: "Your new *agenda*: Be *proactive* and *interface* with customers. Start *networking. Finalize* sales. Rack up the *done deals* that will *impact* the *bottom line.* We've got *world-class, state-of-the-art, user-friendly* products. That's our *competitive edge.*"

BIG WORDS are often hard to resist. We like to sound impressive. But the person who lives in a *residence* instead of a house, or prefers to *commence* something instead of to start it, is on the wrong track. "Write to express, not to impress." Your first goal is to be clear.

WRONG WORDS must be corrected, of course, by checking a dictionary. "The teacher ~~inferred~~ implied that I had copied the paper."

SPOTCHECK 9-9

Correct the underlined examples of slang, clichés, jargon, big words, and wrong words.

                                    nervous
    EXAMPLE: Rudy is really ~~uptight~~ about tomorrow's game.

1. Sally is the most <u>pulchritudinous</u> woman I know.

2. George wants to <u>interface</u> with me at lunch.

3. The City Council wasn't <u>crazy</u> about the mayor's idea.

4. Most critics said the movie was <u>gross</u>.

5. Please <u>inquire of</u> your boss if you can leave early.

6. Despite her long trip, Amy <u>was the picture of health</u>.

7. Someone stole Peter's new <u>wheels</u> last night.

8. The Petersons have bought a new <u>domicile</u>.

9. <u>Irregardless</u> of Tim's feelings, the family will vacation again at Lac Edouard.

10. Samantha was <u>green with envy at</u> Julia's success.

Compare your answers with those in the Answer Key.

CHECKPOINT 9-1

Some of the sentences below contain comma errors. Find the kind of error on this list and write the identification number of the rule being illustrated in the blank to the left of each sentence.

1. Use commas with *and, but, or, for, nor, yet,* and *so* to join two independent clauses (complete thoughts).

2. Use commas after introductory elements that lead up to the main clause of a sentence.

3. Use commas to separate items in a series.

4. Use commas to set off nonessential words that interrupt a sentence.

5. Use commas to separate geographical names and items in addresses and dates.

6. If a sentence contains no error, write *6* in the blank.

_____   1. Giovanni's restaurant which serves great spaghetti is on Main Street.

_____   2. It will be closed next Monday and Tuesday.

_____   3. The office lunch gang will be unhappy but they will just have to find another restaurant.

_____   4. It wouldn't hurt them of course to fix a lunch and bring it to work.

_____   5. A person who won't eat a bag lunch is going to spend a lot of money on food.

_____   6. When I worked at Weston and Co. nearly everyone brought a bag lunch.

_____   7. We ate our sandwiches in the company cafeteria or we took them to the little park across from the office.

_____   8. I have been working for Darwin and Associates which is a big law firm for six months.

_____   9. I joined the company on Monday April 16.

_____   10. What I like about the company are the flexible work hours the medical benefits and the lunches at Giovanni's.

No answers are given for Checkpoint quizzes.

10

THE PERSUASION
PARAGRAPH

◆ READING

PERSUADING OTHERS TO SHARE
ONE'S VIEWS

PRECHECK

Writers often try to persuade readers to think or act a certain way. In this article, writer Kate Tavender urges the members of Generation X to take more control of their lives.

Earth to Generation X: Quit Whining

—Kate Tavender

devoured ate up

So the Me generation devoured all the money and jobs in the 1980s 1 and left those of us unfortunate enough to be born in the late 1960s and early 1970s with a big mess to clean up.

apathy lack of interest

Many of us overqualified, eager twentysomethings can't even get a 2 job. Perhaps this is the root of our frustration and apathy. Doors have been slammed in our faces so often that we stop thinking we can make an impact. We stop dreaming our dreams because they'll never come true. We might even stop caring about anything at all.

Sound familiar? It should, because it's the trendiest new ideology 3 being spouted by authors, the media and, of course, all those unemployed university graduates, otherwise known as Generation X.

I should know, I'm one of them. And I think it's time Generation X 4 stopped feeling bitter and started putting things in perspective.

Being one of these disillusioned slackers, I am fully fluent in the 5 Generation X discourse. I can see it as an empowering force. It has helped to form a community around those who have to re-evaluate their expectations and learn to survive in the post-1980s era.

woeful pitiful

But I can also see the power this label has to lull us into inaction. 6 The Generation X attitude allows us to justify our woeful situations by blaming the baby boomers.

We're angry at them because the endless opportunities they had 7 have now ceased to exist.

We're angry at them because the success and optimism they en- 8 joyed is for us, at best, dicey.

We're angry at them for letting the fairy tale of security crumble 9 before we had a chance to try it out for ourselves.

And we're angry at them for abandoning us to fend for ourselves in 10 the middle of a depression that they created.

It makes sense that as well as feeling angry and betrayed, we're 11 also fearful in the face of all this cold, hard reality.

scapegoat object of blame

We all agree, the age of idealism is over. Our confidence has been 12 shattered and maybe we can use the baby boomers as a scapegoat for our cruel predicament.

But instead of continuing to mourn over the past and all the things 13 that we missed by being born at the wrong time, isn't it time to move forward and concentrate on the things we do have that make us unique and, yes, even fortunate individuals?

wrapped up absorbed
ethnic cleansing killing all members of a race

Living in Canada as a young adult, I have the luxury of getting so 14 wrapped up in my own Generation X self-pity that I might overlook troubles in other parts of the world such as ethnic cleansing, war and starvation.

Awareness of these horrors forces me to look outside myself and 15 put things in perspective. So it's tough, really tough, for me to find a job despite my years of education. So I may feel disillusioned with notions like success and security. So I may feel a bit lost at times, afraid of failure and even more afraid of just giving up.

atrocities horrors

Yet when I compare my worries to the daily atrocities people expe- 16 rience elsewhere in the world, I feel ashamed.

I don't know exactly when the idea that life ought to be a breeze 17 became so instilled in the minds of North Americans. I think my generation, at last, has a chance to see through this myth.

diminished lessened

Yet, although we may be aware of the truth, we don't like it one bit. 18 So we are prone to bitterness and cynicism. And what a pathetic waste of our youth and energy it is, to feel so hard done by when we should be feeling vitalized and blessed that we live in a time of relative peace and freedom; a time when our opportunities, however diminished, are not inhibited by war or starvation.

tenacity determination

It's time to drop the self-pity and begin to embrace our futures, 19 however uncertain, with more courage and tenacity than those in the past.

We have the freedom to make our mark on society, and though it 20 will be a struggle, it's up to us to find the will.

Forget the boomers.   21

This is our time.   22

CHECKING MEANING AND STYLE

1. Where do the terms "boomers" and "Generation X" come from?

2. What does Kate Tavender think is "the trendiest new ideology"?

3. What stylistic device does Tavender use to impress the reader?

4. Why does she think her generation should stop whining?

5. What are the consequences for her generation of not moving forward?

CHECKING IDEAS

1. With what points in Tavender's article do you agree?

2. Do you think that the boomers have "devoured all the money and jobs"?

3. Why are many members of Generation X frustrated?

4. Do you personally have faith in your future?

5. Do you think this article will persuade some members of Generation X to "stop whining"?

◆ WRITING MODELS

THE PERSUASION PARAGRAPH

Writers often want to persuade others to share their views or to take a certain course of action—to buy a Spitfire SX auto, to vote for Candidate Doe, to oppose or support offshore oil drilling. Kate Tavender wanted to wake up her generation, spurring its members to action in the world.

In the following paragraph (condensed and paraphrased from an actual advertisement), the Planned Parenthood Federation tries to persuade readers to pressure the television industry to change the way it handles commercials and programs that deal with sex.

Model Persuasion Paragraph #1

Television is irresponsible in its treatment of sex, and viewers should complain to the networks. Teenage viewers see thousands of sexual scenes each year that promote the idea of frequent and unprotected sex. The scenes rarely if ever suggest that the lovers are concerned about unintended pregnancies. These programs contribute to the more than one million teen pregnancies a year and to the resulting school drop-outs, broken families, welfare costs, and abortions. Network executives should be told they have other responsibilities in using the public airwaves besides pushing products and making money.

The following paragraph is taken from the original Planned Parenthood Federation advertisement. Notice how the writer persuades by using both statistics and an example.

Model Persuasion Paragraph #2

A recent Louis Harris Poll showed exactly what the public wants. Most Americans believe that television portrays an unrealistic and irresponsible view of sex. And 78% would like to see messages about contraception on TV. A similar percentage wants more sex education in schools. So it's not the public that resists more responsible sexual imagery. It's the television executives who resist it. Why? Maybe it's just a creative problem for them. We think they can solve it. Right now they don't even mention birth control when it's exactly appropriate. Why can't J. R. ask his latest conquest if she is prepared? Why can't she ask him? The screenwriters can work it out.

Note: J. R. was a character on the TV series *Dallas*.

1. What is the source of the statistics?

2. What statistic indicates that the public wants messages about contraception on TV?

3. What example of responsible behaviour does the writer suggest?

The following persuasive paragraph gives specific details to show what may be wrong with a vegetarian diet.

Model Persuasion Paragraph #3

The topic sentence has been underlined.

A vegetarian diet is not always as healthful as vegetarians claim. Vegetarians that I know usually eat a lot of fat, which doctors link to clogged arteries and heart disease. Although my vegetarian friends avoid the fat found in meat, they more than make up for it by eating large quantities of cheese which is often about 50 percent fat. They also favour nuts and seeds, foods high in fat. Vegetarians can eat all the sugar they want without violating their beliefs. But sugar isn't healthful, and the honey that they often substitute isn't much better. Some doctors don't favour a strictly vegetarian diet for pregnant women and babies. While most people would probably be healthier if they ate less meat and more vegetables and grains, a vegetarian diet has its pitfalls too.

1. What point is this paragraph persuading the reader to believe?

2. State one example of what is wrong with a vegetarian diet.

3. Name three foods on a vegetarian diet that are not necessarily healthful.

◆ Writing Assignment

A Persuasion Paragraph

In their ad, Planned Parenthood officials urge readers to pressure television executives to take a more responsible attitude toward sex in programming. You might one day want to persuade income tax officials that you really do not owe more taxes, or to convince a sweetheart in a distant city to marry you. In other classes you may need to "prove" in a term paper or exam that John Lennon was a greater composer than Mozart, or that the United States should not send troops to settle disputes in other countries.

Suppose you wanted to write a paper showing that grades in college should be abolished. Here are some techniques of persuasion that might be used:

• Cite <u>facts or statistics</u> on student health problems or suicides blamed on grade worries.

• Quote <u>expert authorities</u> who argue that grades inspire negative competition rather than positive cooperation.

• Give <u>examples from history</u> showing that college students have not always been graded.

• Offer <u>current examples</u> of colleges that don't assign grades.

• Present a <u>narrative (anecdote)</u> about a rich and famous inventor who flunked out of college.

• Give a <u>description</u> of a classroom full of students agonizing over an exam.

• Describe a <u>personal experience</u>—the time you got a rash over a "D" in algebra.

WRITE A PERSUASION PARAGRAPH

Write a paragraph in which you argue for or against one of the following:

1. Sex education in schools
2. Legalizing marijuana
3. A speed limit of 100 kilometres per hour
4. Vegetarianism (Model #3)
5. Legal drinking at 18
6. Government-sponsored child-care centres
7. Limiting children's TV watching

Start with a topic sentence that says clearly what you want your reader to believe or do.

_____

_____

_____

Develop your argument with specific details and other techniques of persuasion just discussed.

Try to look at your argument through another's eyes. Would you be convinced?

In revising, check especially for run-together sentences and fragments and for errors in the use of verbs, pronouns, and commas.

◆ Sentence Punctuation

Part II: More on Using Punctuation

The Problem: Knowing When and How to Punctuate

The previous chapter devoted an entire section to the correct use of the comma, perhaps the most confusing punctuation mark. This section covers the following ten punctuation marks:

period	.
exclamation mark	!
question mark	?
quotation marks	" "
underlining	____
apostrophe	'
semicolon	;
colon	:
dash	—
parentheses	( )

Solution #1: Periods, Exclamation Marks, and Question Marks

Show that a sentence is completed by using a period, an exclamation mark, or a question mark.

A period marks the end of a statement.

Good grief! I thought you knew that an exclamation mark shows strong emotion.

Do you always remember to put a question mark at the end of a question?

Be sure to note the difference between a direct question and an indirect question. An indirect question is actually a statement and ends with a period, not a question mark.

(**direct**) Lee asked me, "Are you going home?"

(**indirect**) Lee asked me if I was going home. (This statement tells what Lee asked.)

A sentence may contain both a question mark and a period.

"Are you going home?" Lee asked me.

SPOTCHECK 10-1   *Supply the correct end punctuation.*

1. Did Frank remember to fill the gas tank

2. Look out   That gun is loaded

3. Jerome asked Julie if she had a spare dime

4. "What time is it" William asked

5. William wondered what time it was

Check the Answer Key before continuing.

Solution #2: Quotation Marks with Written and Spoken Language

Use quotation marks around direct quotations—the *exact* words of a speaker or writer. Do not use quotation marks around indirect quotations—the idea of the speaker or writer put into your own words.

(**direct**) "Reading is to the mind what exercise is to the body," said Sir Richard Steele. (his exact words)

(**indirect**) Sir Richard Steele said that reading develops the mind in the way that exercise develops the body. (his idea, your words)

(You will often find the word *that* before an indirect quotation.)

Study the use of quotation marks in the following examples. Note especially the relation of the marks to other punctuation and to capital letters.

1. "The plane will be 20 minutes late," the flight attendant said.

• The words identifying the speaker (*the flight attendant said*) are separated from the quotation by a comma.

• All commas (and periods) go *inside* the ending quotation marks.

2. The captain said, "Prepare to abandon ship."

• The quotation begins with a capital letter if it is a complete sentence.

3. "The time to relax," wrote Sydney J. Harris, "is when you don't have time for it."

• If the quotation is interrupted, the next part doesn't begin with a capital letter unless it is a complete sentence.

• Be sure to put quotation marks around the quoted words only, not around the words naming the speaker.

4. Angela protested, "That's not fair. You should have told me that I was expected to attend class. I don't want to flunk."

• When the quotation goes on for more than one sentence without interruption, use quotation marks only at the beginning of the first sentence and at the end of the last.

SPOTCHECK 10-2   *Supply quotation marks and any other needed punctuation.*

1. According to Northrop Frye literature is conscious mythology.

2. Marriage is a great institution said Mae West. But I'm not ready for an institution.

3. I did it for Canada said Marilyn Bell after her marathon swim.

4. No Mr Speaker said Elijah Harper.

5. In the seventeenth century John Comenius said We are all citizens of one world; we are all of one blood. To hate a man because he was born in another country, or because he speaks a different language, or because he takes a different view on this subject or that, is a great folly.

Check the Answer Key before continuing.

Solution #3: Quotation Marks, Italics, and Underlining in Titles

Use quotation marks around the titles of short works such as essays, short stories, songs, book chapters, and magazine or newspaper articles.

Underline (or type in *italics*) the titles of longer works, such as books, magazines, plays, movies, and television or radio shows.

Wanda read an article titled "Buying Your First Home" in the September issue of Canadian Living.

For Monday, the class is supposed to read the short story "The Painted Door" in the book Best Canadian Stories.

Use single quotation marks for a quotation or title within a quotation.

"We read the poem 'Cat Dying in Autumn' in class," Mario said.

SPOTCHECK 10-3   *Supply quotation marks, underlining (italics), and commas. Remember that quotation marks go outside commas and periods.*

1. What are you doing tonight? Mary asked.

2. Oh, I don't know Cathy answered. I'll probably just stay home and watch a rerun of Star Trek on TV.

3. Mary said that she thought television was a waste of time.

4. So what are you going to do, Miss Intellectual? Cathy wanted to know.

5. Mary said I'll probably do some reading. There's an article called Lipstick and You in the new Teen World that looks good.

Check the Answer Key before continuing.

Solution #4: Apostrophes in Contractions

An apostrophe is used to show where one or more letters have been left out in a contraction of two words into one. Some examples:

isn't = is not   can't = cannot   they've = they have

I'm = I am   here's = here is   won't = will not

Do not confuse the following contractions with other sound-alike words.

it's = it is   we're = we are   they're = they are

you're = you are

(The sound-alikes *its, were, their, there,* and *your* have other meanings—see Appendix E.)

✓

SPOTCHECK 10-4

In the blanks, write the contractions of the words shown in parentheses. Be sure to put the apostrophe where one or more letters have been left out.

1. (I have) My boss was surprised at how much _____ learned in English class.

2. (cannot) I _____ believe that final exams are here already.

3. (has not) Lyman is worried because he _____ had a letter from his fiancée in three weeks.

4. (they are) When the baseball teams finish spring training, _____ ready for action.

5. (you are) If _____ ready, we'll leave now.

6. (there is) _____ a new drugstore on the corner.

7. (could not) Tim _____ remember where he had left the car keys.

8. (you have) Congratulations! _____ won first prize.

9. (will not) The dog _____ surrender the bone.

10. (we will) Unless it rains, _____ return Tuesday.

Check the Answer Key before continuing.

Solution #5: Apostrophes to Show Possession

Apostrophes are also used to show possession or ownership.

Alec's book   children's games

two mothers' opinions   the car's brakes

A common problem is not knowing whether the apostrophe comes before or after the -s. Why is it *Bill's book* (apostrophe before the -s) but *mothers' opinions* (apostrophe after the -s)?

You can solve the problem by asking yourself this question: Whom (or what) does it belong to? If the answer does not end in -s, add -'s to the word. If the answer does end in -s, add only an apostrophe.

Whom does the book belong to? (Alec)

Since *Alec* does not end in -s, add -'s: It is <u>Alec's</u> book.

Whom do the games belong to? (the children)

Since *children* does not end in -s, add -'s: They are the <u>children's</u> games.

Whom do the opinions belong to? (the two mothers)

Since *mothers* ends in -s, add only an apostrophe: They are the <u>mothers'</u> opinions.

What do the brakes belong to? (the car)

Since *car* does not end in -s, add -'s: They are the <u>car's</u> brakes.

Be sure to place the apostrophe clearly in front of or behind the -s. Don't cheat by putting it on top of the -s!

The following possessive pronouns, although they end in -s, never take apostrophes:

his   hers   yours   ours   theirs   its

Almost all nouns form the plural by adding an -s. Be sure a word shows ownership before giving it an apostrophe.

Two <u>cats</u> sat on the fence. (no ownership, no apostrophe)

SPOTCHECK 10-5   *Put apostrophes in the possessive words.*

1. the mens wages
2. three horses stalls
3. a weeks work
4. the countries borders
5. the radios volume
6. both flowers petals
7. the two cars headlights
8. a lifetimes effort

Check the Answer Key before continuing.

SPOTCHECK 10-6   *Add apostrophes where needed.*

1. The history books cover was worn from hard use.
2. Duncans attitude has improved since he got a raise.
3. These notebooks belong to Monica.
4. Both boys wagons were on the sidewalk.

5. The caddies brought the womens golf carts to the clubhouse.

Check the Answer Key before continuing.

SPOTCHECK 10-7 ✓

Write sentences using the words in parentheses.

1. (men's)_____

_____

2. (farmers') _____

_____

3. (Jennifer's) _____

_____

4. (players) _____

_____

Compare your answers with those in the Answer Key.

DOUBLECHECK 10-1 ✓

Add quotation marks, apostrophes, and underlining (italics) as needed.

1. Why are you calling me at three in the morning? he yelled into the phone.

2. The college drama class is putting on Shakespeares The Taming of the Shrew.

3. Im sure I saw you last night at Joes party.

4. We had to memorize John McCrae's poem In Flanders Fields in the third grade.

5. Surely, Joyce said, you don't expect me to drink day-old coffee.

6. Is that bicycle yours, or is it ours?

7. That used to be Charles car, but now it belongs to Karen.

8. The two cowboys horses were tied to the hitching post.

9. Look before you leap is an old saying.

10. Dwight says that he will never forget the goal he scored in his high schools hockey game.

Check the Answer Key before continuing.

Solution #6: The Semicolon

A semicolon may be used between two closely related independent clauses that are not joined by *and, but, or, for, nor, yet,* or *so.* (You may want to review the discussion of independent clauses in Chapter 3.)

The rain stopped; we decided to continue our walk.

A semicolon may also be used when the second clause contains a transition word such as *however* or *consequently.*

The rain stopped; therefore, we decided to continue our walk.

Periods could have been used instead of the semicolons. In fact, a good test of the semicolon is to ask if a period might have been used instead.

Another use of the semicolon (in which the preceding test does not apply) is to separate series items that already contain commas.

The new club officers are Hilda Jones, president; Franklin Hill, vice-president; and Rick Okamura, secretary-treasurer.

SPOTCHECK 10-8   *Put semicolons in the following sentences.*

1. The sun came up the dew quickly dried.

2. Michael Jordan wanted to play major-league baseball however, he never made the grade.

3. The highest-paid entertainers for 1990 and 1991 were pop musicians New Kids on the Block, $115 million TV comic Bill Cosby, $113 million talk-show host Oprah Winfrey, $80 million and singer Madonna, $63 million.

Check the Answer Key before continuing.

Solution #7: The Colon

Use a colon *after a complete statement* to introduce one of the following: a list, an explanation, or a long quotation.

(list) Everyone should bring these items to class: the text, a notebook, and a pen.

(explanation) There are two things I like about Gerry: his sense of humour and his loyalty to his friends.

(quotation) The commencement speaker quoted Mark Twain: "When I was a boy of 14, my father was so ignorant I could hardly stand to have the old man around. But when I got to be 21, I was astonished at how much he had learned in seven years."

SPOTCHECK 10-9   *Supply colons as needed.*

1. Here's what you should bring to the picnic paper plates, paper cups, and plastic forks.

2. Monica has a quality I really admire enthusiasm.

3. Before you leave home, be sure to turn off the lights, turn down the furnace, and put out the cat.

Check the Answer Key before continuing.

Solution #8: Dashes and Parentheses

Use a *dash* to show an abrupt change in thought or to provide emphasis.

(abrupt change) We were married in 1982—no, in 1981.

(emphasis) Our neighbour—the scoundrel—still hasn't returned our lawn mower.

Use *parentheses* to set off extra information that is not emphasized.

Jason said weight training (which he took up in January) helped him with the batting title.

The battle is discussed in Chapter 6 (pages 123 to 134).

SPOTCHECK 10-10

Add dashes and parentheses as needed.

1. I'd like a girlfriend just like Marsha a knockout!

2. The construction of the St. Lawrence Seaway completed in 1959 was an exceptional engineering feat.

3. My wife Mildred I mean Agnes went to visit her mother.

4. My friend Brad who owes me money by the way was just named a vice-president at the bank.

5. Tina's brother in fact her whole family is a little odd.

Compare your answers with those in the Answer Key.

DOUBLECHECK 10-2

Add semicolons, colons, dashes, and parentheses as needed.

1. Among the largest cities of the world are Bombay, India Cairo, Egypt Jakarta, Indonesia London, England and Tokyo, Japan.

2. Uncle Alfred he's my mother's late brother once went over Niagara Falls in a barrel.

3. The curtain rose the performance began.

4. Be sure to bring these on the camping trip a knife, a first-aid kit, and a can of bear repellent.

5. Ludwig van Beethoven 1770–1827 was probably the greatest composer ever known.

6. Allison lost would you believe it? ten pounds in two weeks.

7. Jan lost ten pounds in two months however she gained them back in one.

8. Everything the Garcias owned furniture, clothing, family keepsakes was destroyed in the fire.

9. The Blue Jays won the World Series in 1992 moreover they won it again in 1993.

10. Katharine Hepburn do you remember her? won the Academy Award for best actress in 1981.

Compare your answers with those in the Answer Key.

◆ WRITING PROCESS

REVISING: FAULTY LOGIC

Your writing should be logical. If your reader's response is "That doesn't make sense," you have lost your reader. Here are five common logical fallacies or errors in reasoning:

1. **Hasty Generalization**—A sweeping statement about a group that doesn't take into account likely exceptions; a conclusion based on little evidence ("jumping to a conclusion").

    (illogical) Women workers are underpaid.

    (illogical) French bread is the best in the world.

    Yes, *some, many, a few* women are underpaid. But the sentence implies that *all* are underpaid, and the reader knows that isn't true. As for the second example, it seems unlikely the writer has sampled all the breads in the world.

    Watch out for sentences that use or imply the words *all, every, none, always, never*. Instead use qualifiers such as *many, some, most, the average, sometimes*.

2. **Non Sequitur**—These Latin words mean "it doesn't follow." Here's an argument in which the conclusion "doesn't follow" the evidence offered:

    (illogical) Maria had a frown on her face yesterday, so she must have flunked her history exam. (Her frown has many possible explanations.)

3. **Bandwagon**—The fact that most people favour something is not necessarily a reason for everyone to "get on the bandwagon."

    (illogical) Senator Godfrey is leading in the polls, so I guess I should vote for him.

4. **Either–Or Fallacy**—Saying there are only two choices or possibilities when there are actually more.

(**illogical**) Unless my parents buy me a car, I'll never get a girlfriend.

5. **Circular Reasoning**—"Proving" a point by restating it (going around in a circle).

   (**illogical**) Professor Jones is a poor teacher because his classes are no good.

SPOTCHECK 10-11

Identify the type of logical fallacy in each of the following examples.

1. Everyone else cuts class, so why shouldn't I do it?

   Fallacy: _____

2. Either everybody stops using paper products, or we soon won't have any more trees.

   Fallacy: _____

3. The reason I like that band's music is that it sounds so good.

   Fallacy: _____

4. You just know that anyone on welfare is lazy.

   Fallacy: _____

5. Angela has a nice smile, so she will be good in sales.

   Fallacy: _____

6. Football players advertise beer, so drinking must improve athletic performance.

   Fallacy: _____

7. If we don't go to a movie tonight, the evening will be wasted.

   Fallacy: _____

Check the Answer Key before continuing.

CHECKPOINT 10-1

One sentence in each of the following pairs contains a punctuation error. Place a check mark in front of the correct sentence.

_____ **1a.** Who is that at the front door?

_____ **1b.** Its probably just the newspaper boy.

_____ **2a.** I asked him if he would put the paper inside the screen door.

_____ **2b.** He said that "he would."

_____ **3a.** I enjoy reading The Edmonton Sun every day, don't you?

_____ **3b.** Well, I'd rather watch The National on TV.

_____ **4a.** I like the special reports, especially the international features, they're really interesting.

_____ **4b.** However, I do wish they would cover more local news.

_____ **5a.** My mother likes listening to Peter Gzowski on Morningside on CBC Radio.

_____ **5b.** She says "He's a very good interviewer."

_____ **6a.** "I don't like the radio; it's boring."

_____ **6b.** "Thats a ridiculous thing to say," James told me.

_____ **7a.** One part of The Toronto Star that I do like is the column Careers.

_____ **7b.** One of the columnists, Janis Foord Kirk, is pretty clever.

_____ **8a.** Did you read her item about what to write in a résumé?

_____ **8b.** It is not appropriate to mention, your marital status, or how old you are.

_____ **9a.** On the other hand she said you must mention your experience.

_____ **9b.** "Your experience," she said, "must be mentioned."

_____ **10a.** She said "we must think of the employers when we write."

_____ **10b.** She told us that we must think of the employers when we write.

No answers are given for Checkpoint quizzes.

THE ESSAY

◆ READING

AN ESSAY WITH INTRODUCTORY, BODY, AND CONCLUDING PARAGRAPHS

PRECHECK Are you a fan of the late John Candy's movies? Did you think he was an exceptionally funny man? The following essay by Jane Merivale looks at Candy's personality and describes three of the characteristics that made him popular not only at home but also internationally. To illustrate these personality traits, the essay uses examples from Candy's life.

We All Love Candy

—Jane Merivale

quintessential most representative

    On March 4, 1994, a well-loved Canadian left us prematurely: 1 John Candy suffered a massive heart attack in Mexico and died peacefully. He had been filming his fortieth movie, *Wagons East*. He was only 43, and most of his enormous potential was still untapped. Many Canadians mourn for this quintessentially Canadian actor, who had three predominant characteristics for which he was so popular: he was well-loved for his geniality, renowned for his generosity, and respected for his genius.

pretensions ways of appearing differently, often richer/smarter than in reality

    There are many stories about John Candy's genial nature. He was 2 an extremely popular person. As Wayne Gretsky said, "He just enjoyed people; he enjoyed life." He was popular not only with actors he worked with, but also with members of the Argonauts football team, which he co-owned with Gretsky, and with ordinary people he came into contact with. John had no pretensions: "I'm the real article. What you see is what you get," as he put it in *Planes, Trains and Automobiles*. He was a family man who was very sensitive to others. As Dan Ackroyd, his long-time friend, said, "Everybody loved John." They appreciated his gentle nature and found something totally Canadian in the contradiction between the famous actor and the gentle, unassuming giant.

Candy's generosity was well-known. A shy, heavy child, he grew up   3
to be extremely aware of and generous toward the needs of others. He enjoyed sharing his gifts with others. Many of his screen characters depicted the sensitive person he really was. He contributed to many charities that involved children, going out of his way once to fulfil a child's last wish by enabling the boy to meet him and Tom Hanks. Many people who knew John refer to his humanity, his compassion, and the way his caring for others made him so generous in spirit. When, on the set of *Only the Lonely,* he discovered that Maureen O'Hara's caravan was smaller than his, he insisted on switching with her immediately—even though, for someone his size, the exchange could not have been easy. He was the kind of person who didn't want to disappoint or hurt others, and this was revealed in his many acts of generosity.

absurd   ridiculous to the point of extraordinary

Although his geniality and generosity are legend, Candy's ge-   4
nius—his comic brilliance—is also sorely missed. When he joined Second City as a comedian, his star rose as he became famous for characters like Yosh Shmenge, the polka bandleader who played the clarinet: the ordinary transformed into the absurd. Thereafter, Candy had several years of acting in movies that bombed, and it is typical of his character and true to his talent that he never lost his audience appeal. His later films remain as much a testimony to his phenomenal comic ability as do the hilarious reruns of *Second City.* The sleeper movie *Planes, Trains and Automobiles,* the highly successful *Uncle Buck,* and *Only the Lonely* are all exceptionally funny movies, fully expressing the genius of John Candy. It is a tribute to this brilliance that Candy was always learning, facing new challenges. He ventured into radio—*Radio Candy*—and the Camp Candy cartoons. His versatility led him to direct a TV movie, *Hostage for a Day,* shortly before his death. No one knows how he might further have applied his talents in directing.

versatility   ability to do many different jobs

Canadian icon   symbol of being Canadian

We all know, however, that a Canadian icon has left us and that we   5
feel his absence. We miss this man, who was a star, a fabulous star, in America—not an easy achievement, especially for a Canadian. Yet with all his fame and fortune, he remained a simple, accessible Canadian man. We cannot forget Candy's geniality, his generosity, and his enormous capacity for comic genius.

CHECKING MEANING AND STYLE

1. What are the three traits that, according to this essay's author, Candy is loved for?

2. What examples does the essay's author give of his generosity?

3. What did Candy say that made it clear that he was a man without pretensions?

4. Find the sentence in the introduction that states what the essay will be about.

5. Where are the topic sentences in Paragraphs 2, 3, and 4?

6. What does the conclusion state?

CHECKING IDEAS

1. Do you agree with this description of John Candy?

2. Are there other Canadian actors who are now internationally famous who are different from, or similar to, Candy?

3. Do you think it is easy for a Canadian actor to "make it" in the United States and elsewhere?

4. Does a man like Candy reflect Canadian culture or humour? In what way?

◆ WRITING MODELS

THE ESSAY

"We All Love Candy" is a well-organized essay. It has a one-paragraph introduction that states the main idea of the essay, three body paragraphs that develop that idea, and a one-paragraph conclusion. The student essay that follows is an example that is worth analyzing in detail.

Model Five-Paragraph Essay

A Double Standard

Introduction: The final sentence is the thesis statement for the whole essay.

The Women's Movement has helped improve the lives of women in 1 North America in many ways. We can work at jobs formerly closed to us. We are more likely to get pay comparable to that of men. We are less likely to hear men call us "baby" and more likely to have them treat us as adults. But the Women's Movement hasn't had much impact on my family, especially on the way my brother and I are treated. Just because he is male, he has many privileges and advantages that are denied me just because I am female.

Body I: The first sentence is the topic sentence for the paragraph.

Even though he is two years younger than I, he is much more free 2 to stay out late and to come and go as he pleases. If I come home after midnight, my dad throws a fit. He wants to know where I've been, who I was with, and who drove me home. Even if I tell him I went to a church meeting and had a pizza afterwards with several girlfriends, he tells me that if it happens again I won't be allowed out of the house after dark for a month. Meanwhile, my brother's coming home at one or two in the morning, and all my dad says the next day is, "Well, did you have a good time last night?"

Body II: The first sentence is the topic sentence for the paragraph.

It irritates me that my brother doesn't have to do nearly as much   3 work around the house as I do. I'm expected to set the table for all meals, help Mom with the cooking, and wash the dishes by myself. On Saturdays, it's my job to mop and wax the kitchen floor and vacuum all the rugs. And what does Little Brother do? Once in a while he carries out the garbage. He's supposed to keep the lawn mowed, but somehow he always seems to have baseball practice or some other crucial activity just when the grass gets a bit long. So Dad does it, saying he needs the exercise anyway.

Body III: The first sentence is the topic sentence for the paragraph.

Then there's the matter of the car. You can guess who gets to use it   4 and who doesn't. He drives to classes. I take the bus to my morning job and the bus to my afternoon classes. I told my friend Shauna that I thought I could get the car to take us to the new Spielberg movie on Saturday night. But Brother gets the car to drive his buddies to a rock concert at the auditorium. Mother said it was too dangerous for him to take the bus to that part of town.

Conclusion: The first sentence summarizes the three body paragraphs.

It isn't fair that my brother has more freedom than I, that he gets   5 out of household chores, and that he monopolizes use of the car. Whoever said it's a man's world must have been peeking into our house.

Until now we have concentrated on writing paragraphs. It is time to tackle the larger challenge of writing the essay. If you have been having success with paragraphs, you should not have much trouble with the essay. A paragraph is a brief development of one idea. An essay is a longer development of one idea or subject.

You have been urged to use a topic sentence to express the main idea of each paragraph. You are now urged to use a thesis sentence to express the main idea of the entire essay.

We will focus on writing the kind of essay that is standard in many college composition courses: the five-paragraph essay. The five paragraphs look like this:

PARAGRAPH 1

The introduction, including a thesis sentence that states the main point of the essay.

PARAGRAPH 2

First support paragraph to back up the thesis sentence. Starts with a topic sentence.

PARAGRAPH 3

Second support paragraph, with a topic sentence.

PARAGRAPH 4

Third support paragraph, with a topic sentence. (Paragraphs 2, 3, and 4 make up the body of the essay.)

PARAGRAPH 5

The concluding paragraph, which brings the essay to a satisfying end, perhaps with a summary or restating of the main points.

Here is the essay in diagram form:

Introductory Paragraph

> Thesis Sentence

First Body Paragraph

> Topic Sentence
>
> Support

Second Body Paragraph

> Topic Sentence
>
> Support

Third Body Paragraph

> Topic Sentence
>
> Support

Concluding Paragraph

> Conclusion

Now let's apply the outline to the essay "A Double Standard."

INTRODUCTION — Thesis sentence: "Just because he is male, [my brother] has many privileges and advantages that are denied me just because I am female." (The purpose of the next three paragraphs is to support or show the truth of the thesis sentence.)

FIRST SUPPORT — Topic sentence: ". . . [He] is much more free to stay out late and to come and go as he pleases." (This idea is *developed* by using specific examples and comparison. The next two paragraphs are developed in the same way.)

SECOND SUPPORT — Topic sentence: ". . . [M]y brother doesn't have to do nearly as much work around the house as I do."

THIRD SUPPORT — Topic sentence: (implied) He gets to use the car more than I do.

CONCLUSION — (implied) It's a man's world.

Of course, not every essay is organized in just this way. An essay might have fewer or many more paragraphs to support the thesis. Essays written by professionals often do not contain a written-out thesis sentence; the thesis is only implied. But all essays have a thesis—a central point the writer wishes to make.

Why a thesis sentence? Using a thesis sentence forces a writer to decide ahead of time just what point is to be made. It helps the writer stay on track once the writing begins. On a smaller scale, the topic sentence offers the same kind of help in writing the paragraph. Of course, the thesis sentence also helps the reader by stating the main point of the essay.

Some writers (and instructors) like an essay to start with a thesis sentence that outlines the entire essay. Using that approach, the essay "A Double Standard" could have had the following thesis sentence:

> Just because he is male and I am female, my brother has more freedom, has fewer household chores, and has first call on the family car.

That clearly sets up an essay with three developing paragraphs: one on freedom, one on chores, and one on use of the car.

Whichever method you use, it is important that you know before you begin your first draft just what it is you want to say. If you do not make a formal outline, at least jot down the main idea and the points you will use to support it, using the prewriting techniques discussed earlier.

◆ Writing Assignment

An Essay

Let's examine the three parts of the essay a little more closely.

The <u>introduction</u> (first paragraph) serves two purposes. One, as we have already seen, is to present the thesis or main idea of the essay. The other is to arouse interest so that the reader will want to continue. Perhaps the thesis sentence alone will do that. But often a more complex introduction is effective. The introduction to "A Double Standard," for example, puts one young woman's problems in the framework of recent progress made by women in general in North America.

Any introduction that sets the stage for the rest of the essay can be used. It might be a brief anecdote or description that leads into the thesis sentence. It might be an interesting quotation or a startling fact. A question can be an effective opener—but be sure it implies very clearly what point you intend to make in the essay and is not just a way of postponing that decision.

The <u>body</u> is the main part of the essay. It should be at least two or three paragraphs long. It is in these paragraphs that you support the thesis sentence. You prove your point with specific details, illustrations, examples, comparisons, and the other methods of paragraph development already studied. Each paragraph will consider one particular aspect of the general subject announced in the thesis sentence. Look again at "A Double Standard" for examples.

How long should a paragraph be? This is the logical answer: long enough to develop the idea it expresses in a way that satisfies or convinces the reader. In general, if a paragraph doesn't have at least four to six sentences, it needs more development.

The concluding paragraph should bring the essay to a satisfying close. Often it will summarize the main points made, as in "A Double Standard," although in a short essay this reminder of what has just been read may not be thought necessary. It might be appropriate to suggest actions based on what has been said or to predict future developments.

The title (for example, "A Double Standard") is usually a short, catchy phrase intended to capture the reader's interest and perhaps to give a hint about the subject of the essay. Centre the title about 1½ inches (4 cm.) from the top of the first page (on the top line of notebook paper). Capitalize the first word and other important words. Do not underline the title or put quotation marks around it (unless it is a quotation). The title is not really part of the main essay; any essential information it contains must be repeated in the essay itself.

WRITE AN ESSAY WITH INTRODUCTION, BODY, AND CONCLUSION PARAGRAPHS

Write an essay with two or three paragraphs of development on one of the following subjects:

1. Causes of family arguments

2. Why I would (not) want to be a police officer (or other occupation)

3. Two or three things (not people) I would hate to do without

4. Two or three desirable characteristics in an employee

5. Two or three types of pets—good and bad points

Use this outline planning form to help organize your essay:

INTRODUCTION

1. (The thesis statement for the essay) _____

_____

_____

BODY I

2. (The topic sentence for the first body paragraph) _____

_____

_____

BODY II

3. (The topic sentence for the second body paragraph) _____

_____

_____

BODY III

4. (The topic sentence for the third body paragraph) _____

_____

_____

CONCLUSION   **5.** (Summary of the body paragraphs or a final statement) _____

_____

_____

_____

Be sure your essay

- has a thesis sentence in the introductory paragraph.
- has a topic sentence at the beginning of each paragraph of the body.
- develops the thesis with interesting and convincing details.
- has a concluding paragrah.
- has a title centred at the top of page 1.

◆ SENTENCE MECHANICS

USING CAPITALS, FIGURES, AND ABBREVIATIONS

The Problem: Knowing When to Use Capitals, Figures, and Abbreviations

Can you identify the error in each of the following sentences?

> Ruth is majoring in History.
> Tom shouted, "we won the game!"
> 12 percent of the police force was sick.
> She had two hundred twenty-one old records.
> That dog must weigh at least fifty lbs.
> Dr. Cooper spoke after the dinner.

Knowing when and when not to use capital letters, figures, and abbreviations will make you feel more confident about your writing.

Solution #1: When to Use Capital Letters

Capitalize the first word of a sentence and the first word of a direct quotation that is a complete sentence.

> The store manager said, "We close at midnight."

Capitalize names and nicknames of persons and the word *I*.

> Do you remember that I called you "Elephant Breath" Smith in high school?

Capitalize names of specific places, structures, and school subjects.

Asia	Yellowknife	Biology 256
Gardiner Expressway	St. John's	Gaspé Bay
John A. Macdonald High School	Modern Greek 101	Prince Edward Island

Don't capitalize names that are general rather than specific.

He went to <u>high school</u> near here.

They lived on an <u>island</u> last summer.

Ruth is majoring in <u>history</u>.

The Finleys live <u>east</u> of town.

Capitalize names of races, nationalities, languages, and religions.

Caucasian	Russian	Swahili
Presbyterian	Buddhism	Jewish

Capitalize names of organizations.

Reform Party	Senate	Rotary Club
Red Cross	General Motors	Mafia

Capitalize days of the week, months, holidays, and historical events.

Tuesday	July	Canada Day
New Year's Eve	Thanksgiving	Korean War

Capitalize the first word, the last word, and every important word in a title.

"She Don't Get the Blues"	*War and Peace*	*The Maple Leaf Forever*
Northern Exposure	*Anne of Green Gables*	

Capitalize a person's title only if it appears before a name.

We saw <u>Professor</u> Mehta in the cafeteria.

Alfred Mehta is a <u>professor</u> of economics.

SPOTCHECK 11-1 *Supply capital letters as needed.*

1. college of the jesuits is in quebec.

2. her father is catholic, and her mother is baptist.

3. my language professor can speak six languages, including tagalog.

4. the olsons vacationed on an island in lake superior.

5. the kids in elementary school called sam "sparky."

6. the band named loud and funky performed the beatles song "norwegian wood."

7. dave flunked math 1a, so i guess he won't major in accounting.

8. mr. and mrs. mcdonald saw the grand canyon when they went to arizona in june.

9. the salvation army building is on the corner of elm street and pine avenue.

10. vickie declared she would "never set foot in this town again."

Check the Answer Key before continuing.

Solution #2: When to Use
Figures

In general, spell out numbers from one to ten, and use figures for the others. Ordinals are almost always spelled out.

ten cookies	11 cookies	fourth
three miles	162 miles	thirteenth

But always use figures to show times, dates, addresses, decimals, percentages, fractions, and statistics.

We have tickets for Flight 7, leaving at 3:15 a.m. on September 1.

Megan lives at 4 Spruce Street, Apartment 2.

Only 8 percent of the students know that in math *pi* equals 3.1416.

The Latin Club elected Liz president, 10–8.

Always spell out a number that begins a sentence. If the result is too long and awkward, rephrase the sentence.

(wrong) 123 bands marched in the parade.

(awkward) One hundred and twenty-three bands marched in the parade.

(rephrased) Members of 123 bands marched in the parade.

If two or more related numbers in a sentence call for different styles, use numbers for all.

The dictator's wife left behind 6 fur coats, 87 dresses, and 203 pairs of shoes.

SPOTCHECK 11-2

Cross out any incorrect uses of numbers and write the correct forms.

eight

EXAMPLE: There were at least ~~8~~ **eight** chipmunks in the yard.

1. The mayor laid off three secretaries, 22 street cleaners, and 112 firefighters.

2. 12 percent of the police force was out sick.

3. Mimi wears shoe size six and a half.

4. Our candidate got only 9 percent of the vote.

5. The bus leaves at three p.m.

6. Ricky's birthday is on August third.

Check the Answer Key before continuing.

Solution #3: When to Use
Abbreviations

Only a few abbreviations are acceptable in formal writing. Here are some of them:

A.M. and P.M. (or a.m. and p.m.)   B.C.   A.D.

Mr.   Mrs.   Ms.   Dr.   (before a name)

Jr.   Sr.   M.D.   (after a name)

B.A.   M.A.   Ph.D.   (academic degrees)

GST   MPH

If any of these abbreviations are unfamiliar, you can see the danger in using abbreviations: Your reader may not understand them.

It is generally safer to spell out a name once before switching to the abbreviation.

> We took poor Poochie to the Society for the Prevention of Cruelty to Animals. The workers at the SPCA said . . .

Some names are perhaps better known in abbreviated form: *CAA, CBC, RCMP, TV, VCR, IQ.* Use your judgment. Check a dictionary to see if periods are used with the abbreviation.

You may abbreviate titles like *Gen., Gov., Prof.,* and *Dr.* when they appear before a full name. Spell them out when they appear with the last name alone.

> Sen. Amanda Cross will speak at the rally.

> Senator Cross will seek a fourth term next year.

Spell out (do not abbreviate) the names of provinces, countries, months, days, and units of measurement (ounces, pounds, feet, yards).

SPOTCHECK 11-3

Cross out any abbreviations that would be inappropriate in formal writing, and substitute full forms.

> **Manitoba**
> **EXAMPLE:** Phoebe was born in ~~Man.~~

1. The police academy will hear a speaker from the CSIS on Nov. 12.

2. The baby weighed seven lbs., three ounces (3.25 kg), at birth.

3. I've heard that Prof. Parsnip trains attack dogs.

4. The college will offer a new poli sci course next semester.

5. Two-thirds of the land in downtown T.O. is used for driving, parking, or servicing cars.

6. Singer Maureen Forrester was born in Montreal, Que., in 1930.

Check the Answer Key before continuing.

DOUBLECHECK 11-1

Correct errors in capital letters, numbers, and abbreviations. Each sentence has one error.

1. 12 years ago I moved to Regina.

2. Carrie is attending a University in the West.

3. Gilbert has studied spanish for four years.

4. Nick still owes me thirty-six fifty for a sports coat.

5. Did world war II end in 1945 or 1946?

6. Joey lives at seventy-three Main Street.

7. Fatima earned a B.A. degree in Economics.

8. She attended High School in Moncton, New Brunswick.

9. That dog must weigh at least 20 kg.

10. The bartender told the boys to return "When you're 21."

Check the Answer Key before continuing.

DOUBLECHECK 11-2

Correct errors in capital letters, numbers, and abbreviations. Each sentence has one error.

1. The Earth's five billionth person was born in 1987, just 13 years after the 4 billionth person was born.

2. At that rate, there will be 6 billion people by the year 2000.

3. According to statistics Canada, the population of Canada was 26,833 million by the first day of 1991.

4. That was an increase of more than one million since new year's day, 1986.

5. Many canadian cities continued to grow, according to the Census Figures.

6. The Statistics show that, between 1981 and 1986, St. John's grew by 3%.

7. During the same time period, Sault ste. Marie declined by 0.4%.

8. According to Statistics Canada, as many women have their first baby after age 30 as those in their mid-20s.

9. In 1986, 63.1% of the Canadian population spoke english.

10. In the same year, 24.3% of Canadians listed French as their first language.

Check the Answer Key before continuing.

DOUBLECHECK 11-3

Edit the following paragraph, correcting any errors in capital letters, numbers, and abbreviations.

[1]The Flea is a remarkable insect, says the magazine *national geographic*. [2]If there were olympic games for insects, fleas would win most of the gold medals. [3]Some fleas can jump one hundred and fifty times their own length. [4]That's equivalent to a human jumping nearly

a thousand ft (300 metres). ⁵One flea was observed jumping thirty thousand times without stopping. ⁶Fleas are fast too. ⁷A flea can accelerate 50 times faster than an Astronaut in a space shuttle after liftoff. ⁸Except for the creatures' athletic skills, Humans don't admire fleas. ⁹3 plague epidemics, spread by rats and their fleas, have ravaged the World, killing more than 200 million people. ¹⁰the last plague epidemic started in china in 1855 and was carried by steamships to all parts of the world. ¹¹In the U.S. in 1987 there were 12 cases of plague and 2 deaths.

Check the Answer Key before continuing.

◆ WRITING PROCESS

REVISING: UNITY IN THE PARAGRAPH AND IN THE ESSAY

Unity is important both in paragraphs and in essays. A unified paragraph deals with only one idea or topic and does not wander into unrelated matters. In the same way, an essay is also unified. The thesis statement announces what the essay is about, and all the paragraphs stick to that subject.

PARAGRAPH UNITY

A helpful way to gain paragraph unity is to start the paragraph with a topic sentence that states what the paragraph is about. The other sentences in the paragraph then provide details and examples that *support* or *develop* the topic sentence.

Here is an example of a paragraph that lacks unity, that does not stick to the (underlined) topic sentence. Which sentences should be left out?

¹Cats have stirred strong feelings in people for thousands of years. ²Ancient Egyptians treated cats almost like gods, and someone who killed a cat could be punished with death. ³People who like cats often don't like dogs, and vice versa. ⁴In Europe in the Middle Ages, cats became associated with witchcraft and black magic and were persecuted by the Christian church. ⁵In the nineteenth century, sentimental Victorians restored the cat as a household favourite. ⁶It is clear that cats are minor gods in many North American homes today. ⁷We spend more money on cat food than on baby food—$2 billion a year. ⁸Birds and fish are also popular in many homes.

Checking Sentences 3 and 8 against the topic sentence, we see that they have gotten off the track and should be omitted.

The topic sentence sometimes appears in the middle or at the end of a paragraph. Sometimes it is only implied—not written out. But inexperienced writers will find it most helpful to make the topic sentence the first sentence. That approach is emphasized in this text.

ESSAY UNITY

Unity in an essay occurs when all the paragraphs relate to the thesis statement. In the model essay "A Double Standard," the paragraphs were about how the writer's parents treat her brother and her differently. The essay is unified because all of its paragraphs support its thesis statement.

✓

CHECKPOINT 11-1   *Each of the following sentences has an error in the use of capital letters, abbreviations, or numbers. Underline the error and write the correct form in the blank.*

_____   **1.** Dalhousie university is in Halifax, N.S.

_____   **2.** Fred graduated from the University of Alberta, but his brother never went beyond High school.

_____   **3.** The scenery is interesting along the Trans-Canada Hwy.

_____   **4.** Cynthia jumped 17 ft, 6 inches, in the track meet Saturday.

_____   **5.** Next fall, we hope to visit jasper Park.

_____   **6.** Mary hopes Dr. Bell will be able to perform the operation.

_____   **7.** I enjoyed the course "Theory of Capitalism," but I don't plan to take another course in Economics.

_____   **8.** If I take a shower after P.E., I'm late for my English class.

_____   **9.** Alejandro was born in Peru and still speaks fluent spanish.

_____   **10.** Did you remember that Nov. 29 is Allison's birthday?

No answers are given for Checkpoint quizzes.

THE PROCESS ESSAY

◆ READING

EXPLAINING A PROCESS

PRECHECK

Have you ever skated on a homemade garden rink? In this process essay, Paul Quarrington shows us how to make such a skating rink.

Home Ice

—Paul Quarrington

Think of it as wintry gardening. Focus on the magical aspects, for on a more worldly level, we are about to discuss standing outside on the most bitter of nights with a spurting garden hose in your hand, likely frozen there forever. We are about to discuss how to make a backyard skating rink.

It seems to me that the backyard rink ranks right up there with frozen duck ponds and ice-locked rivers. Which is to say, they have a home not only on earth but also in our frostbitten imaginations. Dreams of Stanley Cups and figure-skating championships are born there. Local arenas are nice enough places, I suppose, but the important thing is the sense of community. When I think of local arenas, I think of the benches, the snack bars, the people huddled together eating cold hot dogs and blowing on cups of hot chocolate. The ice itself is nothing special—it is quiet and subdued, not like the unruly ice you find in a backyard rink. The ice of a backyard rink is welted and scarred and unable to smooth the wrinkled face of the planet. It is elemental, having as much claim to the land as rocks or wind.

elemental fundamental

mundane ordinary

That is why the process is not really so much "making" or "con- **3** structing" a backyard rink; it is more along the lines of allowing one to come into being, a sort of shivering midwifery. Some people conceive of the process as imposing the rink on the ground, which results in the most mundane and dreary objection to the backyard skating rink: it will ruin the grass. That is not true. I even checked with a landscape gardener who assured me that although the grass may grow in opposite directions for a time the rink won't ruin the grass.

quintessential most typical

I propose to pass on the recipe for the definitive, the quintessen- **4** tial, the perfect backyard skating rink. I did not arrive at such a recipe without a lot of help. I turned to my friend Peter Hayman, a Toronto filmmaker and father of three young boys. I have skated on Hayman's rink and know it to be first-class (I have a simple test: any ice that does not immediately flip me onto my dustcover is first-class). Also, I went to Ronn Hartviksen, the creator of perhaps the most ambitious and beautiful rink in the world, and I also consulted the guru of the backyard rink, Walter Gretzky.

The first step in making the rink is to find the right site. If you are **5** going to make a rink, decide early in the season, well before winter is actually in sight. This is the easy part, walking outside and choosing the likeliest spot. It may be that you have a smallish backyard and are simply going to flood the whole thing. The guiding principle should arise from the fact that you are going to have to shovel, resurface and otherwise groom your backyard rink, so you should keep it to a manageable size. Twenty by forty feet seems reasonable: large enough for skaters to manoeuvre, even to play a spirited, congested, game of shinny, but small enough to care for.

A prime consideration is flatness. It is not necessary that the **6** ground be perfectly smooth (you will be surprised at how hilly and full of cavities your lawn really is), but there is no getting around the fact that it must be level. Some depressions can, of course, be built up with snow, and small rises will just become part of the rink.

proximity nearness

The last consideration is proximity to a water source. Tapping into **7** an inside source is best. If you can run a hose into the basement, for example, and hook up with the washing-machine taps, you will reap a number of benefits. Remember that no nozzle/hose connection is perfect, and imagine some of the nasty things that could happen at an outside connection—such as finding the thing encased in block of ice. Even if you avoid nightly chipping and hacking, any outside terminal is going to require a bucket or two of hot water just to get the tap cranked. So, if you can get to the water inside, so much the better, especially because in the maintenance stages, you can employ the hot water for resurfacing, a technique I call "the poor man's Zamboni" (a machine used to resurface the ice in arenas).

But let's not worry about maintenance right now; let's get the **8** thing started. Just a couple of quick points here: make sure you have plenty of good-quality, thick, heavy rubber hose. Having selected the site, and got the hose, make sure the ground is properly tended, which means mowing and raking. If you don't you may face what proved to be the bane of my childhood backyard rinks: errant blades of grass popping through the ice surface. I know this does not seem likely or even possible, but, believe me, little green Ninjas will sprout up and flip you onto your backside. So give your lawn a marring cut late in the fall.

Here is an optional step. In Thunder Bay, Hartviksen hoses down the naked earth in late fall but in more southerly climes, watering your lawn in fall serves no purpose except to demonstrate to the neighbours that you are fairly strange, so they will not think twice the first time you are out there at midnight and 40 below. 9

Now you wait. You wait for cold temperatures. You are more than likely going to have to wait for the cold temperatures in January. So you wait for the requisite cold temperatures, and you wait for snow. Wait until there is a whole lot of snow, maybe two or three good dumpings. Then clear some of it away from your rectangle, leaving behind anywhere from four to six inches. This clearing supplies you with a little border, something to aid in water retention while flooding. It also gives a comfortable sense of containment and might even keep a puck on the ice, although you and I both know that the puck will hit your little ridge of snow, pick up torque and be gone into the neighbour's yard. 10

Now you are ready to make your base. It is best to flatten the snow. Hartviksen sends out troops of kids to play "boot hockey." He also possess a heavy piece of wood that he can drag behind him, smoothing the surface. The foundation of the base you are making is snow. Snow plus water and the chilly, chilly air. I am going to advocate the "slush" approach to base building. I am the proponent of the most active sort of base building, getting out there with a hose and creating slush, which is then smoothed flat. You want the slush to be more solid than a slurpee, just watery enough that snowball construction is out of the question. Do small sections at a time: water the ground, work it into slush with a snow shovel, use the back of the shovel to smooth it out, move along, do it again. Work lanes, walking backward across the rink-to-be. Once you get that done, have someone carry you inside to thaw you out in a dry, warm corner. In the morning, it will be slightly hilly—well, let's face it, your rink at this point would baffle most topographical mapmakers. But that's all right. You have done most of the heavy human work now; it is time to turn things over to Mother Nature and let her smooth everything out. 11

The next night, go out there armed with your hose. Just the hose, no fancy nozzle or sprayer: you have to have the open-ended hose because you want to get as much water on the ground in as short a time as possible. You should be able to hit most places without stepping on the ice surface, but if you can't, go ahead and step on it. Depending on how cold it is you might be able to do two or even three floodings that first night. When you have finished, do yourself an enormous favour: take the coil of hose inside the house with you. 12

The next morning, you will find a vaguely flat sheet of ice, although it might be alarmingly pitted, cracked and ravined. Now, in Peter Hayman's words, you "make like a referee." No, don't get small-minded and petty and order people around for no good reason (just joking); he means that you get out there on hands and knees—as referees often do during games—grab handfuls of snow and start stuffing 13

topography study of landsurface

tamping   *packing down*   the cracks and holes. Stuffing and tamping, tamping and stuffing. It's amazing how much snow even the smallest crack can hold, so don't imagine this is the work of a few moments. However, the more patching you do the better your rink will be.

Now you have to do your flood that evening, taking care to find the 14 air pockets that undermine the structure and correct them at this stage. In the morning, you have something that looks like a skating rink. There is still some patching to do, but it seems less fundamental—more like polishing than anything else—and after another couple of floodings that evening you will have, if not a proper skating rink, what Hayman refers to with caution as "a skateable situation."

Put the lightest family member out there. Hold your breath. As the 15 person skates around the outer edges there will be some creaking and cracking. Make like a referee and flood again that evening. And the next. And the next. You need an ice thickness of perhaps six inches to survive sudden thaw. In time you will not have to flood every evening, or even every other night, but many nights will find you out there, hose in hand, practising some wintry gardening.

**CHECKING
MEANING AND
STYLE**

1. Where is the thesis statement in Paul Quarrington's essay?

2. How does Quarrington introduce many of the steps in the home-made-rink process?

3. What factors should you consider in choosing the site?

4. Why must you make sure the ground is "properly tended"?

5. What steps are involved in making the base?

6. What do you do when you "make like a referee"?

7. What is the tone of this essay? Where would you be likely to find an article of this kind?

CHECKING IDEAS

1. In making a backyard rink, why is it advisable to focus on the magical aspects?

2. How does Quarrington view the backyard rink?

3. Why is skating so popular in Canada?

4. Do you participate in winter sports?

◆ WRITING MODELS

THE PROCESS ESSAY

"Home Ice" is a process essay that gives detailed and lively instructions on making a backyard skating rink. The thesis statement is in the introductory paragraph, and in each paragraph where a step in the rink's construction is explained, the topic sentence introduces the instruction, which is then followed by any relevant details.

INTRODUCTION PARAGRAPH	We are about to discuss how to make a backyard skating rink.
PARAGRAPH 5	The first step in making the rink is to find the right site.
PARAGRAPH 8	But let's not talk about maintenance right now; let's get the thing started.
PARAGRAPH 9	Here is an optional step.
PARAGRAPH 10	Now you wait.
PARAGRAPH 11	Now you are ready to make your base.
PARAGRAPH 12	The next night, go out there armed with your hose.
PARAGRAPH 13	Now, in Peter Hayman's words, you "make like a referee."
PARAGRAPH 14	Now you have to do your flood that evening. . . .
PARAGRAPH 15	Put the lightest family member out there.

In a process essay, the thesis statement introduces the subject and the topic sentences make the instructions extremely clear.

The instructions are often written in the imperative, or command, form where "you" is understood rather than written. Here is an outline of "Home Ice" as it might appear in the five-paragraph format, using the imperative voice.

INTRODUCTION	We are about to discuss how to make a backyard skating rink.
BODY 1	The first step in making the rink is to find the right kind of site.
BODY 2	Now wait for the cold temperatures before making the base.
BODY 3	Hose the area at night; patch it during the day.
CONCLUSION	Put the lightest family member out there.

◆ WRITING ASSIGNMENT

A PROCESS ESSAY

Choose a topic from the list below. Read the example process essay outline on "How to make a marriage succeed," and then write a plan for your own essay topic before you write the assignment.

INTRODUCTION	How do you make a marriage succeed?
BODY 1	Learn how to communicate your feelings. (Give personal example with details.)
BODY 2	Compromise; give more than you get. (Give personal example with details.)
BODY 3	Trust each other enough to allow freedom. (Give personal example with details.)
CONCLUSION	Communication, compromise, and trust can help couples survive the trials of marriage.

Topics:

1. How to wash a car
2. How to train a pet
3. How to study successfully
4. Buying a car
5. Being a good parent

◆ SENTENCE STRUCTURE

BEING CONSISTENT

The Problem: Being Consistent in Time, Person, and Tone

You will probably sense right away that there is something wrong with each of the following sentences. (The underlined words will give you some clues.)

1. The waiter puts our hamburgers on the counter and then returned to the kitchen.

2. When one drives into the Cabot Trail, you are overwhelmed by the magnificent scenery.

3. The prime minister walked slowly to the lectern, carefully adjusted his glasses, and delivered a nifty address on the state of the economy.

Each of the above sentences is inconsistent; each contains a confusing or annoying *shift*.

• Sentence 1 shifts from the present-time verb *puts* to the past-time verb *returned*. This is called a *shift of tense*.

- Sentence 2 shifts from the third-person pronoun *one* to the second-person pronoun *you*. (This use of *person* will be explained in a moment.)

- Sentence 3 shifts from a formal tone or style to the casual style *nifty*.

Solution #1: Be Consistent in Verb Tense

Be consistent in your use of the time (tense) of verbs unless there is a good reason to shift. Sentence 1 could have been written in either of these two ways:

The waiter <u>puts</u> our hamburgers on the counter and then <u>returns</u> to the kitchen. (Both verbs are in present time.)

The waiter <u>put</u> our hamburgers on the counter and then <u>returned</u> to the kitchen. (Both verbs are in past time.)

Sometimes a shift in time is necessary:

Rosalia remembers [present time] that her parents owned [past time] a Plymouth station wagon when she was [past time] a little girl.

SPOTCHECK 12-1

Make the second verb in each sentence consistent in time with the first.

> **EXAMPLE:** Jackie Robinson <u>was</u> an outstanding athlete who opened the door to professional sports for other black athletes.

1. Robinson joined the Brooklyn Dodgers in 1947 and becomes the first black player in modern major-league baseball.

2. Robinson went to high school in Pasadena, California, where he is a star in track, football, and baseball.

3. He attends the University of California at Los Angeles on a football scholarship and, in 1939, gained more yards than any other college player.

4. After service in World War II, Robinson joined the Kansas City Monarchs and plays for $400 a month in the Negro American League.

5. When Dodgers general manager Branch Rickey signs Robinson, he warned him to expect acts of prejudice from other players and the fans.

6. During the ten years he plays for the Dodgers, Robinson batted .311 and helped the team win six National League championships and a World Series in 1955.

Check the Answer Key before continuing.

SPOTCHECK 12-2   *Rewrite the seven sentences in Spotcheck 12-1 (including the example) as a paragraph, leaving out the numbers. Make the verbs consistent— all in past time.*

_____

_____

_____

_____

_____

_____

_____

_____

_____

Check the Answer Key before continuing.

SPOTCHECK 12-3   *Cross out any verbs that are inconsistent, and write in the correct form above the crossed-out words.*

[1]The first tinted glasses were not intended to protect eyes from the sun. [2]Darkened with smoke, the glasses are worn by judges in China in the fifteenth century. [3]The idea was to conceal a judge's eyes so that witnesses couldn't tell if the judge thinks they are lying. [4]The earliest dark glasses were not vision-corrected, but by around 1430 judges are taking advantage of that feature too. [5]Outside the courts, others start wearing tinted glasses to reduce glare from the sun. [6]In America, the military played a major role in the development of sunglasses. [7]In the 1930s, the Army Air Force commissions Bausch & Lomb to develop glasses to protect pilots from high-altitude glare.

[8]The resulting dark-green glasses became available to the public as Ray-Ban aviator glasses.

Check the Answer Key before continuing.

Solution #2: Be Consistent in Personal Pronouns

Pronouns are said to be in the first, second, or third *person*, depending on whether they refer to the person speaking, the person spoken to, or the person spoken about.

	Singular	*Plural*
First person	I, me, my, mine	we, us, our, ours
Second person	you, your, yours	you, your, yours
Third person	he, him, his	they, them,
	she, her, hers	their,
	it, its	theirs

(Third person also includes the names of persons, places, and things and indefinite pronouns such as *one, everyone,* and *anybody.*)

The point to remember is to avoid unnecessary pronoun shifts. Let's revise our earlier example.

(shift) When <u>one</u> drives into the Cabot Trail, <u>you</u> are overwhelmed by the magnificent scenery.

(consistent) When <u>one</u> drives into the Cabot Trail, <u>one</u> is overwhelmed by the magnificent scenery.

Watch out especially for the most common shift—from the first- or third-person pronoun to the second-person *you.*

SPOTCHECK 12-4

Eliminate shifts in person by making the second pronoun in each sentence agree with the first. Also, change verbs when necessary.

EXAMPLE: I used to think Lola was perfect, but as ~~one gets~~ **I get** to know her ~~one sees~~ **I see** she has a few faults.

1. People can usually solve a problem if you are willing to work at it.

2. In history class we had to bring the teacher an apple before one could get an "A."

3. Oscar buys his clothes at flea markets because you can save money that way.

4. We tried to cheer Mike up, but there was only so much you could do.

5. When one watches television a lot, you get depressed at the poor quality of many of the programs.

Check the Answer Key before continuing.

Although newspaper and magazine writers often use the word *you* to address the reader directly, this informal approach is seldom appropriate in college writing. The only exception is the use of *you* in instructional writing as in textbooks.

(weak) You could easily understand the president's problem.
(better) A person could easily understand the president's problem.
(better) The president's problem was easily understood.

SPOTCHECK 12-5   *Rewrite each of the following sentences to eliminate the inappropriate* you. *Make the sentences as short as you can without leaving out information.*

1. You don't need a ticket to attend the Blue Rodeo concert.

   _____

   _____

2. After eating at Shopsey's restaurant, you feel you got your money's worth.

   _____

   _____

3. You can imagine how glad I was to see Ralph again.

   _____

   _____

4. Foreign travel helps you understand your own country.

   _____

   _____

5. If you drove to the sun at 100 kilometres per hour, it would take you 171 years to travel the 149.6 million kilometres.

_____

_____

Compare your answers with those in the Answer Key.

Your writing in college and later in your career will usually have a fairly serious or formal tone. Avoid slipping into overly casual and slangy language. Such shifts in tone are jarring to the reader, as in the case in our original example:

Solution #3: Be Consistent in Language Tone

(shift) The prime minister walked slowly to the lectern, carefully adjusted his glasses, and delivered a <u>nifty</u> address on the state of the economy.

(consistent) The prime minister walked slowly to the lectern, put on his glasses, and delivered a <u>stirring</u> address on the state of the nation.

Of course, if you are jotting a note to a good friend, you can be as informal as you want to be.

SPOTCHECK 12-6

Change the italicized words to keep a fairly formal tone.

    EXAMPLE: Students who enrol in English 100 should expect to

~~keep their noses to the grindstone~~ all semester.

1. Anyone who thinks Canadian schools will ever operate year-round is *full of beans.*

2. This year's top student is not only intelligent, she is a *foxy chick.*

3. The orchestra gave a *swell* performance of Beethoven's Third Symphony.

4. The members of the Seniors' Club *boogied* until midnight after installing their new officers.

5. Mr. Alberts was pleased to receive a raise of fifty *bucks* a week.

Compare your answers with those in the Answer Key.

DOUBLECHECK 12-1

In the blanks, write time, person, *or* tone *to identify the shift in each sentence. One of the sentences is correct as it stands.*

_____   1. If someone has visited Quebec City, they will have admired the interesting architecture.

_____ **2.** Quebec City is originally called Stadacona and was one of the oldest settlements in Canada.

_____ **3.** The beautiful city is a really cool place to vacation.

_____ **4.** It was always a tourist attraction because of its fascinating history.

_____ **5.** Anyone visiting Quebec will certainly see the famous Château Frontenac and they will also see the Legislative Assembly.

_____ **6.** Eating out in Quebec has been a gourmet experience because there is a variety of cuisine.

_____ **7.** Quebec is also famous for its yummy seafood dishes.

_____ **8.** Of course, visitors should speak French in Quebec if he wants to get around easily.

_____ **9.** Most Canadians learn French when they were at school.

_____ **10.** Even with only a little knowledge of French, visiting Quebec is an awesome experience.

Check the Answer Key before continuing.

◆ WRITING PROCESS

REVISING: COHERENCE

When sentences and paragraphs follow each other in a clear and logical way, we say they have <u>coherence</u>—they "stick together." When revising your writing, be sure to present your ideas in the most effective order.

✓

SPOTCHECK 12-7

Number the following lists of items in the most coherent order.

1. An essay on your experience as a student

_____ High school

_____ Elementary school

_____ College

(This is an example of time order.)

2. A descriptive essay about Orchestra Hall

_____ Auditorium

_____ Lobby

_____ Stage

(This is an example of space order.)

3. A narrative essay about Little League

_____ Striking out

_____ Getting up to bat

_____ Pitcher throwing ball

(This is an example of climax order.)

4. An essay with the following thesis statement: "It isn't fair that my brother is allowed to stay out later, do nothing around the house, and take over the car."

_____ Chores

_____ Car

_____ Curfew

(This is an example of logical order.)

Compare your answers with those in the Answer Key.

Another way to tie your ideas together is to use <u>transition words</u> such as these:

Time-Order Words

first   before   then   next   during   meanwhile
afterward   finally

Space-Order Words

next to   nearby   across from   to the left   to the right
above   below

Climax-Order Words

consequently   thus   therefore   as a result   in the end

Logical-Order Words

first of all   moreover   in addition   furthermore   finally

✓

SPOTCHECK 12-8   *Write appropriate order words in each of the blanks.*

1. An essay on your experience as a student (time order)

_____ I attended grade school.

_____ I attended high school.

_____ I attend college.

2. An essay on the view from your front door (space order)

_____ I see the Quicks' house.

_____ I see the Baptist Church.

_____ I see Leech Lake.

3. An essay on your uncle's career (time and climax order)

_____ He was a grocery bagger for 18 months.

_____ He worked hard.

_____ He became assistant manager.

4. An essay with the following thesis statement: "It isn't fair that my brother is allowed to stay out later, do nothing around the house, and take over the car." (logical order)

_____ He has no curfew.

_____ He does no chores.

_____ He uses the car.

Compare your answers with those in the Answer Key.

✓
CHECKPOINT 12-1   *Cross out the word causing a shift in time, person, or tone and write the correct or appropriate word in each blank at the left.*

___crashed___   **EXAMPLE:** The car sped around the corner and ~~crashes~~ into an ambulance.

_____   1. As we neared the Rockies, you could see the snow on the mountain peaks.

_____   2. If people have a real desire to win, you will often succeed.

_____   3. Anthony came to church wearing his new threads.

_____   4. After he had studied most of the night, Curtis falls asleep during the exam.

_____   5. Twice in the past week, I took the bus to school and arrive late.

_____   6. The judge sentenced the car thief to six months in the slammer.

————————— **7.** You should always eat a good breakfast because one's mind doesn't function right when the stomach is empty.

————————— **8.** When you jogged a lot, do your knees ever get sore?

————————— **9.** Whenever Karen saw Kirk talking to another girl, she gets angry.

————————— **10.** I never have trouble finishing my homework; the first thing you do is turn off the TV set.

No answers are given for Checkpoint quizzes.

THE EXAMPLE ESSAY

◆ READING

GIVING EXAMPLES TO SUPPORT A THESIS STATEMENT

PRECHECK

Joy Kogawa's family were moved out of their home and into a camp during World War II, when the government classified Japanese Canadians as "enemy aliens." In her novel *Obasan,* Kogawa describes the family's ordeal; the following selection is about their forced work in Alberta's sugar-beet fields. Among her Aunt Emily's belongings, the novel's protagonist comes across a file with the label "Facts About Evacuees in Alberta." In this she finds a newspaper clipping about how industrious and productive the Japanese workers had been. Below the picture is the caption "Grinning and happy." In the following extract, Kogawa cites many examples of just how unhappy the evacuees really were.

Evacuees in Alberta

—Joy Kogawa (extract from Obasan)

evacuees persons moved from their homes, in this case by law

pervasive spreading everywhere

Facts about evacuees in Alberta? The fact is I never got used to it and I cannot, I cannot bear the memory. There are some nightmares from which there is no waking, only deeper and deeper sleep. 1

There is a word for it. Hardship. The hardship is so pervasive, so inescapable, so thorough it's a noose around my chest and I cannot move any more. All the oil in my joints has drained out and I have been invaded by dust and grit from the fields and mud is in my bone 2 marrow. I can't move any more. My fingernails are black from scratching the scorching day and there is no escape.

Aunt Emily, are you a surgeon cutting at my scalp with your folders and your filing cards and your insistence on knowing all? The memory drains down the sides of my face, but it isn't enough, is it? It's your hands in my abdomen, pulling the growth from the lining of my walls, but bring back the anaesthetist turn on the ether clamp down the gas mask bring on the chloroform when will this operation be over Aunt Em? **3**

Is it so bad? **4**

Yes. **5**

Do I really mind? **6**

Yes, I mind. I mind everything. Even the flies. The flies and flies and flies from the cows in the barn and the manure pile—all the black flies that curtain the windows, and Obasan with a wad of toilet paper, spish, then with her bare hands as well, grabbing them and their shocking white eggs and the mosquitoes mixed there with the other insect corpses around the base of the gas lamp. **7**

Obasan Grandmother
(Japanese)

It's the chicken coop "house" we live in that I mind. The uninsulated unbelievable thin-as-a-cotton-dress hovel never before inhabited in winter by human beings. In summer it's a heat trap, an incubator, a dry sauna from which there is no relief. In winter the icicles drip down the inside of the windows and the ice is thicker than bricks at the ledge. The only place that is warm is by the coal stove where we rotate like chickens on a spit and the feet are so cold they stop registering. We eat cloves of roasted garlic on winter nights to warm up. **8**

hovel shack

It's the bedbugs and my having to sleep on the table to escape the nightly attack, and the welts over our bodies. And all the swamp bugs and the dust. It's Obasan uselessly packing all the cracks with rags. And the muddy water from the irrigation ditch which we strain and settle and boil, and the tiny carcasses of water creatures at the bottom of the cup. It's walking in winter to the reservoir and keeping the hole open with the axe and dragging up the water in pails and lugging it back and sometimes the water spills down your boots and your feet are red and itchy for days. And it's everybody taking a bath in the round galvanized tub, then Obasan washing clothes in the water after and standing outside hanging the clothes in the freezing weather where everything instantly stiffens on the line. **9**

galvanized made of iron
sheeting

Or it's standing in the beet field under the maddening sun, standing with my black head a sun-trap even though it's covered, and lying down in the ditch, faint, and the nausea in waves and the cold sweat, and getting up and tackling the next row. The whole field is an oven and there's not a tree within walking distance. We are tiny as insects crawling along the grill and there is no protection anywhere. The eyes are lidded against the dust and the air cracks the skin, the lips crack, Stephen's flutes crack and there is no energy to sing any more anyway. **10**

It's standing in the field and staring out at the heat waves that waver and shimmer like see-through curtains over the brown clods and over the tiny distant bodies of Stephen and Uncle and Obasan miles away across the field day after day and not even wondering how this has come about. **11**

There she is, Obasan, wearing Uncle's shirt over a pair of dark **12**
baggy trousers, her head covered by a straw hat that is held on by a
white cloth tied under her chin. She is moving like a tiny earth cloud
over the hard clay clods. Her hoe moves rhythmically up down up
down, tiny as a toothpick. And over there, Uncle pauses to straighten
his back, his hands on his hips. And Stephen farther behind, so tiny I
can barely see him.

It's hard, Aunt Emily, with my hoe, the blade getting dull and mud- **13**
caked as I slash out the Canada thistle, dandelions, crab grass, and
other nameless non-beet plants, then on my knees, pulling out the ex-
cluster group   tra beets from the cluster, leaving just one to mature, then three hand
spans to the next plant, whack whack, and down on my knees again,
pull, flick flick, and on to the end of the long long row and the next and
the next and it will never be done thinning and weeding and weeding
and weeding. It's so hard and so hot that my tear glands burn out.

And then it's cold. The lumps of clay mud stick on my gumboots **14**
and weight my legs and the skin under the boots beneath the knees at
the level of the calves grows red and hard and itchy from the flap flap
of the boots and the fine hairs on my legs grow coarse there and ugly.

I mind growing ugly. **15**

I mind the harvest time and the hands and the wrists bound in **16**
rags to keep the wrists from breaking open. I lift the heavy mud-clot-
ted beets out of the ground with the hook like an eagle's beak, thick
and heavy as a nail attached to the top of the sugar-beet knife.
Thwack. Into the beet and yank from the shoulder till it's out of the
ground dragging the surrounding mud with it. Then crack two beets
together till most of the mud drops off and splat, the knife slices into
the beet scalp and the green top is tossed into one pile, the beet heaved
onto another, one more one more one more down the icy line. I cannot
tell about this time, Aunt Emily. The body will not tell.

We are surrounded by a horizon of denim-blue sky with clouds **17**
clear as spilled milk that turn pink at sunset. Pink I hear is the colour
of llama's milk. I wouldn't know. The clouds are the shape of our new
prison walls—untouchable, impersonal, random.

There are no other people in the entire world. We work together all **18**
day. At night we eat and sleep. We hardly talk anymore. The boxes we
brought from Slocan are not unpacked. The King George/Queen Eliza-
muffled silenced   beth mugs stay muffled in the *Vancouver Daily Province*. The camera
phone does not sing. Obasan wraps layers of cloth around her feet and
her torn sweater hangs unmended over her sagging dress.

Down the miles we are obedient as machines in this odd ballet **19**
without accompaniment of flute or song.

"Grinning and happy" and all smiles standing around a pile of **20**
beets? That is one telling. It's not how it was.

CHECKING
MEANING AND
STYLE

1. Where is this essay's thesis statement?

2. Where do the examples of what Joy Kogawa's protagonist couldn't
bear about the evacuees' life in Alberta start?

3. What is the effect of starting many paragraph with "It's"?

4. Why is Paragraph 15 only one sentence?

5. What other devices does Kogawa use to make the extract affect the reader? For example, why are there few commas in Paragraph 3?

CHECKING IDEAS

1. During World War II, did this kind of discrimination happen to any other group of people?

2. Do you think that treating a group of people this way can ever be justified?

3. Have you, your family, or your friends ever experienced discrimination because of race or religion?

◆ WRITING MODELS

THE EXAMPLE ESSAY

Joy Kogawa's essay is full of examples of the terrible hardships endured by the evacuees. The essay could be reorganized into the five-paragraph format using Kogawa's own words. In each paragraph, the topic sentence has been underlined.

Model Example Essay #1

Evacuees in Alberta

Introduction with thesis statement underlined

Facts about evacuees in Alberta? The fact is I never got used to it ₁ and I cannot, I cannot bear the memory. There are some nightmares from which there is no waking, only deeper and deeper sleep. There is a word for it. Hardship. The hardship is so pervasive, so inescapable, so thorough it's a noose around my chest and I cannot move any more. Do I really mind?

Body with 1st support; topic sentence underlined

Yes, I mind. I mind everything. Even the flies. The flies and flies ₂ and flies from the cows in the barn and the manure pile—all the black flies that curtain the windows, and Obasan with a wad of toilet paper, spish, then with her bare hands as well, grabbing them and their shocking white eggs and the mosquitoes mixed there with the other insect corpses around the base of the gas lamp.

Body with 2nd support; topic sentence underlined

It's the chicken coop "house" we live in that I mind. The uninsu- ₃ lated unbelievable thin-as-a-cotton dress hovel never before inhabited in winter by human beings. In summer it's a heat trap, an incubator, a dry sauna from which there is no relief. It's the bedbugs and my having to sleep on the table to escape the nightly attack, and the welts over our bodies.

Body with 3rd support; topic sentence underlined

Or it's the work we had to do. It's standing in the beet field under ₄ the maddening sun, standing with my black head a sun-trap even though it's covered, and lying down in the ditch, faint, and the nausea in waves and the cold sweat, and getting up and tackling the next row.

It's standing in the field and staring out at the heat waves that waver and shimmer like see-through curtains over the brown clods and over the distant bodies of Stephen and Uncle and Obasan miles away across the field day after day and not even wondering how this has come about.

"Grinning and happy" and all smiles standing around a pile of 5 beets? That is one telling. <u>It's not how it was.</u>

Conclusion with final message underlined

The three body paragraphs in the rewrite of Kogawa's essay give examples to support her thesis statement. The following two outlines give examples of the ways advertisements influence our lives.

Model Example Essay #2 (Outline)

THESIS
Television commercials encourage people to buy things they don't need or can't afford.

FIRST SUPPORT
(topic sentence) My bedroom dresser is covered with worthless lotions, creams, and oils that commercials promised would make me a beauty.

SECOND SUPPORT
A young man at work has taken a second job to try to make the payments on a fancy car that was promoted on TV by a local football star.

THIRD SUPPORT
Parents that I know are constantly fighting off demands from their children for toys advertised on the Saturday morning kiddie programs.

CONCLUSION
Tobacco ads have been eliminated from TV; now we need to eliminate all TV advertisements.

A writer would bring those topic sentences to life with examples and specific details, referring to actual TV commercials.

Another writer might write an example essay on advertising in which each of the body paragraphs focuses on a different medium for presenting ads:

Model Example Essay #3 (Outline)

THESIS
Wherever we turn, we are bombarded with advertisements.

FIRST SUPPORT
Television and radio commercials

SECOND SUPPORT
Print advertisements in newspapers and magazines

THIRD SUPPORT
Advertisements on billboards and buildings

CONCLUSION
Advertisements are taking over our lives and should be completely eliminated.

◆ WRITING ASSIGNMENT

AN EXAMPLE ESSAY

WRITE AN EXAMPLE ESSAY

Think of an essay to write based on Kogawa's writing. Have you ever experienced discrimination in your neighbourhood or in society? Think of three examples of the kinds of prejudice you see around you. Decide on an appropriate thesis statement. Develop your thesis with at least two or three supporting paragraphs.

Your thesis statement: _____

_____

_____

First support (topic sentence): _____

_____

_____

Second support (topic sentence): _____

_____

_____

Third support (topic sentence): _____

_____

_____

Your conclusion: _____

_____

_____

Remember that when you write an essay on prejudice or any other topic, you should follow these four steps:

STEP #1

Prewriting: Think about the topic and make some notes. (You have already done prewriting about prejudice.)

STEP #2

Writing: Write the first draft of your essay.

STEP #3 Revising: When possible, lay the essay aside for a while; later read the essay and identify the parts that do not work well; write a second draft making changes in content and phrases.

STEP #4 Editing: Proofread the second draft looking for errors in spelling, punctuation, capitalization, and word choice.

◆ SENTENCE STRUCTURE

SOLVING SENTENCE PROBLEMS

The Problem: Solving Problems That Weaken Sentences

We will now consider an assortment of problems that can weaken sentences: misplaced modifiers, dangling modifiers, nonparallel construction, other mixed constructions, faulty comparison, and passive constructions.

Notice what happens when we move the word *only* around in the following sentences:

> Stan only borrowed five dollars. (He didn't steal the money.)
>
> Stan borrowed only five dollars. (He would have liked more.)
>
> Only Stan borrowed five dollars. (His friends had enough money already.)

We see that it is important to position words in a sentence carefully, especially words that change the meaning of other words. Such words are called *modifiers.*

Solution #1: Avoiding Misplaced Modifiers

A modifier should usually be near the word(s) it describes to avoid what is called a *misplaced modifier.* Sometimes the error is unintentionally amusing.

> **(misplaced)** Antonia bought a used car from a local dealer with weak headlights. (The *dealer* had weak headlights?)
>
> **(revised)** Antonia bought a used car with weak headlights from a local dealer.
>
> **(misplaced)** Tony was given a horse by the rancher that was old and swaybacked. (The *rancher* was old and swaybacked?)
>
> **(revised)** The rancher gave Tony a horse that was old and swaybacked.

The lesson is clear: Put modifiers near the words they modify.

Be especially careful with the modifiers *almost, only, just, even, hardly,* and *nearly.* They go in front of the words they modify.

> Roderick ~~almost~~ ate almost the entire pizza by himself.
>
> Kimberly ~~nearly~~ saved nearly six dollars by buying the dress on sale.

SPOTCHECK 13-1   *Rewrite each of the following sentences to correct misplaced modifiers.*

1. Leah bought a new handbag at a downtown store with a silk lining.

    _____

2. A cowboy's 10-gallon hat only holds 1½ gallons of water.

    _____

3. Min saw an accident driving home from work.

    _____

4. Gloria even likes her new baby when he cries.

    _____

5. The average marriage in Canada only lasts 12.4 years.

    _____

Compare your answers with those in the Answer Key.

Solution #2: Avoiding Dangling Modifiers

    A modifier is said to "dangle" if it lacks a clear connection to the word it is supposed to modify.

> **(dangling)** Arriving home from work, the dog greeted Elena at the front door.

    Of course it was Elena, not the dog, who arrived home. The modifier "arriving home from work" dangles. A modifier that begins a sentence should usually be followed immediately by the word it modifies.

> **(revised)** Arriving home from work, <u>Elena</u> was greeted at the front door by the dog.

> **(option)** When Elena arrived home from work, the dog greeted her at the door.

> **(option)** The dog greeted Elena at the door when she arrived home from work.

SPOTCHECK 13-2   *Rewrite the following sentences to eliminate dangling modifiers.*

1. Growing careless, the wrong name was entered by the clerk.

    _____

    _____

2. Although 21 years old, my father expected me to be in by midnight.

_____

_____

3. Able to bend steel bars with ease, I watched Mighty Mo in awe.

_____

_____

4. Vacation rushed to an end, playing tennis during the day and dancing at night.

_____

_____

5. Contentedly eating grass, Solomon took a photo of the cows.

_____

_____

Compare your answers with those in the Answer Key.

Solution #3: Using Parallel Construction

Similar ideas are easier to read if they are in the same grammatical form—that is, if they have *parallel construction*. Compare the following pairs of sentences:

Not parallel	**Parallel**
Seeing is to believe.	Seeing is believing.
Kimberly likes to sail, to swim, and skiing.	Kimberly likes to sail, to swim, and to ski.
Naomi is not only smart, she has a lot of luck.	Naomi is not only smart, she is lucky.
Aspiring models should be attractive, tall, and not be overweight.	Aspiring models should be attractive, tall, and slender.

If the topic sentence of a paragraph or the thesis sentence of an essay lists several points, be sure to put them in parallel form.

(not parallel) Among the advantages of attending a community college are the low tuition, the small class size, and because it is close to my home.

(parallel) Among the advantages of attending a community college are the low tuition, the small class size, and the convenient location.

The first example has two nouns (*tuition* and *class size*) before switching to a dependent clause (*because it . . .*). The correction replaces the clause with a third noun, *location*.

✔️

SPOTCHECK 13-3   *Revise the underlined segments to achieve parallel construction.*

1. Whether right or when he is wrong, Larry likes to argue.

    _____

    _____

2. After playing soccer all afternoon, Matty was tired, thirsty, and he needed a bath.

    _____

    _____

3. Henry believes having a good family life is more important than to have a lot of money.

    _____

    _____

4. Working at Ajax Repair has taught me not only how to fix cars but also getting along with people.

    _____

    _____

5. Terrie was bright but being lazy.

    _____

6. Many industries are moving from the North to the South in the United States because wages are lower, the climate is often more pleasant, and offers greater recreational opportunities.

    _____

    _____

Compare your answers with those in the Answer Key.

Solution #4: Avoiding Mixed Constructions	Do not start a sentence off in one direction and then, without reason, go off in another.

> **(mixed)** Because he was bored caused him to sleep in class.
> **(better)** Because he was bored, he slept in class.
>
> **(mixed)** When Tony gets home early pleases his wife.
> **(better)** When Tony gets home early, his wife is pleased.
>
> **(mixed)** The best part of a baseball game is where [is when] they hit home runs.
> **(better)** Home runs are the best part of a baseball game.

✅ **SPOTCHECK 13-4**   *Revise the following sentences to eliminate mixed constructions.*

1. Because she was hungry caused her to eat a late-night snack.

   _____

2. When Sally gets a raise pleases her family.

   _____

3. Although sunshine is forecast, but Rocky has his umbrella.

   _____

4. A good sale is when I am happy

   _____

Compare your answers with those in the Answer Key.

Solution #5: Avoiding Faulty Comparisons	Be sure comparisons are completed.

> **(incomplete)** Puffy cigarettes have less nicotine. (less than what?)
> **(better)** Puffy cigarettes have less nicotine <u>than Gaspers do.</u>
> **(or)** Puffy cigarettes have less nicotine <u>than tar.</u>
>
> **(incomplete)** Plumbers charge more.
> **(better)** Plumbers charge more <u>than they should.</u>

Be sure comparisons are clear.

> **(unclear)** The days in July are longer than December. (*Days* is compared to the month *December.*)
> **(better)** The days in July are longer than <u>those</u> [or <u>the days</u>] in December.

Watch out for incomplete comparisons using the words *so, such,* and *too.* Careful writers will not stop short of the bracketed words in these sentences.

It was <u>so</u> hot yesterday [that I went swimming.].
He is <u>such</u> an intelligent student [that he should do well in college].
The sunset was <u>too</u> beautiful [for me to describe].

(or) The sunset was beautiful.

SPOTCHECK 13-5   *Revise the following sentences to eliminate faulty comparisons.*

1. Polly is a lot smarter.

   _____

2. The trees in the spring are greener than the fall.

   _____

3. A Jeep Comanche looks better and goes faster.

   _____

4. The summers in Victoria are hotter than Vancouver.

   _____

Compare your answers with those in the Answer Key.

Solution #6: Active vs. Passive Voice

Compare these two sentences:

Spike Owen hit two home runs Sunday.
Two home runs were hit by Spike Owen Sunday.

In the first sentence, the subject (Spike Owen) *acts;* in the second, the subject (home runs) *receives* the action of the verb *were hit.* The first sentence is in the *active voice,* the second in the *passive voice.*

You should generally use the more vigorous active voice. However, you may prefer the passive voice if the receiver of the action is more important than the doer. For example, the first of these two sentences might be preferred in some cases.

(passive) Thirty-two home runs were hit by American League batters in games Sunday. (emphasizes the home runs)
(active) American League batters hit 32 home runs in games Sunday. (emphasizes the American League batters)

✓

SPOTCHECK 13-6   *In the blanks, write* A *if the sentence is in active voice,* P *if it is in passive voice.*

_____   1. The country road was littered with bottles and paper.

_____   2. Marietta read three novels during summer vacation.

_____   3. The tire was removed by Robert.

_____   4. The grass has been cut by Thomas only twice.

_____   5. The fishermen repaired their nets.

Check the Answer Key before continuing.

✓

SPOTCHECK 13-7   *Change the following sentences from passive voice to active voice.*

1. The holdup was seen by two customers.

    _____

2. Carrie was praised by the teacher.

    _____

3. All employees were notified of the layoffs by the company.

    _____

    _____

4. People over 65 were offered discounts at the store.

    _____

    _____

5. The essays were all written by students.

    _____

Compare your answers with those in the Answer Key.

DOUBLECHECK 13-1   *Use the lettered items to identify the problem in each of these sentences.*

A. Misplaced or dangling modifier   D. Faulty comparison

B. Nonparallel construction   E. Passive voice

C. Mixed construction

_____   1. The wings of hummingbirds travel much faster.

_____   2. Although the sun had gone down, the lake still shining in the distance.

_____   3. The guide showed us the waterfalls, the lake, and where the trails went to the caves.

_____   4. The window was closed by Raymond.

_____   5. While studying in the library, the lights went out.

_____   6. Ernie is good at ping-pong, chess, and playing backgammon.

_____   7. The movie *Black Robe* was a lot longer.

_____   8. The concert was attended by 10,000 fans.

Check the Answer Key before continuing.

◆ WRITING PROCESS

EDITING: SPELLING TROUBLEMAKERS

When you revise a paper you are rethinking your approach to writing the essay. The order and content of entire paragraphs may change. On the other hand, in editing or proofreading your paper, you are looking only for small errors in spelling, punctuation, capitalization, or word choice. If it will not affect the appearance, you can sometimes write these last-minute improvements neatly on the final draft.

Probably because the words sound alike, people often have trouble with little words such as *its* and *it's* or *their, there,* and *they're.* Since the words come up so often in everyday writing, it's worth knowing how to get them right.

IT'S/ITS

Use *it's* only as a short form or contraction of the words *it is* or *it has*. The apostrophe (') means that one or more letters have been left out.

It's [It is] time to go home.

It's [It has] been a week since the lawyer called.

Use *its* without an apostrophe when you don't mean *it is* or *it has*.

The dog wagged its [not *it is*] tail when it saw the bone.

The car lost its [not *it is*] left headlight in the collision.

Its is an example of a *possessive pronoun*. Here are some other pronouns that show possession or ownership:

his   hers   ours   theirs   yours

Notice that none of the possessive pronouns has an apostrophe.

SPOTCHECK 13-8

Underline the correct word in parentheses. Remember to use it's *only if you could write* it is *or* it has.

1. Look at that old house. (Its/It's) roof is sagging.

2. The weather report says (its/it's) unlikely to rain.

3. (Its/It's) been a great party, Rebecca.

4. Wear a hat. Your body loses 80 percent of (its/it's) heat through the head.

5. The lacrosse team has won (its/it's) fifth game in a row.

Check the Answer Key before continuing.

THEY'RE/THEIR/THERE

They're is a contraction of *they are*. Notice that the apostrophe goes where the letter *a* has been left out.

They're [They are] building a theatre on that corner.

Jason and Tamara said they're [they are] in the same biology lab.

Their is a possessive pronoun; it shows ownership.

The Chevy convertible is their car.

Their three sons are all in the Navy.

There shows location (not *here*) and is also a frequent sentence starter: *There is . . . There are . . .*

The deer was standing right over there.

There was no way to solve the riddle.

✓ SPOTCHECK 13-9

Fill in the blanks with they're, their, *or* there.

1. The Changs are selling _____ house.

2. _____ planning to buy a new one in Victoria.

3. _____ son and his family live _____.

4. _____ may be a delay while _____ house is in escrow.

5. But before long _____ sure _____ new home will be _____ in Victoria.

Check the Answer Key before continuing.

✓ CHECKPOINT 13-1

Use the lettered items to identify the problem in each of these sentences.

A. Misplaced or dangling modifier   **D.** Faulty comparison

B. Nonparallel construction   **E.** Passive voice

C. Mixed construction

_____   **1.** Stacy put the cookies back in the box she hadn't eaten.

_____   **2.** The tennis player is slender and moves gracefully.

_____   **3.** I would rather play bridge than to play chess.

_____   **4.** While driving to work, the radio announced a fire on Front Street.

_____   **5.** Reginald Foster is the smartest.

_____   **6.** Because he was tired was the reason Mr. Flores left the office early.

_____   **7.** While away from the desk, the phone rang and rang.

_____   **8.** The award was accepted by Jocelyn gratefully.

_____   **9.** Nine out of ten car owners say Shiny is better.

_____   **10.** Nguyen is a loyal friend, a diligent student, and good at tennis.

_____   **11.** The exam was passed by most of the students.

No answers are given for Checkpoint quizzes.

THE COMPARISON AND CONTRAST ESSAY

◆ READING

AN ESSAY COMPARING SIMILARITIES (AND CONTRASTING DIFFERENCES)

PRECHECK

In this essay, writer and reviewer Philip Marchand argues that underneath Canadians' mask of docile civility there's a tremendous amount of suppressed vitriol, which comes out in surprising ways. To make his point about Canadians, he compares their character, their literature, and their deference to that of Americans.

Those Nasty Canadians

—Philip Marchand

Two years ago, a *Star* reporter interviewed Molly Ivins, the well-known political columnist from the state of Texas. Ivins, a tart-tongued liberal, forever appalled by the antics of her state and national politicians, was marvelling, as American liberals are wont to do, at the niceness of Canada. 1

"There's nothing weird here, is there?" she said. 2

The reporter kept silent, but afterward he felt complicit in a lie. He 3 felt as if he had made his small contribution to the preservation of a myth, like the notion that Italians, unfailingly, are great singers and adore *bambini*.

He had the feeling that Ivins would go back to the United States 4 and enjoy a chuckle with fellow journalists about good old Canada.

wont accustomed

complicit involved

bambini children (Italian)

Did you know that Canadians won't cross a street against a red 5
light even if there's not a single car in sight? And don't you love the way
Canadians always apologize when you *bump into them?*

Haw, haw. Maybe these journalists should take a look at Canadian 6
playwright John Gray's recent book, *Lost in North America: The Imag-*
inary Canadian in the American Dream. In this book of reflections on
the state of being Canadian, Gray discusses the myth, as he puts it,
that "Canadians are a docile people."

docile obedient

truculent silently aggressive

Here is Gray's answer: "We are not. We are a truculent, rather vio- 7
lent people, and know it—which is why we have tougher gun laws
than the United States, a country that takes a more naively optimistic
view of human individuality. Gun laws or not, I would far rather wander the streets of New York on a Saturday night than the streets of
Stellarton, Nova Scotia. In both World Wars, Canadian soldiers were
feared for their ruthlessness. In international tournaments, Canadian
hockey players are regarded as skillful thugs."

The Canadian journalist Carsten Stroud currently lives in West 8
Vancouver but spends a lot of time in "the most dangerous urban territory" in the U.S. today, a section of southeast Washington, D.C., called
District Seven. There he sits in an unmarked police car, researching
his next book, about a federal fugitive pursuit unit.

He witnesses a lot of violence around him, but it's a kind of *busi-* 9
nesslike violence.

"I don't see the same kind of brainless, mean violence that I do 10
with the kids who hang out at 15th and Marine Dr. here in Vancouver,"
Stroud comments.

"There's a certain kind of order [in District Seven] that's compre- 11
hensible, once you know what's going on. Not so on Marine Dr. There,
the kids are just as rude and threatening as they can be to anybody
who comes along."

Gray insists that "Canadians are not a docile people, we are a *con-* 12
quered people." Being conquered often does give a society a reputation
for being polite and self-effacing and—outwardly at least—deferential
to authority.

self-effacing modest

deferential respectful

But Richard Nixon—who spoke in a moment of candor in the Oval 13
Office, while the fatal tape recorders were rolling—was right. Underneath that Canadian niceness, that civility, is a tremendous amount of
suppressed vitriol, nastiness, which comes out in surprising ways.

vitriol bitterness

It comes out in the way kids hang around 7-Eleven stores in cer- 14
tain neighborhoods. It comes out in our art and literature—and literature does not lie. The late 20th century likes to think of itself as the
most enlightened and progressive era in history, for example, but its
literature is the gloomiest ever written.

Similarly, Canadian literature is not nice. It is not polite. One 15
might even say it's deliberately the opposite. Mordecai Richler, Margaret Atwood—not exactly known for their sweetness, are they?

depictions portraits

ruthlessly mercilessly

Richler's novels are justly famed for their depictions of savage 16
male rivalry, in which weaklings are ruthlessly crushed.

No reader can forget the opening of *The Apprenticeship of Duddy* 17
Kravitz, for example, in which the well-meaning schoolteacher, Mr.
MacPherson, is destroyed by his tough students.

In Richler's most recent novel, *Solomon Gursky Was Here,* the 18 founder of the fictional Gursky clan, Ephraim Gursky—"tough" is too mild a word to describe his kind of hardihood—follows this tradition.

impregnating making pregnant

Saved as a youth from drudgery in British coal mines by the 19 benevolent Mr. Nicholson, Ephraim repays his benefactor by impregnating [the latter's] wife and stealing his valuables.

The novel's attitude is indulgent toward, if not admiring of, this be- 20 havior, since Nicholson—a repressed homosexual, if you please, who yearns for young Ephraim—is clearly another fool and weakling.

internecine destructive to all parties

In this fictional world of internecine male warfare, revenge is a fre- 21 quent theme.

Richler, in fact, has perfected his own unique formula for portray- 22 ing revenge. The formula involves somebody who once bullied or ignored the hero coming to that hero later in life for help with his literary ambitions.

The fictional world of Margaret Atwood is not much gentler. The 23 tone of that world was set by her early novels.

Her second novel, *Surfacing,* for example, set in the woods and 24 lakes of Northern Ontario, displays a characteristic pattern—a heroine, reasonably complex and appealing, surrounded by characters

etched engraved

etched in acid.

In Atwood's later novels, the men still cling to their ridiculous pre- 25 tensions, but the women characters change. At least some of them be-

vicious mean

come truly vicious.

Cordelia in *Cat's Eye,* Zenia in *The Robber Bride,* are terrifying 26 partisans in the internecine war between women.

Even Robertson Davies—who, on first glance, seems to possess a 27 much more genial sensibility—is not immune from the suppressed-vitriol syndrome.

His novel *World of Wonders,* for example, is one long revenge 28 tale—its hero, the magician Magnus Eisengrim, spends most of the novel reminiscing about his past career before a small group of listeners.

In the process, he fully exposes the shabby behavior of one of the 29 listeners, a movie producer named Roland Ingestree.

At the end of his story, Eisengrim sits down to dinner and is very 30 polite to Ingestree, having "trampled his old enemy into the dirt," as the novel's narrator contentedly observes.

Sorry, Roland. 31

Given the huge space Richler, Atwood and Davies occupy in our lit- 32 erary culture, their emphasis on the sadistic humiliation of characters—humiliation inflicted either directly by themselves, as authors, or by other characters—is remarkable.

There simply is no parallel with it in American literature. 33

No American author displays quite so much satisfaction in corro- 34 sive depiction of characters.

splenetic spiteful

Not tough guy Norman Mailer, not splenetic Philip Roth. Not Bel- 35 low or Malamud or Updike or Oates or Styron or Doctorow or Cheever.

adduced given as evidence

Parallels to this situation in other areas of life could be adduced— 36 the fact, for example, that we defer to our politicians and authority figures more than Americans do, but despise them more thoroughly.

All this seems to indicate that, as a society, we're both terrifically 37 polite and deeply resentful. And that our fabled civility cannot be relied upon, if circumstances bring out the latter aspect of the national character.

Think about this, Molly Ivins: We're friends with you now, but we 38 can't afford not to be.

If the unimaginable ever happened, and open hostility ever devel- 39 oped between the two countries, remember what Richard Nixon told you.

CHECKING MEANING AND STYLE

1. How does Philip Marchand begin his essay?

2. Where is the thesis statement?

3. What, according to the sources Marchand cites, is the difference between American and Canadian violence?

4. What examples does Marchand give to make his point about Canadians?

5. In what way, according to Marchand, does Canadian literature differ from American literature?

CHECKING IDEAS

1. Is it easy to define a "Canadian"?

2. Have you read any works by major Canadian writers? Do you agree with Marchand's view?

3. In what other ways do you believe that Canadians differ from Americans?

4. What impressions of Canadians do you think other people have?

◆ WRITING MODELS

THE COMPARISON AND CONTRAST ESSAY

In his essay, Philip Marchand uses the point-by-point method to compare Canadians and Americans. Here is how his arguments might look in a five-paragraph essay.

Introduction, with thesis sentence underlined

Recently, when a reporter was asked whether Canadians really are as nice as they seem, he kept silent. Later he felt complicit in a lie. He had been guilty of preserving the myth about the niceness of Canadians. In fact, underneath their docile civility, there's a tremendous amount of suppressed vitriol that make Canadians nastier than Americans.

1st paragraph of development, with a topic sentence underlined, specific details, and description

Canadians are a truculent, rather violent people, according to author John Gray, and they know it. As a result, Canada has tougher gun laws than the United States does. They also had a more fearful reputation in both World Wars. Journalist Carsten Stroud describes American violence as "businesslike," whereas, he insists, Canadian violence is "brainless and mean."

2nd paragraph with a topic sentence of comparison

The literature produced by Canadians in the late twentieth century is the gloomiest ever written; it is much less polite and nice than American literature. One might even say it's deliberately the opposite. Mordecai Richler and Margaret Atwood are not exactly known for their sweetness. There is simply no parallel with it in American literature.

3rd paragraph with a topic sentence and specific detail

Parallels to this situation in other areas of life could be adduced. For example, we Canadians defer to our politicians and authority figures more than Americans do, but despise them more thoroughly.

Conclusion, summarizing main argument

All this seems to indicate that, as a society, Canadians are both terrifically polite and deeply resentful. If the unimaginable ever happened, and open hostility ever developed between the United States and Canada, Americans would do well to remember what Richard Nixon said—"All Canadians are tough."

◆ Writing Assignment

A Comparison and Contrast Essay

An essay about Canadians can contain description, narration, opinion, comparison, and example paragraphs. Note how Marchand used narration and examples as well as comparison to make his point in "Those Nasty Canadians."

Write a Comparison and Contrast Essay

Choose one of the essay topics below:

1. Western Canada and Maritime Canada

2. Canada now and one hundred years ago

3. Eating in Canada and in another country

4. Canadian wildlife on the west coast and on the east coast.

A helpful step in writing an essay is to develop an outline. The following is an outline for Topic 3, using the point-by-point method.

Introduction

Eating out in Canada and in China is very different.

Point 1

Food in China is cheaper than in Canada.

Point 2

There is more variety in Chinese food.

Point 3

Many more restaurants serve food outside in China than in Canada.

Conclusion

The lower cost, the greater variety, and the open-air accessibility of food in China make eating there more pleasurable than in Canada.

Write a comparison essay about Canadians. Before you begin, think of three features for comparison and choose the block or point-by-point method.

Plan your own essay by completing the following outline.

INTRODUCTION   (Thesis statement) _____

_____

_____

BODY I   (Topic sentence) _____

_____

_____

BODY II   (Topic sentence) _____

_____

_____

BODY III (OPTIONAL)   (Topic sentence) _____

_____

_____

CONCLUSION   (Final statement) _____

_____

_____

Before you submit your final draft, proofread/edit it for the kinds of errors marked on your most recent papers.

◆ SENTENCE STRUCTURE

ACHIEVING SENTENCE VARIETY

The Problem: Varying Sentences in Your Essay

A speaker who always uses the same tone of voice becomes boring. A writer who uses the same sentence patterns over and over can also become boring. The ability to construct sentences in a variety of ways makes our writing more interesting and allows us to express our ideas more effectively.

Notice how the repetition of short sentences makes the following paragraph boring and even irritating:

> More than a million earthquakes may take place in any one year. Most of them take place under the oceans. They usually don't cause any damage. Some earthquakes occur on land. Earthquakes near large cities may cause extensive property damage. They may even cause deaths.

With a variety of sentence patterns, the paragraph becomes smoother, more concise, and more interesting.

> More than a million earthquakes may take place in any one year. Most of them take place under the oceans, so they usually don't cause any damage. When they occur near big cities, however, they may cause extensive property damage and even deaths.

We will study three of the basic sentence patterns: simple, compound, and complex sentences.

Solution #1: Using Simple Sentences

The simple sentence is made up of one independent clause, with no dependent clauses. Recall from Chapter 3 that a clause has a subject and a verb. The clause is independent if it expresses a complete thought.

The <u>detective</u> *left.*

Describing words (modifiers) may be added to form the complete subject. Words added to the verb make up the complete predicate.

The uniformed <u>detective</u> *left in a blue car.*

A simple sentence can have a compound subject (more than one) or a compound verb.

The <u>detective</u> and the <u>burglar</u> *left.* (compound subject)
The <u>detective</u> *left* but *returned.* (compound verb)

A simple sentence can combine all these elements.

The uniformed <u>detective</u> and the <u>burglar</u> *left* in a blue car but *returned* within half an hour and *entered* the interrogation room.

That is a long sentence, but it is still, grammatically speaking, a simple sentence because it has only one independent clause and no dependent clause.

SPOTCHECK 14-1

Combine the short simple sentences into one longer simple sentence containing a single independent clause.

EXAMPLE: The apple was ripe. It fell. It fell to the ground.

The ripe apple fell to the ground.

1. The ripe apple fell. It fell with a crashing sound.

2. Lucinda washed dishes. Martin washed dishes.

_____

3. Martin washed the dishes. He did it without complaining.

_____

4. Martin washed the dishes. He dried them.

_____

5. The baby was happy. The baby smiled. The baby gurgled. It was in the bathtub.

_____

_____

Compare your answers with those in the Answer Key.

Solution #2: Using Compound Sentences

A compound sentence is made up of two or more independent clauses.

The moon came up, and we set off through the woods.
Anthony got a raise, so he decided to celebrate.

As in the examples above, the two clauses are usually joined by a comma and one of the connecting words *and, but, or, for, nor, yet,* or *so.* The two parts of a compound sentence are considered equal in importance.

✓

SPOTCHECK 14-2   *Change the simple sentences into compound sentences by joining them with one of the connectors* and, but, or, for, nor, yet, *or* so. *Don't forget a comma after the first clause.*

1. Calgary has a population of 600,000. Edmonton has a population of 540,000.

_____

_____

2. An early Greek named Stentor had a loud voice. Today we call a booming voice *stentorian.*

_____

_____

3. A penguin may look clumsy. It can swim faster than many fish.

_____

_____

4. Waldo couldn't do his homework. He had broken his glasses.

_____

_____

5. Roderick might go fishing. He might go sailing.

_____

_____

6. You should learn to swim. Almost three-fourths of the earth is covered by water.

_____

_____

Compare your answers with those in the Answer Key.

Solution #3: Using Complex Sentences

A complex sentence has an independent clause and one or more dependent clauses.

> **dependent clause**   **independent clause**
> Because Mrs. Larson was sick, her husband fixed breakfast.

> **independent clause**   **dependent clause**
> Marian netted the fish while Bill steadied the boat.

A dependent clause begins with a dependent word such as *because, although,* or *since.* It needs an independent clause to complete its meaning. (See page 44 for a longer list of dependent words.)

In a compound sentence, the ideas in both clauses are given equal emphasis. In a complex sentence, the idea in the dependent clause is emphasized less than the one in the independent clause. In the second example just given, more importance is given to Marian netting the fish (in the independent clause) than to Bill steadying the boat. If we put Bill in the independent clause, his actions become more important:

> **dependent clause**   **independent clause**
> While Marian netted the fish, Bill steadied the boat.

Remember to put a comma after a dependent clause that starts a sentence.

SPOTCHECK 14-3   *Draw one line under the dependent clause and two lines under the dependent word.*

> **EXAMPLE:** Ruth is tired <u>because</u> <u>she studied until three.</u>

1. While one American died on-screen in *Rambo*, 75 Russians and Vietnamese were killed.

2. Antonio will get a raise unless his sales decline.

3. Mr. Eden is the neighbour who owns two Dobermans.

4. Although many young baseball players are signed to professional contracts, 90 percent never appear in a major-league game.

5. The local team will win the pennant because their pitching staff is strong.

Check the Answer Key before continuing.

SPOTCHECK 14-4   *Combine the two simple sentences to make a complex sentence. The result will contain one independent clause and one dependent clause. Start some sentences with the independent clause and some with the dependent clause. Put a comma after the dependent clause if it starts the sentence.*

1. The dentist was upset. Sean missed his appointment.

   _____

   _____

2. Lisa was nervous. She was to meet her new in-laws.

   _____

3. Jousuf Karsh is a great photographer. He photographed Winston Churchill.

   _____

   _____

4. Gambling was legalized in Windsor. The crime rate went up 275 percent.

   _____

   _____

5. That is the bus driver. He returned my lost wallet.

_____

Compare your answers with those in the Answer Key.

• Don't assume that long sentences are always better than short ones. A mixture of long, short, and medium-length sentences is usually the most effective approach.

SPOTCHECK 14-5   _Change these compound sentences into complex sentences._

> **EXAMPLE:** Martin repaired his bicycle, and Claudette read a novel. (compound)
>
> While Martin repaired his bicycle, Claudette read a novel. (complex)

1. The floor of the house shook, and Jack knew it was an earthquake.

_____

_____

2. The bank will give you a loan, and you can buy a car.

_____

_____

3. Yolanda got many Christmas gifts, but she didn't give any.

_____

_____

4. Claudette enjoys nature, so she spends her weekends camping.

_____

_____

5. Kimberly began giving money to friends, for she had won a lottery.

_____

_____

Compare your answers with those in the Answer Key.

Quickcheck on Sentence Patterns

✓   A simple sentence has one independent clause and no dependent clause.

✓   A compound sentence has two or more independent clauses and no dependent clause.

✓   A complex sentence has one independent clause and one or more dependent clauses.

✓

DOUBLECHECK 14-1   *Identify each sentence as simple (S), compound (C), or complex (X).*

_____   1. The giraffes and the bears are at the east end of the zoo.

_____   2. The giraffes are fenced in, and the bears are surrounded by a moat.

_____   3. Although the giraffes are interesting, I could watch the bears for hours.

_____   4. My real favourites are the monkeys that live on Monkey Island.

_____   5. Their antics amuse everyone but are a particular delight to the children.

Check the Answer Key before continuing.

◆ WRITING PROCESS

EDITING: MORE SPELLING TROUBLEMAKERS

Editing your paper to identify and correct small errors is the final step in the writing process. Here are some more everyday words that cause many people problems. Be sure you can use them correctly.

A/AN

Use *an* before a word that begins with the *sound* of a vowel (*a, e, i, o, u*): *an* apple, *an* opportunity, *an* hour (silent *h*).

     Use *a* before a word that begins with the *sound* of any other letter (a consonant): *a* book, *a* Pontiac, *a* university (the *u* sounds like *y*).

ARE/OR/OUR	*Are* is a verb: "They *are* happy." *Or* separates two possibilities: "Sara *or* Cathy will drive the truck." *Our* is a word showing ownership: "That is *our* house on the corner."
HAVE/OF	Don't use *of* for *have*: "They should *have* [not *of*] phoned first."
HEAR/HERE	*Hear* is what you do with your *ear*: "We can *hear* a bird singing." *Here* means "this place": "Bring the book *here*."
THAN/THEN	Use *than* in comparisons: "Wanda is taller *than* Edith." *Then* refers to time: "If I had known *then* what I know now, I wouldn't have bought the car."
THERE'S/THEIRS	*There's* is a shortened form of *there is*: "*There's* a full moon tonight." *Theirs* shows ownership: "That poodle is *theirs*."
TO/TOO/TWO	*To* is a preposition: "Robert is going *to* college." *Too* means "excessively": "Sam is *too* tired to study for a test." *Too* can mean "also": "Besides the ketchup, bring some mustard *too*." *Two* is a number: "The Coles own *two* houses."
WERE/WE'RE/WHERE	*Were* is a verb: "The cats *were* frisky." *We're* is a shortened form of *we are*: "We'll leave when *we're* ready." *Where* indicates place: "*Where* are you going?"
YOU'RE/YOUR	*You're* is a shortened form of *you are*: "Let us know if *you're* uncomfortable." *Your* shows ownership: "Is that *your* basketball?"

✓ SPOTCHECK 14-6

Underline the correct words in parentheses.

1. (Are/Our/Or) you going to the lake in (are/or/our) car (are/our/or) in Franklin's?

2. We should (have/of) planned ahead.

3. I (hear/here) that Judith forgot her swimsuit.

4. I have mine (here/hear) in my tote bag.

5. Monica is more excited (than/then) Karen about the trip.

6. But Karen will be excited (to/too/two) when she arrives at the lake.

7. (Were/Where) are Dwight and Mary? They (were/where) supposed to roast the hot dogs.

8. (You're/Your) supposed to bring ice for the soft drinks.

9. Let's use this picnic table over (hear/here).

10. (Then/Than) everything will be just about perfect.

Check the Answer Key before continuing.

DOUBLECHECK 14-2　　*Underline the correct word in parentheses.*

1. The human brain is almost (to/too/two) amazing to be believed.

2. (Its/It's) unlikely that a computer will ever do all that the brain can do.

3. The brain tells us what is happening in (are/or/our) world by processing messages from the eyes, ears, nose, and skin.

4. It controls bodily functions (to/too/two), such as the beating of the heart.

5. The brain stores information and memories, so (there's/theirs) a chance of learning and benefiting from experience.

6. Without a developed brain, the human species might (have/of) disappeared as the dinosaurs did.

7. By the time you were about 15, (your/you're) brain had reached (its/it's) full size.

8. By (than/then) it weighed about 1.5 kg.

9. The brain of a genius is not necessarily bigger (than/then) that of an average person.

10. (There's/Theirs) no direct relationship between human intelligence and the size of the brain.

Check the Answer Key before continuing.

CHECKPOINT 14-1　　*Identify each sentence as simple* (S), *compund* (C), *or complex* (X).

————————　1. People have been trying to hide or get rid of body odour for a long time.

————————　2. After taking a scented bath, the early Egyptians applied scented oils under their arms.

————————　3. Citrus and cinnamon applications were favoured because they did not turn rancid in the tropical heat.

————————　4. The body uses perspiration to cool off, and in hot weather humans have secreted up to 15 litres of sweat in 24 hours.

————————　5. Because the armpits stay warm and damp, they provide a good environment for the bacteria that cause odour.

———————————— **6.** It wasn't until 1888 that a product was marketed to fight underarm odour.

———————————— **7.** Named *Mum,* the product worked, and other manufacturers hurried to enter the competition.

———————————— **8.** Body odour was not a topic that North Americans liked to discuss.

———————————— **9.** They used hushed voices in requesting their favourite brand of deodorant at pharmacies.

———————————— **10.** Deodorants for men were not advertised until the 1930s.

No answers are given for Checkpoint quizzes.

THE CAUSE AND EFFECT ESSAY

◆ READING

THINKING ABOUT CONSEQUENCES

PRECHECK

Do you listen to the weather forecast? Have you noticed any changes in our weather patterns? In this essay, environmentalist Ian Burton writes that our behaviour is having drastic effects on the weather.

Individual Actions Can Have Huge Consequences*

—Ian Burton

affects   influences

It is easy to accept the idea that the large-scale affects the small. What is not always so obvious is that the small-scale affects the large. Take the weather. "Everybody talks about the weather, but nobody does anything about it." This has long been a common complaint. The weather affects us in many ways. Too little rain and farmers are clamoring for drought relief. Too much rain and they are complaining again. The success of the office picnic, the garage sale, the baseball game, the weekend at the cottage, is affected by the weather. Our very moods reflect the weather—the ennui of a dull, rainy afternoon; the spring in our step on a warm, sunny morning. The large-scale affects the small. We are creatures of the weather.

ennui   feeling of inactivity, listlessness

*Editor's title.

It's not true, however, that nobody does anything about it. Environment Canada goes to great lengths to try to predict it. The weather forecast is the news with the highest number of listeners. 2

Evidence shows that we act on this information. Farmers choose the time to plant and the time to harvest depending upon the weather. Tour operators, managers of ski resorts, golf courses, marinas, in fact the whole leisure, vacation and tourist industry responds in critical ways to weather forecasts. The whole economy is strongly influenced by weather. So we have been "doing something about it," even if it has been largely linked to attempts to predict. 3

But now we are discovering something new in the weather equation. People are actually changing the weather, and in a really big way. 4

elaborate sophisticated

This has been a long-standing human ambition. Traditional societies developed elaborate rituals, such as rain-dances, to influence the weather. Greek sailors in classical times made sacrifices for a favorable wind. In modern times, cloud seeding has been tried to produce rain or deflect the track of hurricanes. Smoke canisters are used in Florida to prevent frost, and burners were once used at London's Heathrow airport to try to disperse fog. 5

All these attempts have had minimal results. But in the next 50 years or less we are set to transform our weather beyond recognition. By the middle of the next century the weather in southern Ontario will probably be like that of Kentucky today. The Maritimes could be more like southern New England or New Jersey; southern British Columbia like Oregon or northern California, and the Prairies like Nebraska or Kansas. And all this the result of human behavior. The small-scale is affecting the large. 6

aggregate total

The mechanism for all this is the well-known emission of carbon dioxide from the use of fossil fuels like oil, coal and natural gas, as well as other greenhouse gasses. The aggregate effect of our innumerable small-scale decisions is changing our world. 7

Is this bad or good? Many Canadians might relish shorter and less severe winters. Heating bills would be down but air-conditioning bills would be up. Drought might become more frequent in the Prairies, the level of the Great Lakes might fall, and the level of the sea rise on all three coasts—Atlantic, Pacific and Arctic. 8

Economic impact studies carried out by the Canadian Climate Centre suggest that, on balance, the costs would be greater than the benefits, the risks greater than the opportunities. But all the evidence is not yet in. 9

What should we do in the meantime? Many nations, Canada included, are moving toward an approach that will try to change people's behavior as a precaution against changing the weather. But it's a far cry from international agreements to the behavior of the person on Main Street. 10

This means that the small has to begin to think seriously about how it affects the large. Our everyday behavior has suddenly become powerful enough to change the weather. 11

Who says nobody is doing anything about it? It's rather like casting a vote in a democratic election. One single vote appears to matter 12 very little. But good citizens take the responsibility to vote very seriously, and that changes governments and the direction of the country.

Changing the weather is something we each do every day. As prophets and philosophers have told us for millennia, the behavior of each individual is significant. Now science is showing us a new version of this eternal message.

millennia thousands of years

13

CHECKING MEANING AND STYLE

1. What does Ian Burton mean by "the large-scale affects the small"?
2. What have we mainly attempted to do about the weather?
3. What have we suddenly discovered?
4. In what way has changing the weather "been a long-standing human ambition"?
5. Why is the weather going to change "beyond recognition"?
6. What are the effects of the changed climate going to be?

CHECKING IDEAS

1. What is Burton's attitude toward the way we are influencing the weather?
2. Have you noticed any differences in your environment over the past few years?
3. In what ways are you personally affecting the environment?

◆ WRITING MODELS

THE CAUSE AND EFFECT ESSAY

A cause and effect essay may explore the *reasons* for phenomena (like acid rain), behaviour or events, or the *results* (of not studying hard, for instance), or the essay may combine both causes and effects. In his essay, Ian Burton explores the results, the consequences, of our behaviour on the environment.

Model Cause-and-Effect Essay #1

Ian Burton's essay could be written in five paragraphs that follow this plan:

Introduction—The weather affects people, who don't usually think they affect the weather.

Body 1—Weather predictions are most listened to and acted upon.

Body 2—Individuals' actions are causing changed weather conditions.

Body 3—Results of the change in weather are drastic.

Conclusion—Solution is to alter our behaviour

Model Cause-and-Effect Essay #2

In an essay that she wrote in high school, Erica Van Gorder used an anecdote to introduce her thesis about the consequences of not informing teenagers realistically about alcohol abuse.

Let's Get Realistic About Teenage Drinking

Introduction with thesis statement

A few weeks ago, a younger friend of mine decided to have a little fun and get drunk before going to a high school dance. Her parents were away, so she consumed an entire 26-ounce [750 mL] bottle of vodka. When her friends got her to the hospital, she spent the night being closely monitored in case her heart stopped beating, a result of the tremendous amount of alcohol that had invaded her body. We as teenagers are all aware that alcohol isn't exactly "healthy," but when we think of death and alcohol, we think of drinking and driving and alcoholics. What many teenagers need to be informed about is that alcohol has a lethal limit, and the consequences if they pass it.

1st support with topic sentence and consequences

Drinking is associated with the "good times," like partying and just letting loose. Yet we are bombarded with messages from parents, teachers, and the media that unless we are 19 years old in this country we should "just say no." The result is we react by "just saying yes."

2nd support with topic sentence and reasons

I ask you, is this a realistic request? Teenagers have been drinking before our generation and they will after our generation, and all the public service messages in the world aren't going to change it. When are the media and government going to wake up to reality? Teenagers are going to drink, and that is why we should start to inform them about drinking responsibly.

3rd support with topic sentence and specific details

What many teenagers are not aware of is that drinking has a lethal limit. I'm not talking about the hangover in the morning or "puking the night of." I'm talking about the dangers of overdoing it. Many teenagers who have their first excessive drinking experience, which usually occurs at a house party, have no idea what their personal "limit" is. Many will drink themselves into oblivion until they either vomit or pass out. All of them are unaware of how close they are to possibly putting their lives at serious risk.

Conclusion with solution

I'm not here to condone teenage drinking; I'm here to say that teens are not made aware of the realities of excessive drinking and the dangers associated with it. Let's get realistic about teenage drinking because if we are more aware of the possible outcomes, then maybe we'll make more informed choices.

◆ WRITING ASSIGNMENT

A CAUSE AND EFFECT ESSAY

WRITE A CAUSE AND EFFECT
PARAGRAPH

Choose one of the following topics to write a five-paragraph cause and/or effect essay: Your essay should have an introduction, two or three support paragraphs, and a conclusion.

1. Protecting our environment

2. Alcohol or drug abuse

3. The use of anabolic steroids

   During revision and proofreading, watch especially for the kinds of problems marked on recent papers.

◆ SENTENCE STRUCTURE

BUILDING EFFECTIVE SENTENCES

The Problem: Building Varied
Sentences

Many times, two or more short sentences can be combined to form a single sentence that provides variety, saves words, and gives more exact emphasis. **Prepositional phrases, participial phrases,** and **appositives** can be used in sentence combining.

Solution #1: Using
Prepositional Phrases

   Phrases, you'll recall from Chapter 3, are groups of related words that do not contain both a subject and a verb. A prepositional phrase begins with a preposition and ends with a noun or pronoun: *to the beach, with them, under the gnarled oak tree.* See page 13 for a review.

   Notice how prepositional phrases (underlined) are used in the following two examples:

   The mechanic finally started the car. It took him about five minutes.

   The mechanic finally started the car <u>after about five minutes.</u>

   The lieutenant picked up the grenade. He didn't give it a second thought.

   <u>Without a second thought,</u> the lieutenant picked up the grenade.

Remember to put a comma after a phrase that starts a sentence.

SPOTCHECK 15-1

Combine the following pairs of sentences by making one of each pair a prepositional phrase.

   EXAMPLE: The trail guide built a campfire. She built it near a stream.

Near a stream, the trail guide built a campfire.

(or) The trail guide built a campfire near a stream.

1. The mechanic had grease all over his face. He looked like a creature from another galaxy.

_____

_____

2. The magazine had a picture of Marie. It was on page 34.

_____

_____

3. The rabbit hid. It hid between two boulders.

_____

_____

4. It had been a hectic day. Mrs. Farnaby was tired.

_____

_____

5. Crows were in the tree's highest branches. They were holding a meeting.

_____

_____

Compare your answers with those in the Answer Key.

Solution #2: Using Participial Phrases

A participle is a word made from a verb. A *present participle* adds -*ing* to the verb. A *past participle* usually adds -*d* or -*ed*.

Verb	Present Participle	Past Participle
move	moving	moved
jump	jumping	jumped

Past participles of *irregular* verbs, you may recall, do not end in -*d* or -*ed*. Examples of irregular past participles are *begun, fought, eaten, sent, taught,* and *written.* (For a longer list, see page 82.)

A participial phrase consists of a participle and its modifiers. Here are examples:

<u>moving</u> into position
<u>encouraged</u> by his parents
<u>having risen</u> to the top
<u>written</u> by a secretary

A phrase must be joined to an independent clause to make a sentence.

<u>Moving into position</u>, the wrestlers await the referee's signal.
<u>Encouraged by his parents</u>, Whitney did well in school.
<u>Having risen to the top</u>, the new president turned his back on those who had helped him.

The first noun or pronoun after a participial phrase usually must name the person or thing referred to by the phrase. Otherwise, the error called a *dangling modifier* results.

(wrong) <u>Having risen to the top</u>, those who had helped him were ignored by the new president.

(right) <u>Having risen to the top</u>, the new president ignored all those who had helped him.

A phrase may appear before or after the word it describes.

(before) <u>Checking his watch frequently</u>, the nervous bridegroom waited for the bride.

(after) The nervous bridegroom, <u>checking his watch frequently</u>, waited for the bride.

Use commas to separate the participial phrase from the rest of the sentence.

An *-ing* word may also be used as a noun (the name of something). Then it is called a *gerund*.

<u>Walking</u> is good exercise.

SPOTCHECK 15-2 *Underline the participial phrases in these sentences.*

1. The mail carrier, terrified at the dog's snarling, retreated to the sidewalk.

2. Singing in the rain, Mark and Christine enjoyed their walk.

3. He remembered a poem taught to him by his mother.

4. Finished with his homework, Adrian went to bed.

5. Searching for a route to Asia, Cartier reached the St. Lawrence River.

Check the Answer Key before continuing.

SPOTCHECK 15-3   *Underline the participial phrases in these sentences.*

1. Played in India in the sixteenth century, the game we call Parcheesi was originally not a board game at all.

2. The game, enjoyed by the emperor Akbar the Great, took place in the royal garden.

3. Moving from bush to bush in the garden, the "pawns" were the most beautiful young women in India.

4. Their progress, determined by the throw of shells, finally brought them "home" to the emperor's throne in the center of the garden.

5. The English, changing the Indian name *pacisi* to *Pachisi,* moved the game indoors and replaced the beautiful maidens with ivory pawns to mark progress around the board.

Check the Answer Key before continuing.

SPOTCHECK 15-4   *Use participial phrases to combine the following pairs of sentences.*

> **EXAMPLE:** Norman backed the car out of the garage. He ran over Tim's bike.
>
> Backing the car out of the garage, Norman ran over Tim's bike.

1. Paul was exhausted from his hike. He wanted a hot bath.

   _____

2. The Selvadurais saved 10 percent of their salaries for ten years. They were finally able to make a down payment on a house.

   _____

   _____

3. The players were excited at the victory. They held their trophy for all to see.

   _____

   _____

4. Mrs. Ward was pleased with her garden. She gave some tomatoes to her neighbours.

   _____

   _____

5. Richard was playing volleyball in the gym. He met his future wife.

_____

_____

Compare your answers with those in the Answer Key.

Solution #3: Using Appositives

An appositive helps identify a noun or pronoun ahead of it.

Dr. Eugenia Wilson, a dentist, needs a technician. (identifies Dr. Wilson)

The Ashleys saw a statue of Sir John A. Macdonald, the first prime minister of Canada. (identifies John A. Macdonald)

Appositives are set off by commas if they are not essential to the meaning, as in the examples just given.

No commas are used if the appositives contain information essential to the sentence.

(no commas) The store Top Banana sells expensive toys.

(no commas) The movie Wayne's World stars Mike Myers.

SPOTCHECK 15-5

Underline the appositives in these sentences.

1. Vlad the Impaler, a fifteenth-century Romanian prince, was the inspiration for *Dracula*.

2. The seventeenth-century story "Bluebeard" was based partly on an actual Frenchman who killed several wives.

3. According to New England legend, the original Mother Goose of nursery rhyme fame was a Boston widow, Elizabeth Goose.

4. The first mechanically recorded human speech were the words of the nursery rhyme "Mary Had a Little Lamb."

5. The words were spoken in 1877 by Thomas Edison, inventor of the phonograph.

Check the Answer Key before continuing.

SPOTCHECK 15-6

Use appositives to combine these sentences.

EXAMPLE: Whitehorse is the largest city in the Yukon Territory. It has a population of about 15,200.

Whitehorse, the largest city in the Yukon Territory, has a population of about 15,200.

1. Elizabeth Kenny was an Australian nurse. She developed a method for treating polio.

_____

_____

2. The quartet played bebop. Bebop is a style of jazz developed in the late 1940s.

_____

_____

3. Elvis Presley was the "King" of rock 'n' roll. He died in 1977.

_____

_____

4. Alice Munro wrote *Open Secrets*. It is a collection of short stories.

_____

_____

5. The Toronto Skydome has a retractable roof. The arena can hold 50,516 people.

_____

_____

Compare your answers with those in the Answer Key.

✔

DOUBLECHECK 15-1

Identify the underlined words as a prepositional phrase (Prep), *a participial phrase* (Part), *or an appositive* (Ap).

_____ 1. <u>Under her bed</u>, Mary kept all her childhood dolls.

_____ 2. Doctor Peterson, <u>a sprinter in college</u>, now runs marathons.

_____ 3. Renata, <u>one of four sisters</u>, had three brothers.

_____ 4. <u>Having lived on a farm all his life</u>, Milton was eager to attend college in a city.

_____ 5. The Ricardos, <u>annoyed by the poor sound quality</u>, left the performance after the first act.

_____ 6. <u>Clinging to a teddy bear</u>, the child climbed into her mother's lap.

_____ 7. Michael got a souvenir from his brother, <u>a centre fielder for the Expos</u>.

_____ 8. <u>Encouraged by the appearance of the sun</u>, the boys went to the beach.

Check the Answer Key before continuing.

◆ WRITING PROCESS

EDITING: SPELLING ERRORS

Proofreading the final draft of your essay and correcting small errors is the last step in the writing process. This section considers spelling problems.

SPELLING WITH SUFFIXES

A suffix is one or more letters added at the end of a word to form a different word. Some suffixes are *-ing, -ed, -ent,* and *-ance.* Three rules will help you spell words with suffixes.

1. When a word ends in *-y,* change the *y* to *i* before adding a suffix—except in the case of *-ing.*

   happy—happier
   study—studies
   easy—easily
   but study—studying

2. Usually, drop a final *-e* when adding a suffix that begins with a vowel.

   drive—driving
   sincere—sincerity
   desire—desirable

3. Generally, if a word is accented on its first syllable, double the final consonant before adding a suffix.

   permit—permitted
   occur—occurring
   regret—regrettable

THE "*I* BEFORE *E*" RULE

The old rhyme usually goes "*i* before *e*, except after *c*, or when sounded like *a*, as in *neighbour* and *weigh*."

Thus we have *field*, *grief*, *niece*, and *relieve*.
And we have *ceiling*, *deceive*, *conceit*, and *freight*.

Some common exceptions to the rule: *science*, *efficient*, *leisure*, *either*, *neither*, and *height*.

SPOTCHECK 15-7

In each blank, write the correct form of the word in parentheses.

1. (move) The Petersons are _____ to Corner Brook.
2. (control) Despite the blowout, Patrick _____ the car.
3. (silly) Denise is the _____ member of the club.
4. (regret) The accident was very _____.
5. (satisfy) We had a _____ meal.
6. (hope) We were all _____ Gloria would win.
7. (occur) Last night's accident _____ at an intersection.
8. (happy)) Eugene seemed _____ when he lived in New Brunswick.

Check the Answer Key before continuing.

SPOTCHECK 15-8

Underline the word in each pair that is spelled correctly.

1. The merchant (decieved/deceived) the tourists.
2. The butcher cut a (vien/vein) in his arm.
3. The farmer drove through the (field/feild).
4. We were (relieved/releived) when the drought ended.
5. The three teenagers met their (friends/freinds) at the mall.
6. Can you guess the (wieght/weight) of that pony?
7. Mark will never (believe/beleive) Brent again.
8. William (recieved/received) an "A" in botany.

Check the Answer Key before continuing.

CHECKPOINT 15-1

Identify the underlined words as a prepositional phrase (Prep), *a participial phrase* (Part), *or an appositive* (Ap).

_____ 1. One of the earliest eye drops, <u>used in China 5,000 years ago</u>, was made from the mahuang plant.

_____ 2. It contained ephedrine hydrochloride, <u>an ingredient still used today to treat eye irritations.</u>

_____ 3. <u>In Germany in the late nineteenth century</u>, Hermann von Helmholtz made an important contribution to eye care.

_____ 4. He invented the ophthalmoscope, <u>a device for examining the eye's interior.</u>

_____ 5. In 1890, Otis Hall, <u>a banker in Spokane, Washington</u>, accidentally helped bring about one of the best-known eye solutions.

_____ 6. <u>Looking at a horse's broken shoe</u>, Hall was struck in the eye by a flick of the horse's tail.

_____ 7. His cornea, <u>lacerated by the blow</u>, became infected.

_____ 8. His injury was treated by two eye specialists, <u>brothers James and George McFatrich.</u>

_____ 9. <u>Impressed by his quick recovery</u>, Hall joined the brothers in a firm to market their eye drops, which contained muriate of berberine.

_____ 10. They combined the first and last syllables of the medicine for the market name <u>Murine.</u>

No answers are given for Checkpoint quizzes.

APPENDIX A
WRITING A SUMMARY

WHAT IS A SUMMARY?

After you have seen a good movie, you tell your neighbour what it was about—that is a summary. Giving a brief account of something is making a summary. To summarize is to concentrate on the main points rather than on the details of a piece. It could be a summary of a news item, a novel, a film, or a scientific feature in a newspaper for instance. A summary does not change the meaning of the original or re-interpret the author's view in any way. It is generally one-third the length of the original and includes only the essential points—the main ideas—and NOT the specific examples or details of the article. Unless quotation marks are used to indicate where the author's actual words are quoted, in a summary, writers use their own words.

WHY SUMMARIZE?

An ability to summarize is a very useful study skill. It helps in recalling the main details of a textbook. For students, a quick summary on index cards can reinforce a text's or lecturer's main points and provide an easy review before finals. Summaries convey essential information about material to others who have not read or seen what the writer has. In research papers, a summary of a writer's work or opinion is essential if the report is an argument, a discussion, or an opinion about particular material. In addition, summaries are useful in writing comparisons of the plot, or characters or style, in novels or films. Lastly, summaries help students focus concisely on the main ideas.

◆ READING

In her article "Lack of English, Not Good Will, Is the Culprit," Anna Nike Mineyko explains why many immigrants have problems. Read the article and then examine the model summary, which has been taken from the main points of the article.

Lack of English, Not Good Will, Is the Culprit

—Anna Nike Mineyko

Did you ever have to look for a job in a new, unfamiliar environment, especially during a recession, while hardly being able to understand English, your second language?

A lot of immigrants in Canada could answer yes. They are afraid to make phone calls and are frightened by interviews because they lack communication skills. They are unsure if their resume was written correctly or whether a covering letter might contain errors. Many of these new Canadians are educated, some with university degrees. They are proud of their knowledge but are shy about what they perceive to be their poor English.

They seek employment because they are motivated and responsible. They have not arrived in Canada to collect welfare.

In Poland, I was a journalist and an editor. When I came to Canada three years ago, I didn't know English at all. During my first year, I learned by myself and then I took courses. One day I realized, "Okay, I am not a journalist right now. I can't write because I don't know sufficient English, but I can stay in my chosen field and experience the special, exhilarating tension involved in the print and publishing environment."

Today, my first Canadian job in a printing store came to an end. I found this job placement after completing a desktop publishing course. Because I also worked in Poland as a graphic designer, it wasn't difficult to change tools—from drawing by pencil to drawing by computer software. Much more difficult to learn, however, was how to understand the customers who visited the store.

Clients would order letterheads, business cards, envelopes, logos, invitations, résumés, newsletters and flyers. They wanted to be advised by a designer and needed professional artwork.

It took time until I understood why the customer was the most important thing in the world. I remember one customer who stood over me while I created two complicated forms for him and a logo using CorelDraw.

The whole time he advised me that this job was supposed to take only 15 minutes. To behave properly in this context I should have smiled and been polite. I didn't smile. Instead, I asked him to go for coffee and come back after 20 minutes. Should I feel guilty? Yes; because the customer was paying for my work.

Customers expect not only nice, appropriate behavior but also excellent communication skills. The Polish language expresses itself differently from English. We shear words; I make small breaks after each word I speak. My parents and teachers taught me how to speak properly in Poland because educated people have to speak Polish very clearly.

But English is a river. Words flow together. If somebody is nervous, or excited, he or she may speak in the same clipped manner, but I do that because English is my second language, not because I am nervous. The result is that Polish people often are thought to be aggressive because they speak English the same way they speak Polish.

A nice woman visited our store quite frequently. After a few visits, I felt she barely tolerated contact with me. One day I understood why: I sounded rude.

It happened when I couldn't open her electronic file in the software memory. I told her about my difficulties simply: "I can't open your file." I said this sentence clearly. As usual, I sheared words. My accent caused what I said to sound harsh. Even though I smiled, she may have thought I meant, "I won't open your file."

I wanted to say, "Although I can't open your file, don't worry. I will redo this job quickly. I'll give you a call, when I am finished."

Unfortunately, she did not give me enough time to communicate further. The woman was furious. "You know what?" she said, "I'll come back at 6 o'clock to pick up this job!" The work ended up being done well and on time, but I felt the woman now thought I was her enemy. This was a terrible misunderstanding.

It's very important to understand and to be aware of why new immigrants might appear as if they're from outer space. No one is at fault. Each culture is beautiful. And here in this wonderful country we can meet and enjoy people from other cultures.

If a woman from Jamaica doesn't speak before a man during a meeting at work, it doesn't necessarily mean that she is passive. If a Polish man doesn't smile too often, it doesn't mean he doesn't like people. It's important to be aware of these differences.

"Take it easy, Anna," my friend, a designer at the print shop, said after a discussion about my artwork. "I will," I said, but I was upset the whole weekend before I came to realize that there is nothing wrong with me.

Many other immigrants have the same problem—we suffer from culture shock.

◆ WRITING MODELS

THE SUMMARY

Following is an example of a summary, taken from the Reading about the importance of understanding the language and cultural problems many immigrants experience. The main points of the article have been selected, paragraph by paragraph, and the article is shortened to about one-third of its length.

Model Summary

Summary of "Lack of English, Not Good Will, Is the Culprit" by Anna Nike Mineyko

Anna Nike Mineyko, in her article "Lack of English, Not Good Will, Is the Culprit," from *The Toronto Star,* February, 1994, writes about the difficulties of immigrants who speak little English. It is hard to find a job in a "new, unfamiliar environment, especially during a recession."

She maintains that, because of their lack of English, immigrants are hesitant about their job application skills, even though they may be very highly qualified. They want to find work, rather than be on welfare, states Mineyko, who was a journalist in Poland. When she arrived here she had to teach herself English before taking courses. She found a job in a printing store, realizing that she could not be a journalist without adequate English.

Her printing job came to an end, mainly because of her difficulty in understanding the customers. She had no idea of the importance of smiling and being polite to the customer. Mineyko explains that Polish makes sharper sounds than English, which is more flowing, like a river. To the customers, to whom she thought she was being polite, she actually sounded aggressive and rude. In dealing with one particular customer, for example, Mineyko explains that, as a result of her lack of English, a serious misunderstanding arose: the customer thought Mineyko was "her enemy."

Mineyko pleads for understanding of new immigrants' situation. She says that every culture is beautiful and can be enjoyed in our country if we are aware of cultural differences and of the culture shock from which many immigrants suffer.

◆ WRITING ASSIGNMENT

A SUMMARY

Select a reading from *Checkpoints,* and follow these seven steps.

1. Carefully read the passage to be summarized, considering the main topic, the thesis of the article, and the main point of each paragraph. The main point should be conveyed in the *topic sentence* in each paragraph. If you cannot find the main point in one sentence, imagine you are telling a friend about what you have just read, without going into great detail: what you say will be the main point.

2. Read the passage again and highlight the topic sentence, or main point, of each paragraph.

3. Take the highlighted parts and write them in sequence into one paragraph on a separate paper.

4. Consider whether or not you need to add any details to make proper sense. Fill in any "gaps," keeping your sentences as lengthy and as complex as possible. Two ideas can often be conveyed in one sentence. This approach will help to keep the summary brief.

5. Count the words to check that you have the desired length, usually one-third of the original.

6. Make sure that your first sentence includes the author's name, the article's title (correctly punctuated), with a present-tense verb, clearly stated before the introduction of the topic of the item.

   EXAMPLE: E. M. Forster, in *Aspects of the Novel,* defines two types of literary characters.

   Or: In "Legalize Marijuana," Frank Jones suggests that the drug should no longer be illegal.

7. Check that you have a sufficient conclusion in the *last* sentence, with no additional, personal opinions.

   EXAMPLE: Tavender concludes with a warning to Generation X about their present attitude. To survive, they must be more positive.

APPENDIX B
WRITING A JOB
APPLICATION LETTER

◆ READING

PREPARING FOR THE JOB MARKET

All successful writers have thought carefully about the kind of audience that will read their writing. What age are they? Young? What do they already know about the subject? Are they well-informed? What does the writer want to communicate to them? What will they learn from reading the writing?

The applicant who is invited for an interview is the one who successfully communicates his or her message in a covering letter. The keys to a winning letter in this competitive marketplace are *voice* and an awareness of *audience*.

It is crucial to visualize the person you are writing to; pretend you are face to face. Speak to that person in your letter with careful consideration of an appropriate level of formality and knowing exactly what you want to communicate about yourself.

In her article "Take a Close Look at Your Letter and Résumé," Janis Foord Kirk has some good advice for the successful candidate. Consider her advice when you follow the steps to writing an excellent covering letter.

Take a Close Look at Your Letter and Résumé

—Janis Foord Kirk

"It's so frustrating. I've never been out of work this long before. I'm starting to wonder about myself. I'm starting to wonder if there's something I'm doing wrong."

Sound familiar? No doubt you've had similar thoughts yourself if you're among the people who can't find work at the moment. Never mind that the statistics say thousands upon thousands are in the same boat. Never mind that, in some fields especially, there are simply no jobs available right now. When months drag by, and nothing happens, the average individual is likely to take it personally.

Quite possibly, there's little more that you can do. Like many people today, you're caught in a waiting game. If you keep doing what you're doing and don't lose heart, you're going to find work.

Then again, maybe your approach to job hunting isn't all that effective, or part of it isn't. If something isn't working, it's up to you to change it.

Either way, after months of job search, a critical and objective review of how you're looking for work is a smart move. A fresh look at your approach and the obstacles that seem to be in your way may help you come up with creative ways to overcome them.

Look first at your written work, at the résumés and letters you send prospective employers. If they're not opening doors for you, perhaps they're closing them.

A résumé can't get you a job. What it's meant to do is generate interest and interviews. If it's not producing close to a 10 percent return on effort (100 résumés sent, 10 indications of interest) it may need some work.

Take a hard look at it. Be brutally objective. What does it say about you? Does it feature your strengths? Does it catch the reader's attention early and encourage one to read on? And, most of all, does it give the reader any reason to screen you out?

Tom, a salesman, and a good one at that, has been out of work for months now. At 55, his age and the fact that he doesn't have a college education work against him in the job market, he believes.

Yet, on the top of the first page, a key spot in any résumé because it's there you either catch someone's interest or begin to lose it, Tom has an EDUCATION section noting his high school diploma and the year he received it.

So, up front, long before reading about Tom's impressive work history and accomplishments, an employer can easily figure out what Tom would prefer not to emphasize—how old he is and that he didn't attend college.

It's not unusual for job candidates to provide too much detail on their résumés, according to one survey of 200 executive employers. They also frequently miss typos and grammatical errors, and fail to consider whether the document has a professional appearance, the executives said.

Even worse, these employers suspect that more than one-quarter of all job applicants lie or intentionally omit information on their résumés.

Finding the middle ground between saying too much on a résumé and not enough can take some effort, says Paul McDonald, president of the recruiting firm Robert Half/Accountemps, which conducted the survey. Job seekers who qualify for more than one type of job should have more than one résumé, McDonald suggests. Each one should be truthful, but emphasize different aspects of experience.

The most impressive résumés, he says, are "factual but brief, sticking to relevant job-related information. They have wide margins and plenty of space between paragraphs."

Employers also want to hear about your achievements on a résumé, the survey found.

Some information shouldn't appear on a résumé, according to McDonald. Never indicate past salaries, reason for termination, names of references or past supervisors, political, fraternal or religious affiliations, race, national origin, sex, or personal characteristics. Don't date your résumé and never include a photograph, he adds.

A review of your résumé against this list of shoulds and shouldn'ts may indicate a need for revisions. If so, take time to do them thoroughly. And, once you've reworked it, take it to three people in your field whose opinions you respect and ask them to give a critique of it.

Don't become defensive when they make suggestions. Keep an open mind. Listen carefully and take notes. When their suggestions are valid, incorporate them into your final draft.

You'll want to do a similar review of the letters you send to employers. Read them objectively. Are they personalized and tailored to each job and each employer? If not, they'll never stand out from the hundreds of others that compete for an employer's attention these days.

One employer put it this way: "I read a lot into the covering letter. It tells me what kind of person an applicant is. If it's a form letter, I generally don't bother to read the rest of the application.

"I look for sincere comments," he added. "And, I look for things that are tailored toward our industry. I want to interview a person who has done some research and who can talk with some industry knowledge."

However important, an assessment of your written material is only the start of a job search review.

◆ WRITING MODELS

THE JOB APPLICATION LETTER

A job application letter is an essay describing why you would be a good choice to fill an available position. It may be one of the most important "essays" you ever write.

Let's say you wanted to write an application for a part-time job in a downtown sporting goods store. Jotting down a list of the reasons why you should get the job, you might end up with something like this:

like sports

good worker

worked three summers in sales—Park's Stationery

neat

good personality

punctual

honest

played basketball, tennis in high school

played Little League baseball

taking weight training in college

20 years old

6 feet tall, 165 pounds

sing in church choir

familiar with cash register, making change

some computer skills

two sisters, one brother

Looking over your list, you notice that some items are about your general qualities and job skills. Others are about special qualities that suit you for sporting goods sales. Still others do not seem important to your application. Crossing some out and rearranging the others, you might come up with a new list like this:

GENERAL QUALIFICATIONS

good worker
good personality
neat
punctual
honest
20 years old
worked three summers in sales—Park's Stationery
familiar with cash register, making change
some computer skills

SPECIAL QUALIFICATIONS

like sports
played basketball and tennis in high school
played Little League baseball
taking weight training in college
~~two sisters, one brother~~
~~6 feet tall, 165 pounds~~
~~sing in church choir~~

You are now prepared to write a four-paragraph essay:

Introduction—name of job you are applying for

Body I—general qualifications

Body II—special qualifications

Conclusion—request interview

Here is what a four-paragraph job application letter might look like:

YOUR ADDRESS

> 100 Johnson Avenue
> Edmonton, AB T2G 1S4
> October 17, 19XX

FIRM'S ADDRESS

> Randall Jones
> Jones Sporting Goods
> 111 Seymour Street
> Vancouver, B.C. V4C 3PI

GREETING

> Dear Mr. Jones:

INTRODUCTION

> I would like to apply for the part-time sales position you advertised in yesterday's *Vancouver Sun*.

BODY I

> I am a good worker who is neat, punctual, and honest. I get along well with others. The last three summers I gained worthwhile experience as a salesclerk at Smith's Stationery. I learned to operate a cash register there, and I have had some experience with a personal computer at home. I am 20 years old.

BODY II

> I feel I would be especially qualified to work in a sporting goods store because of my interest in athletics. After playing Little League baseball as a boy, I was on varsity teams in basketball and tennis in high school. I am now taking a weight training class at Centreville College.

CONCLUSION

> I would be happy to arrange an interview at your convenience. My phone number is 555-1234.

CLOSING

> Sincerely,
>
> *Mark Smith*
>
> Mark Smith

◆ WRITING ASSIGNMENT

A JOB APPLICATION LETTER

Outside of college, most of the writing people do is in the form of business letters, memos, and reports. One of the first business letters most of us have to write is a job application letter. It will probably follow the same four-part format as the model letter:

INTRODUCTION

Tell what job you are applying for and where or how you learned about the job.

BODY I

Give general background information about yourself that makes clear your qualifications.

BODY II

Give specific background information that suggests ways in which you are especially qualified for this position.

CONCLUSION

Request an interview; give your phone number or tell the employer that you will be calling in a few days.

WRITE A JOB APPLICATION LETTER

Write a letter applying for a job that you might actually be qualified for. Make the letter as interesting and convincing as you can. Jot down all the general and special qualifications you have (prewriting). Then follow the format of the model letter.

Your general qualifications: _____

_____

_____

_____

_____

_____

Your specific qualifications: _____

_____

_____

_____

_____

_____

After you have done a first draft of your letter, check it over carefully for spelling, punctuation, capitalization, and complete sentences. It is especially important to make a good impression in your letter. Many people may be applying for the same job. Even one mistake may mean that the employer will not invite you for an interview.

APPENDIX C
USING THE DICTIONARY

One of the most useful tools a writer or speaker can have is a good dictionary. Of course, dictionaries tell us the meanings of words and how to spell and pronounce them, but they also contain a surprising amount of other information.

Let's look at the dictionary entry for an everyday word, *bird*. First, here is an example of an entry from a pocket dictionary. Small paperback dictionaries of this kind can easily be carried to class in a book bag.

> **bird** (berd) *n*. A warm-blooded, egg-laying, feathered vertebrate, with forelimbs modified to form wings.
> [>OE *brid*]

Now let us look at the entry for the same word in the *Gage Canadian Dictionary*. This is a hardback "college size" or desk edition. As a glance will show, it contains much more information than the pocket edition. If you do not have one at home, you can use one in any library. Now let's take another look at the word *bird* and discover just how much a dictionary can tell us.

pronunciation   part of speech

spelling —— **bird** (bérd) *n., v.*—*n.* **1** any of a class (Aves) of warm-blooded, egg-laying vertebrates having a body covered with feathers, and forelimbs modified into wings by means of which most species can fly. All birds have keen vision. **2** a bird hunted for sport; game bird. **3** shuttlecock.

definitions / **4** *Informal*. person: *He's a strange bird.* **5** *Brit. Slang*. a girl or young

usage — woman. **6** *Slang*. ballistic missile. **7** clay pigeon. **bird in the hand,** something certain because one already has it. **birds of a feather,**

idiomatic — people with the same kind of ideas or interests. **for the birds,** not

expression — worth considering; ridiculous, boring, etc.: *The movie was for the birds. I think house cleaning is for the birds.* **give** (someone) **the bird,** jeer or ridicule someone. **kill two birds with one stone,** get two things done by one action.—*v.* engage in bird-watching. [OE] *bridd,* bird]—**bird′like′** *adj.*—**bird′er,** *n.*

part of speech ——

origins

259

Pronunciation

Right after the first entry of the word is a special spelling of the word to show correct pronunciation. The special alphabet used for pronunciation is explained in the key at the bottom of the page (or, perhaps, in a section at the beginning of the dictionary). For example, you may read that the *er* in *berd* is pronounced the same as the *er* in *fern*. The accent mark shows which part of the word—or which syllable, in a word that has more than one syllable—should get the most emphasis when spoken.

Parts of Speech

How a word may be used in a sentence is shown right after the pronunciation guide. You are told that *bird* can be used as a noun (abbreviated *n.*) or as a verb (*v.*). Some other parts of speech discussed in this text are pronouns (*pron.*), prepositions (*prep.*), adjectives (*adj.*), and adverbs (*adv.*). (All of the parts of speech are defined in Appendix G.)

Meanings

The definitions come next. Since more than one meaning is often given, you will have to figure out which one applies in your situation.

Usage

Not all words can be used on all occasions. Your dictionary will probably tell you which words are *slang* or *nonstandard,* for example. Here, you learn that the definitions numbered 5 and 6 are slang, to be used in only the most informal situations.

Inflected Forms

Some words change their endings to show how they are used in a sentence. Verbs, for instance, usually change for the past-time form and the past participle. Noun endings usually change to show the plural. The dictionary will indicate these changes only when they are "irregular"—that is, not made in the usual way.

Origins

The words we use today often have their origins in words used many centuries ago in England or in such languages as Greek, Latin, German, and French. *Bird,* we are told, is derived from Old English (used in the eighth to twelfth centuries).

Other Features

Your dictionary may also give you examples of words used in idiomatic expressions (*for the birds* is one). It may show differences among synonyms (words that mean almost the same thing) and may give usage tips (when to use *which* and *that,* for example).

SPOTCHECK C-1

Eight definitions are included in the definition just given for bird— *seven as a noun* (n.) *and one as a verb* (v.). *In the blanks at the left, write* N *or* V *and the number of the definition that fits each sentence.*

EXAMPLE: __N-3__ The badminton player tossed the bird to his partner and said, "It's your service."

_____ 1. Three birds splashed in the puddle.

_____ 2. Fred and Jason birded at the seashore.

_____ 3. The giant bird blasted off from the launching pad.

_____ 4. The Williams' neighbour is a strange bird.

_____ 5. The trapshooter waited for the release of the bird.

Check the Answer Key before continuing.

Use a dictionary to answer these questions.

1. Which syllable is emphasized in pronouncing *theatre?*
2. Which spelling is correct, *athlete* or *athelete?*
3. What does *itinerant* mean?
4. Is *itinerant* an adjective, a noun, or both?
5. What is the plural form of *leaf?*
6. What language is *clone* derived from?
7. What usage label is given for *bummer?*

APPENDIX D
READING IN COLLEGE

The ability to read well can bring rewards throughout our lives, but as you no doubt already have discovered for yourself, good reading skills are essential in college. It's hard to take part in class discussions, and impossible to do well on tests, if you don't understand the assigned readings.

In addition, reading can make you a better writer. Reading will show you how experienced writers make use of words, sentences, and paragraphs. Reading will improve your vocabulary and spelling skills, often without your even being aware of the change. And it will give you new ideas, information, and insights to add strength to your own writing.

Whether you are zipping through a biker magazine or struggling with a chemistry text, these suggestions can help you understand and remember what you read.

- *Preview* the material. The more you know ahead of time about what you are going to read, the easier and more efficient your reading will be.

  - Is there an *introductory note* with clues about the subject or about what the author's purpose is? This note often appears at the beginning of the piece, before the title or before the first chapter, as in this text.

  - Look at the *title.* Sometimes it reveals or hints at the subject or purpose.

  - What do you know about the *author?* What is he or she an authority on? What ideas or prejudices have come through in earlier writings that you have seen?

  - Are there *subheadings*—short titles within the work, usually set in contrasting type? These may signal points that the author wants to emphasize or show how the ideas are organized.

  - Read the *first and last paragraphs.* Writers often present their main idea at the beginning and restate it at the end.

  - Read the first sentence of each of the other paragraphs. This may be the *topic sentence,* giving a summary of the entire paragraph. (This approach is less useful with the very short paragraphs often found in articles in newspapers and magazines.)

- Read *actively*. Ideas and information are not going to leap off the page into your mind. You have to make an effort. It may be a good idea to turn off the TV and the radio and to take off your headset!

  - Look for the *main idea*. Then keep asking how other details relate to that idea.

  - Decide what the author's *purpose* is in writing. Is it to inform, to persuade, to describe, to entertain? Focus on those details that carry out the purpose.

- Mark up your book! *Underline key points*. When you review the material before a class discussion or a test, the most important details should be obvious. Underlining requires constant thought about what is and isn't important. Those who overdo it—who underline almost every sentence—are missing the point.

- *Read critically*. Just because something is in a book doesn't mean you have to accept it as true or worthwhile. Ask questions. Do the "facts" seem reliable? Are the opinions supported with sound evidence? Is the writer appealing mostly to your emotions or to your reason? Jot down your doubts and disagreements in the margin.

- Understand the *words*. If not knowing a word blocks your understanding of a passage, by all means look it up. But it isn't necessary to turn to the dictionary every time you come to a new word. Often you can guess what the word means from the way it is used, and you can skip over some unfamiliar words for the moment if they aren't essential to understanding. By the way, reading on a wide range of subjects is the best way to build up your vocabulary.

- When you've finished reading, *quiz yourself*. What was the thesis or main point of the material? What were the main supporting points? If necessary, read the material again to find the answers you missed. Rarely will reading the material just once provide the understanding expected in the classroom.

APPENDIX E
WORDS OFTEN MISUSED

ADVICE/ADVISE You get or give *advice,* a noun. *Advise* is a verb. "I advise you to study for the exam."

AIN'T Avoid except in very informal or humorous usage.

A LOT Often misspelled *alot.*

ALREADY/ALL READY *Already* means "by a certain time": "When I arrived, Bill had already left." *All ready* means "completely prepared": "The class was all ready for the exam."

ALRIGHT Misspelling of *all right.*

AMONG/BETWEEN In general, use *among* when discussing three or more items: "flew among the flowers." Use *between* when discussing two items: "between you and me."

AND ETC. Omit the *and,* since *etc.* is an abbreviation of *et cetera,* meaning "and other." Spell it *etc.,* not *ect.* Generally avoid use of *etc.* in formal writing.

AS (IF)/LIKE *As* or *as if* introduces a dependent clause: "It looks as if [not *like*] it will rain." Use *like* as a preposition: "Frank looks like his father."

CAN/MAY In formal writing, use *can* to show ability: "Susan can drive a car." Use *may* to show permission: "Susan may drive her parents' car."

CONSCIOUS/CONSCIENCE *Conscious* means "aware": "conscious of his shortcomings." *Conscience* is the sense of right and wrong: "The thief's conscience bothered him."

SPOTCHECK E-1   *Underline the correct word in parentheses.*

1. My (conscious/conscience) bothered me because of some unkind remarks I had made to Ernest.

2. So I went over to Pete's house for some (advice/advise).

3. Pete said everything would be (alright/all right) if I would always be (conscious/conscience) of Ernest's feelings in the future.

4. "You (can/may) tell Ernest that I said he should forgive you," Pete said.

5. It was (as/like) I knew it would be: Pete would have the answers.

Check the Answer Key before continuing.

More Words Often Misused—2

COULD OF   Write "could *have*."

DESSERT/DESERT   *Dessert* is the after-dinner treat. Use *desert* for other meanings. "Will the soldiers desert their leader?" "The soldiers struggled across the hot desert."

EXCEPT/ACCEPT   *Except* shows exclusion: "everyone except Bill." *Accept* means to receive: "accept the compliment."

FEWER/LESS   *Fewer* is used with plural nouns: "fewer classes," "fewer bananas." *Less* is used with singular nouns: "less cake," "less money."

FIRSTLY, SECONDLY, ETC.   Use *first, second* instead.

FUN   Avoid in formal writing as an adjective: "We had ~~a fun~~ an enjoyable time."

IMPLY/INFER   *Imply* means "to hint at or suggest": "He implied that I took the money." *Infer* means "to guess": "From my guilty look, he inferred that I took the money."

INPUT   Computer jargon adapted to mean "opinion" or "advice." Avoid, as in "Sue wants my input on what car to buy."

IRREGARDLESS   Nonstandard. Use *regardless.*

IS WHEN, IS WHERE   Avoid in definitions: "A good party is when . . . ," "a good friend is where. . . ."

SPOTCHECK E-2   *Underline the correct word in parentheses.*

1. We had a (fun/pleasant) time at Phoebe and Bob's house Saturday night.

2. All our friends were there (except/accept) the Greenes, who had (excepted/accepted) another invitation.

3. Actually, there were (fewer/less) guests than at the Oswalds' New Year's Eve party.

4. I don't mean to (imply/infer) that Phoebe and Bob are less popular than the Oswalds.

5. No friend will (dessert/desert) someone who makes (desserts/deserts) as good as Phoebe's.

6. A good party is (when/an occasion when) good friends get together.

Check the Answer Key before continuing.

More Words Often Misused—3

KNOW/NO   "We *know* that there is *no* free lunch."

LITERALLY   Do not use for emphasis—"I literally cried my eyes out"—unless that is exactly what happened (your eyes *fell out*).

LOSE/LOOSE   *Lose* is a verb: "He will lose. . . ." *Loose* is an adjective meaning "not tight": "a loose sweater."

LOT(S) OF   In formal writing, use *a great deal of, much,* or *many.* "We saw ~~lots of~~ many wildflowers on our trip."

ME AND   Avoid in compound subjects: "~~Me and Bill~~ Bill and I are brothers."

MORALE/MORAL   *Morale* refers to spirit or attitude: "The team's morale was high." *Moral* refers to good character or conduct: "Sue had high moral standards."

MOST   Do not use instead of *almost:* "~~Most~~ Almost everyone liked the movie."

NICE   Replace this vague word with a more exact one, such as *attractive, kind,* or *generous.*

OK, OKAY   Avoid in formal writing.

PASSED/PAST   *Passed* is a verb: "He passed the gravy" or "Our car passed theirs." If it isn't a verb, use *past:* "The car drove past" or "He lives in the past."

PEACE/PIECE   *Peace* is the absence of war. *Piece* means "a part of something": "a piece of pie."

SPOTCHECK E-3   *Underline the correct word in parentheses.*

1. Vic's (morale/moral) was low when he left Donna's house.

2. To (lose/loose) at chess was something he couldn't accept easily.

3. As he (passed/past) through the front door, he (most/almost) blew his top in disgust.

4. "(Me and Donna/Donna and I) have been playing chess for years," he muttered to himself.

5. "I (know/no) she won't beat me next time."

6. With that thought, Vic was once again at (peace/piece).

Check the Answer Key before continuing.

More Words Often Misused—4

QUIET/QUITE *Quiet* is the opposite of *noisy:* "The library was quiet." *Quite* gives mild emphasis: "The book was quite heavy."

REASON IS BECAUSE In formal writing, use *reason is that:* "The reason we are leaving is ~~because~~ that. . . ."

RIGHT/WRITE *Right* means "correct": "ShuJuan had all the right answers." *Write:* "She had to write the paper before Monday."

SIT/SET *Sit* is what you do in a chair. *Set* means "to place": "Mari-ann set the vase on the table."

SUPPOSE TO Be sure to add the *-d:* "I am supposed to work this weekend."

THEIRSELF, THEIRSELVES Use *themselves* instead.

THREW/THROUGH "He *threw* the baseball *through* the window."

TRY AND Write *try to:* "Try ~~and~~ to be home by six."

USE TO Don't forget the *-d* on *used:* "We used to own a convertible."

WEATHER/WHETHER "We didn't know *whether* [if] the *weather* would get better."

WOMAN/WOMEN *Woman* refers to one, *women* to more than one.

SPOTCHECK E-4 *Underline the correct words in parentheses.*

1. Rebecca was (quiet/quite) sure she would see Martin again before long.

2. The reason (was because/was that) they had had spats before and gotten back together.

3. She (suppose/supposed) he would telephone or (write/right) her a note.

4. But she also wondered (weather/whether) it was all right for (woman/women) to call men.

5. She decided to (sit/set) down and (try and/try to) forget Martin for a while.

Check the Answer Key before continuing.

APPENDIX F
150 WORDS OFTEN
MISSPELLED

1. absence
2. acceptance
3. accidentally
4. accommodate
5. acquaintance
6. acquire
7. across
8. address
9. adolescence
10. against
11. all right
12. almost
13. always
14. answer
15. appearance
16. appreciate
17. argument
18. asked
19. athlete
20. basically
21. believe
22. benefit
23. breathe
24. business
25. candidate
26. careful
27. cellar
28. cemetery
29. certain
30. changing
31. choose
32. clothes
33. coming
34. committee
35. competition
36. condemn
37. confidential

38. conscience
39. conscious
40. counsellor
41. courteous
42. criticize
43. deceive
44. decision
45. definite
46. dependent
47. disappear
48. disappoint
49. dissatisfied
50. doesn't
51. easily
52. efficiency
53. eighth
54. eligible
55. embarrass
56. environment
57. equipped
58. especially
59. exaggerate
60. excellent
61. except
62. exercise
63. experience
64. February
65. finally
66. foreign
67. fortunately
68. friend
69. grammar
70. guarantee
71. height
72. hoping
73. immediately
74. intelligence

75. jealous
76. kindergarten
77. knowledge
78. laboratory
79. leisure
80. library
81. license
82. literature
83. loneliness
84. marital
85. marriage
86. mathematics
87. medicine
88. mileage
89. misspell
90. muscle
91. naive
92. necessary
93. neighbour
94. neither
95. ninth
96. occasion
97. occurred
98. paid
99. particularly
100. persuade
101. possess
102. possible
103. practically
104. preferred
105. prejudiced
106. privilege
107. probably
108. proceed
109. professor
110. pronunciation
111. psychology

112. quantity
113. questionnaire
114. receive
115. recognize
116. recommend
117. religious
118. restaurant
119. rhythm
120. ridiculous
121. sacrifice
122. schedule
123. scissors
124. secretary
125. seize
126. separate
127. significance
128. similar
129. sincerely
130. sophomore
131. statistics
132. strength
133. studying
134. succeed
135. surprise
136. sympathize
137. therefore
138. thought
139. through
140. till
141. tragedy
142. truly
143. usually
144. valuable
145. vegetable
146. Wednesday
147. weird
148. whose
149. writing
150. written

Add to the list words misspelled on your own papers:

Appendix G
Grammatical Terms:
The Parts of Speech

Words are classified into eight *parts of speech* based on their use in a sentence.

Noun
A word such as *Patricia, New York, sofa,* or *patriotism* that names a person, place, thing, or idea.

PROPER NOUNS name particular people, places, etc., and are capitalized: *Professor Kinski, Lake Louise, Pepsi, Buddhism.*

COMMON NOUNS name people and things in general and are not capitalized: *doctor, river, soft drink, religion.*

GROUP (COLLECTIVE) NOUNS refer to groups of people or things as if they were a single unit: *team, audience, flock.*

Verb
ACTION VERBS say what the subject does: "The boy *ran* home." **Linking verbs** connect the subject to a word that identifies or describes it: "The boy *was* tired."

TRANSITIVE VERBS have an object that receives the action of the verb: "The car *hit* the hydrant." **Intransitive verbs** do not take an object: "Birds *fly.*"

A **VERB PHRASE** is a verb made up of more than one word: *has run, could have run, will be running.*

A verb in **ACTIVE VOICE** shows the subject acting: "The singer also *played* a guitar." A verb in **passive voice** shows the subject being acted upon: "A guitar *was played* by the singer."

Adjective
A word that describes a noun ("*talented* actress") or pronoun ("she is *talented*"). An adjective tells which one, what kind, or how many.

Adverb
A word that describes a verb ("ran *slowly*"), an adjective ("*very* beautiful"), or another adverb ("moved *rather* quickly"). An adverb tells how, when, where, or to what extent.

Pronoun
A word that takes the place of a noun: "The students entered slowly. *They* dreaded Professor Higgins' exams."

PERSONAL PRONOUNS refer to people or things: *I, we, she, he, it, they.* Besides those subject forms, pronouns also have object forms (*me, us, her, him, them*) and possessive forms (*my, mine, your, yours, our, ours, his, her, hers, their, theirs, its*). Example: "We gave *them our* tickets."

INDEFINITE PRONOUNS (*each, neither, anyone, everybody,* etc.) do not refer to a specific person or thing: "*Nobody* knows the answer."

INTERROGATIVE PRONOUNS (*who, whom, whose, what, which*) begin questions: "*Whose* book is that?"

RELATIVE PRONOUNS (the interrogative pronouns, plus *whoever, whomever, whichever, whatever*) begin dependent clauses: "The books were free to *whoever* needed them."

INTENSIVE PRONOUNS (words ending with *-self* or *-selves*) give emphasis to a noun or other pronoun: "The doctor *himself* said it." "We *ourselves* will pay the bill."

REFLEXIVE PRONOUNS (words ending with *-self* or *-selves*) show the subject acting upon itself: "The carpenter hit *himself* on the thumb."

DEMONSTRATIVE PRONOUNS (*this, that, these, those*) point to a particular person or thing: "*These* are my favourite flowers."

PREPOSITION

A word such as *to, for, of, in, with,* or *between* that connects a noun or pronoun (its object) to the rest of the sentence and forms a prepositional phrase: "They went swimming *in the river.*"

CONJUNCTION

A word that joins other words.

COORDINATING CONJUNCTIONS ("connectors") are *and, but, or, for, nor, yet,* and *so.* They join grammatically equal units, such as two independent clauses: "Sylvia attended the concert, *but* Glenn was out of town."

SUBORDINATING CONJUNCTIONS ("dependent words") include words such as *although, because, since,* and *unless.* They join dependent (subordinate) clauses to independent clauses: "We went by train *because* Ernie doesn't like to fly."

CONJUNCTIVE ADVERBS ("transitional words") join independent clauses: "Bernice got a pay raise; *however,* she remained unhappy." Other conjunctive adverbs include *moreover, nevertheless, finally,* and *meanwhile.*

INTERJECTION

A word showing strong feeling, such as *wow, oh,* or *well:* "*Oh,* I could hardly believe my eyes!"

ANSWER KEY

SPOTCHECK 1-1

1. Our home computer gets a workout from everyone in the family.
2. Alex and I spent a relaxing day at Henderson Lake Sunday.
3. I plan to become a veterinarian.

SPOTCHECK 1-2

1. Larry threw his book on the floor and stomped out.
2. Yolanda has an old four-door Toyota Cressida sedan.
3. Naomi brought a salami sandwich on rye and a can of diet root beer.

SPOTCHECK 1-3

1. good
2. good
3. weak
4. good
5. weak

SPOTCHECK 1-4

1. office work, typing
2. historical buildings, the Parliament Buildings, Ottawa
3. rock 'n' roll, the Rolling Stones
4. biology students, my lab partner

SPOTCHECK 1-5

1. weak
2. weak
3. weak
4. good
5. weak
6. good

SPOTCHECK 1-6

1. My neighbourhood has several attractive gardens.
2. The neighbours' cat has been nothing but trouble for me.
3. My cousin is a fancy dresser.
4. Shopping is Valerie's favourite pastime.
5. My English class was boring Monday.

SPOTCHECK 1-7

1. electricity
2. Swimming
3. Mrs. Jackson

4. calendar
5. plumber

SPOTCHECK 1-8

1. fought—action
2. were—linking
3. looked—linking
4. hit—action
5. cheered—action

SPOTCHECK 1-9

1. between	3. among	5. on	7. from
2. through	4. in	6. into	8. at

SPOTCHECK 1-10

1. ~~Of the three singers,~~ Charles
2. ~~Between the tall buildings, to the sunlight,~~ tree
3. ~~of the ducks, on the pond,~~ One
4. ~~For some reason, to everyone, in the class,~~ instructor
5. ~~Between you and me, to Sylvia,~~ award

DOUBLECHECK 1-1

1. (s) neighbours; (v) have
2. queen removed
3. Chevy is
4. stew tastes
5. Lawrence was

SPOTCHECK 1-11

1. athletes	4. career
2. player	5. You
3. chance	6. athletes

SPOTCHECK 1-12

1. appeared, achieved	5. would have
2. was invented	6. were offered
3. had resembled	7. was taking
4. developed	8. were named

DOUBLECHECK 1-2

1. (s) Education; (v) is	8. status depends
2. 7 percent drop out	9. half attend
3. rate is	10. They worry
4. quality is credited	11. hours is
5. education has been	12. colleges receive
6. schools stress	13. Canadians have been
7. values are reinforced	14. emphasis may hamper

SPOTCHECK 2-1

1. (B) lacks both
2. (B) lacks both
   (D) lacks both
3. (B) lacks verb
   (D) lacks verb (or both)
4. (F) lacks both
5. (C) lacks subject

SPOTCHECK 2-2

1. (B) lacks both
2. (C) lacks subject
3. (D) lacks both
4. (D) lacks verb
5. (B) lacks both
   (E) lacks verb

SPOTCHECK 2-3

1. A small airplane flew overhead.
2. I spilled my soup while eating lunch.
3. After the movie, Jennifer and Jim went dancing.
4. The dog barked at passing cars.
5. A clerk in the shoe department smiled at Annie.

SPOTCHECK 2-4

1. The officer stopped a red convertible.
2. Tim saw a shooting star while driving home.
3. Angelo studied all night before the exam.
4. The plumber fixed the sink.
5. Willie married a cashier at the theatre.

SPOTCHECK 2-5

1. . . . Cheops, the largest. . . .
2. . . . of desert, it is. . . .
3. . . . stone blocks, some weighing. . . .
4. . . . for twenty years to build. . . .
5. . . . made of reeds and their own. . . .
6. . . . being built, the pyramid. . . .

SPOTCHECK 2-6

1. Fragments: 2, 4, 5, 8, 9, 11, 13

Helen Keller provides an inspiring example of a person who overcame great physical handicaps. She was made deaf and blind by illness before the age of two. With the help of a teacher, Anne Sullivan, Helen learned to communicate by spelling out words on a person's hand. She learned to speak by the time she was 16 as a result of her own hard work and Miss Sullivan's patience. Graduating from Radcliffe College in 1904 with honours, she began working to improve conditions for the blind by writing books, lecturing, and appearing before legislative bodies. Two movies tell of her life: *The Helen Keller Story* and *The Miracle Worker*.

Spotcheck 3-1

1. when
2. Although
3. because
4. where
5. Whenever

Spotcheck 3-2

1. F—Because
2. C
3. C
4. F—Even though
5. F—Before
6. C
7. F—Since
8. C
9. C
10. F—Although

Spotcheck 3-3

1. <u>Although</u> the wind was blowing, we went to the beach.
2. Sally planned a party <u>because</u> it was Ahmed's birthday.
3. <u>Whenever</u> Kimberly entered the classroom, Sam smiled.
4. Mary screamed <u>as</u> Curtis picked up the phone.
5. <u>Since</u> it was raining, we cancelled the picnic.

Spotcheck 3-4

1. which is the day taxes are due
2. who knows more and more about less and less
3. that we sing
4. which was scheduled to appear in many cities
5. that has many mountains

Doublecheck 3-1

1. <u>which</u> is the largest country in the Western Hemisphere
2. <u>which</u> is a distance of 5,514 kilometres
3. <u>X</u>
4. <u>which</u> is also known as the Precambrian Shield
5. <u>that</u> the Shield is composed of
6. <u>Although</u> the Shield's rock is ancient
7. <u>X</u>
8. X
9. X
10. <u>Where</u> erosion has not yet worn away the sharp peaks

Doublecheck 3-2

(Sections that have been edited are underlined.)

The term *martial arts* covers a variety of fighting methods based on ancient Asian combat skills. The martial arts are practised today for a number of <u>reasons, including</u> self-defense, physical fitness, and sports competition. Styles, techniques, and teaching methods <u>vary, even</u> within a given branch of the martial arts, such as <u>karate, although</u> adherence to ancient traditions is usually emphasized.

DOUBLECHECK 3-3

Although the exact origins are <u>uncertain, the</u> Asian styles of the martial arts seem to have come to China from India and <u>Tibet where</u> they were used by monks for exercise and protection against bandits. The arts flourished in <u>Japan, although</u> Japan was among the last of the Asian nations to learn them. For a time, the practice of the martial arts was restricted to the Japanese warrior class, but the peasants practised in secret.

DOUBLECHECK 3-4

The martial arts can be divided into two <u>categories, those</u> that use weapons and those that don't. In the weaponless <u>methods,</u> such as karate and kung fu, the contestant depends on kicks and on hand and arm <u>blows, as well as</u> on various holds, chokes, and twists, to subdue an opponent. In one of the branches using weapons, kendo, based on ancient Japanese sword <u>fighting, contestants</u> today use bamboo swords cased in leather.

DOUBLECHECK 3-5

T'ai chi is the most gentle of the martial arts. <u>It uses</u> slow, graceful movements that bear little resemblance to the <u>original</u> blows and blocks on which the movements are based. <u>T'ai chi is used</u> today for conditioning and flexibility. Some use it as a form of meditation.

SPOTCHECK 4-1

1. . . . World War II. Its empire. . . .
2. . . . the English. They hold. . . .
3. . . . in 1952. She has been. . . .

SPOTCHECK 4-2

1. . . . World War II, so its empire. . . .
2. . . . the English, and they hold. . . .
3. . . . in 1952, and she has been. . . .
4. . . . England, for many. . . .
5. . . . in London, or they may. . . .

SPOTCHECK 4-3

1. One brother is a banker, <u>and</u> the other is a forest ranger.
2. Andrea takes vitamins, <u>but</u> she doesn't need them.
3. Sara will move to Victoria, <u>or</u> she will stay in Vancouver.
4. My car is ten years old, <u>so</u> I am looking for another one.

SPOTCHECK 4-4

1. If mother gets home early, we will. . . .
2. The bulldozer knocked down the trees, <u>as</u> the neighbours. . . .
3. <u>Since</u> she was already ten minutes late, Yolanda decided. . . .

4. We always have a good time <u>when</u> we go camping.
5. <u>Because</u> the electricity went out, Terry lit some candles.

SPOTCHECK 4-5

1. The class bell rang <u>before</u> Mark finished the test.
2. We're going skiing·this weekend <u>unless</u> it rains.
3. Bill enjoyed the stew <u>although</u> he hates parsnips.

SPOTCHECK 4-6

1. . . . in education; they believe. . . .
2. . . . "get ahead"; it produces. . . .
3. . . . children; those children. . . .

SPOTCHECK 4-7

1. . . . in education; in fact, they. . . .
2. . . . "get ahead"; moreover, it. . . .
3. . . . small children; as a result, those. . . .
4. . . . in schools; however, we. . . .
5. . . . "educational"; for example, television. . . .

SPOTCHECK 4-8

1. Ricky doesn't eat sweets; furthermore, he avoids fatty foods.
2. You should go to bed; otherwise, you will be tired tomorrow.
3. The loan is due this month; however, I hope to get an extension.
4. Ned usually does well on tests; for example, he got a 96 on yesterday's history quiz.

DOUBLECHECK 4-1

1. C—automobile was introduced
     it brought
2. C—Farmers could drive
     dwellers could go
3. RTS—Highways, motorways made
     motels were built
4. C—families owned
     they could move
5. C—Cars made
     movies, restaurants, banks became

DOUBLECHECK 4-2

1. C—you are
     you eat
2. RTS—Indians brought
     Pilgrims liked
3. C—Popcorn is
     quart contains

4. C—you add
     popcorn compares
5. RTS—popcorn has
     it has

DOUBLECHECK 4-3

Bathing suits did not make an appearance until the middle of the 1800s <u>because</u> recreational bathing was not popular before then; <u>however</u>, at that time doctors began to prescribe the "waters" for a variety of ailments. Europeans flocked to the streams, the lakes, and the ocean <u>where</u> they sought relief from "nerves" or other disorders. Standards of modesty were different in those days, <u>so</u> bathing suits covered more of the body than they do today. Women wore knee-length skirts in the water; <u>in addition</u>, they wore bloomers and black stockings under the skirts. <u>Since</u> a wet bathing suit could weigh as much as the bather, the accent was on *bathing,* not swimming.

<u>If</u> she wanted greater privacy, a woman could use a "bathing machine" at the ocean. Attendants would wheel her and the portable dressing room into shallow waters. <u>After</u> she had changed into a loose head-to-toe gown, she would step down a ramp into the surf <u>while</u> attendants shooed away any interested males.

A Danish immigrant to the United States named Carl Jantzen revolutionized swim wear in 1915 <u>when</u> he invented a knitting machine that yielded a stretch fabric. The fabric resulted in a body-clinging fit; <u>however</u>, swimsuits still had sleeves and reached to the knees. Swimsuits became more revealing in the 1930s <u>when</u> narrow straps and backless models paved the way for the two-piece suit.

It wasn't until 1946 that the bikini made its appearance. World War II had recently ended, <u>and</u> the United States was testing an atom bomb in the Pacific. A French designer was about to introduce a skimpy swimsuit model, <u>but</u> he didn't have a catchy name. <u>Thus</u>, the atomic blast at Bikini Atoll on July 1, 1946, gave him the name for the "explosive" suit he displayed to the world four days later.

DOUBLECHECK 4-4

A1. . . . five years, so she. . . .
A2. Since Mrs. Frisbee has been with the company five years, she. . . .
A3. . . . years; therefore, she will. . . .
B1. . . . worker, but she. . . .
B2. Although Ruth is a hard worker, she will. . . .
B3. . . . hard worker; however, she. . . .

SPOTCHECK 5-1

1. fly, flew, flown
2. eats, ate, eaten
3. forget, forgot, forgotten
4. goes, went, gone
5. hurt, hurt, hurt

SPOTCHECK 5-2

1. bought   4. told
2. given   5. brought
3. threw

SPOTCHECK 5-3

1. taught
2. sung
3. flew
4. eaten
5. drunk

SPOTCHECK 5-4

1. Chandra had never seen a porpoise before.
2. The baby became tired during the baseball game.
3. The phone rang three times.
4. Alan had known Fran in Calgary
5. The owner had driven the car 150,000 kilometres.

SPOTCHECK 5-5

1. excited
2. frightened
3. grown
4. annoyed
5. prejudiced

SPOTCHECK 5-6

1. is   3. has   5. did
2. had   4. does

SPOTCHECK 5-7

1. knows
2. supposed
3. asked
4. says
5. run

SPOTCHECK 5-8

Sam walks over to the library because he needs some information to write a psychology class paper on hypnotism. He asks a librarian for help. He is told that the *Readers' Guide to Periodical Literature* lists articles from about 200 magazines. He looks under "hypnotism" and sees the titles of many articles on the subject. He decides to request the April 1982 issue of *Essence* because he is attracted to an article called "Hypnosis: Put Your Mind Power to Work."

DOUBLECHECK 5-1

1. was	6. goes
2. lived	7. begins
3. went	8. produces
4. returned	9. meets
5. took	10. receives

SPOTCHECK 6-1

1. are
2. play
3. run

SPOTCHECK 6-2

1. plans
2. expects
3. enjoy

SPOTCHECK 6-3

1. (s) one; (v) is
2. cause is
3. banana adds
4. workers are
5. woman thinks

SPOTCHECK 6-4

1. (s) house; (v) is
2. remains are
3. tombstones are
4. quality is
5. feelings are

SPOTCHECK 6-5

1. (s) One; (v) owns
2. Both have
3. Everyone was
4. Each tastes
5. Nobody is

SPOTCHECK 6-6

1. has
2. don't
3. drive
4. love
5. costs

SPOTCHECK 6-7
1. gives
2. plans
3. is

SPOTCHECK 6-8
1. seems
2. has
3. is

DOUBLECHECK 6-1
1. knows	3. are	5. watches	7. was	9. are
2. was	4. were	6. are	8. need	10. has

DOUBLECHECK 6-2
1. people are
2. Which has (C)
3. answer lies
4. first means
5. (sports) that stimulate
6. Activities are (C)
7. They increase
8. Lifting is (C)
9. walking, swimming produces
10. experts say

SPOTCHECK 7-1
1. skinny	3. compulsive	5. youthful	7. flashy
2. rowdy	4. mature	6. talented	8. stubborn

SPOTCHECK 7-2
1. mother
2. cottage
3. ambulance chaser
4. studious
5. intoxicated

SPOTCHECK 7-3
1. him	3. it	5. me	7. you
2. they	4. she	6. we	8. he

SPOTCHECK 7-4
1. IO	3. IO	5. DO	7. IO
2. S	4. OP	6. S	8. DO

SPOTCHECK 7-5

1. They—subject
2. it—direct object
3. him—indirect object
4. him—object of preposition
5. them—direct object

SPOTCHECK 7-6

1. ~~Sam and~~ I
2. ~~Dwight and~~ him
3. We ~~NDPers~~
4. us ~~tourists~~
5. ~~my wife and~~ me
6. ~~the other hikers and~~ us
7. ~~The Schmidts and~~ she
8. ~~the senator and~~ him

SPOTCHECK 7-7

1. I
2. I
3. we
4. he

SPOTCHECK 7-8

1. Whom
2. who
3. who
4. whom

SPOTCHECK 7-9

1. himself
2. me
3. themselves
4. you

DOUBLECHECK 7-1

1. We
2. me
3. I
4. who
5. himself
6. whom
7. themselves
8. I
9. her
10. who
11. they
12. us
13. we
14. who
15. The auditor and I
16. We
17. us
18. who

DOUBLECHECK 7-2

1. Cordelia painted the picture herself.
2. Whom did you recommend for the prize?
3. The bee stung me on the finger.
4. The children gave themselves a party.
5. It was Fred who won the race.
6. Patrick and she shared first place.
7. Last place was shared by Kimberly and me.

SPOTCHECK 7-10

1. A talented musician, Sheila was chosen to play in the concert.
2. Agnes' dress was bright blue.
3. Late in June, rain drenched the city.
4. Eric is a pacifist.
5. Our team should win tomorrow night's game.
6. We often need good advice.

SPOTCHECK 8-1

1. its	3. his	5. his
2. their	4. her	

SPOTCHECK 8-2

1. All the picnickers brought their own lunches.
2. Each of the drivers had to show a license.
3. A person who showers uses only about half as much water as a person who bathes.
4. Fans who bring their ticket stubs from the rained-out game will get in free.

SPOTCHECK 8-3

1. its	3. its	5. its
2. its	4. it	

DOUBLECHECK 8-1

1a	3b	5b	7a	9a
2b	4b	6b	8b	10b

SPOTCHECK 8-4

1. As the umpire and the coach argued, the coach's voice got louder and louder.
2. Frank told the instructor, "You have a poor understanding of the subject."
3. Ms. Stemley gave a big smile when she saw Ms. Wright.
4. The truck wasn't damaged when it hit the police car.
5. The wind that followed the hail caused extensive damage.

SPOTCHECK 8-5

1. Clint did weight training for a year before the change in his body became noticeable.
2. Jeffrey wants to be a rodeo rider, but he has never attended a rodeo.
3. Highway drivers have to stay alert.
4. People always listen to the one who complains the loudest.
5. Not responding to her invitation was impolite of me.

DOUBLECHECK 8-2

1. Visitors to Paris should see the Louvre museum.
2. Don't buy a car that needs premium gasoline.
3. This magazine says the polar ice cap is melting.
4. Anyone suffering dizzy spells should see a doctor.
5. The radio announcer said rainy weather is expected.
6. The Jayanathans did not meet their neighbours until the neighbours invited them to a PTA meeting.
7. The committee finally made its recommendation at 1 a.m.
8. Neither of the golfers lost a ball in the rough on the final round.
9. Emile told Winston, "I am certain to win the race."
10. Not all drivers know their way around the Trans-Canada Highway.

SPOTCHECK 8-6

1. more faded
2. worst
3. happier
4. more
5. most intelligent

SPOTCHECK 8-7

1. quickly
2. easily
3. enviously
4. good
5. well

SPOTCHECK 8-8

1. Amy didn't take any of Susan's advice.
2. The soccer team doesn't have enough money for uniforms.
3. Frank doesn't contribute anything to charity.
4. The Gregorys don't know anyone in Halifax.
5. Since the accident, Mr. Chan can hardly walk.

SPOTCHECK 9-1

1. fact
2. fact
3. opinion
4. opinion
5. opinion
6. fact
7. opinion
8. fact

SPOTCHECK 9-2

1. . . . ready, so you. . . .
2. . . . late, and he. . . .
3. . . . raise, for you. . . .

4. . . . apologize, or I. . . .
5. . . . pets, but they. . . .

SPOTCHECK 9-3

1. Mary has a cold, and Bill has a headache.
2. It's raining, but sunshine is forecast.
3. Jan's shoes were too small, so she gave them to Sonia.

SPOTCHECK 9-4

1. Grown in California and Oregon,
2. To drink the juice of a coconut,
3. Known in the Mediterranean area as "the poor man's fruit,"
4. No,

SPOTCHECK 9-5

1. The Chinese eat kumquats fresh, preserve them, or make them into jams.
2. Most papayas in Canada come from Florida, Texas, Hawaii, Mexico, or Puerto Rico.
3. Answers will vary.
4. Answers will vary.

SPOTCHECK 9-6

1. Bill's Diner, which looks like it survived a tornado, is a favourite student hangout.
2. My history teacher, Mr. Jefferson, has written a book on the Charlottetown Referendum.
3. The mating call of the Mediterranean fruit fly, according to experts, has the same frequency as the musical note F-sharp.
4. Correct
5. Pound cake, which is one of my favourite desserts, got its name from the pound of butter used in making it.
6. That fact, of course, won't keep me from enjoying pound cake—and putting on pounds.
7. Money is a bad master, it has been said, but a good servant.
8. Billy Bishop, who failed RMC, became Canada's ace pilot in 1917.

SPOTCHECK 9-7

1. . . . 45°C, recorded July 5, 1937, at Midale and Yellowgrass, Saskatchewan.
2. . . . −63°C, at Snag, Yukon Territory, on February 3, 1947.
3. . . . Robert Wong, 213 West Pender Street, Vancouver, British Columbia.
4. . . . Lethbridge, Alberta, on January 4, 1962.

DOUBLECHECK 9-1

1. . . . McLuhan, usually known as Marshall McLuhan, was. . . .
2. . . . on July 21, 1911, and . . . on December 31, 1980.
3. . . . media, he became. . . .

4. . . . in 1943, and he was. . . .
5. . . . man, he formulated. . . .
6. . . . significant, but. . . .
7. . . . media where television, for example, conveys. . . .
8. . . . in 1964, he became. . . .
9. In 1967, *The Medium Is the Message* was published, and. . . .
10. . . . at University of Toronto, and . . . in 1983, in his memory.
11. Correct
12. . . . information, but also. . . .

DOUBLECHECK 9-2

1. According to archeologists, . . .
2. . . . men, and graves. . . .
3. . . . bronze, razors. . . .
4. Correct
5. Correct
6. In the New World, Indian. . . .

SPOTCHECK 9-8

1. anyone,   3. is,   5. Correct   7. canoe,
2. admitted,   4. list,   6. found,   8. and,

SPOTCHECK 9-9

1. beautiful   6. looked healthy
2. talk   7. car
3. enthusiastic   8. house
4. poorly acted   9. Regardless
5. ask   10. envious of

SPOTCHECK 10-1

1. . . . gas tank?
2. Look out! That gun is loaded. (or!)
3. . . . spare dimee.
4. "What time is it?" William asked.
5. . . . it was.

SPOTCHECK 10-2

1. . . . Frye, "Literature . . . mythology."
2. "Marriage . . . institution," said Mae West. "But . . . institution."
3. "I did . . . Canada," said . . . swim.
4. "No, Mr. Speaker," said Elijah Harper.

SPOTCHECK 10-3

1. "What . . . tonight?" Mary asked.
2. "Oh, I don't know," Cathy answered. "I'll . . . Star Trek on TV."
3. Correct
4. "So what . . . Miss Intellectual?"

5. Mary said, "I'll probably do some reading. There's an article called 'Lipstick and You' in the new Teen World that looks good."

SPOTCHECK 10-4

1. I've	3. hasn't	5. you're	7. couldn't	9. won't
2. can't	4. they're	6. There's	8. You've	10. we'll

SPOTCHECK 10-5

1. men's	3. week's	5. radio's	7. cars'
2. horses'	4. countries'	6. flowers'	8. lifetime's

SPOTCHECK 10-6

1. book's
2. Duncan's
3. Correct
4. boys'
5. women's

SPOTCHECK 10-7

1. The men's faces were brightened by smiles.
2. The two farmers' trucks collided.
3. Jennifer's dance class meets on Tuesdays.
4. Both players won athletic scholarships.

DOUBLECHECK 10-1

1. "Why . . . morning?"
2. . . . Shakespeare's The Taming of the Shrew.
3. I'm; Joe's
4. McCrae's poem "In Flanders Fields" . . .
5. "Surely," Joyce said, "you don't expect me to drink day-old coffee."
6. Correct
7. Charles'
8. cowboys'
9. "Look . . . leap" is . . .
10. School's

SPOTCHECK 10-8

1. The sun came up; the dew quickly dried.
2. . . . baseball; however, he . . .
3. . . . Kids on the Block, $115 million; TV comic Bill Cosby, $113 million; talk-show host Oprah Winfrey, $80 million; and singer Madonna, $63 million.

SPOTCHECK 10-9

1. . . . picnic: paper plates . . .
2. . . . admire: enthusiasm.
3. Correct

SPOTCHECK 10-10

1. . . . Marsha—a knockout!
2. . . . Seaway (1950 to 1954) was. . . .
3. . . . Mildred—I mean Agnes—went. . . .
4. . . . Brad (who owes me money, by the way). . . .
5. Tina's brother—in fact, her whole family—is a little odd.

DOUBLECHECK 10-2

1. . . . are Bombay, India; Cairo, Egypt; Jakarta, Indonesia; London, England; and Tokyo, Japan.
2. Uncle Alfred (he's my mother's late brother) once. . . .
3. The curtain rose; the performance began.
4. . . . trip: a knife. . . .
5. . . . Beethoven (1770–1827) was. . . .
6. Allison lost—would you believe it?—ten pounds. . . .
7. . . . two months; however, she. . . .
8. . . . owned—furniture, clothing, family keepsakes—was. . . .
9. . . . The World Series in 1992; moreover, they won. . . .
10. Katharine Hepburn (do you remember her?) won. . . .

SPOTCHECK 10-11

1. bandwagon
2. either–or
3. circular reasoning
4. hasty generalization
5. non sequitur
6. non sequitur
7. either–or

SPOTCHECK 11-1

1. College, Jesuits, Quebec
2. Her, Catholic, Baptist
3. My, Tagalog
4. The, Olsons, Lake Superior
5. The, Sam, "Sparky"
6. The, Loud and Funky, Beatles, "Norwegian Wood"
7. Dave, Math 1A, I
8. Mr. and Mrs. McDonald, Grand Canyon, Arizona, June
9. The, Salvation Army Building, Elm Street, Pine Avenue
10. Vickie

SPOTCHECK 11-2

1. 3 secretaries
2. Twelve percent
3. size 6½
4. Correct
5. 3 p.m.
6. August 3

SPOTCHECK 11-3

1. November
2. pounds
3. Professor
4. political science
5. Toronto
6. Quebec

DOUBLECHECK 11-1

1. Twelve
2. university
6. 73
7. economics

3. Spanish   8. high school
4. $36.50   9. kilograms
5. World War II   10. "when

DOUBLECHECK 11-2

1. four
2. six
3. Statistics Canada, first
4. New Year's Day
5. Canadian, census figures

6. statistics, percent
7. Ste., percent
8. Correct
9. percent, English
10. percent

DOUBLECHECK 11-3

1. flea, *National Geographic*
2. Olympic Games
3. 150
4. feet
5. 30,000
6. Correct

7. astronaut
8. humans
9. Three, world
10. The, China
11. United States, two

SPOTCHECK 12-1

1. (joined) became
2. (went) was
3. (attends) gains
4. (joined) played
5. (signs) warns
6. (plays) bats, helps

SPOTCHECK 12-2

(past time) Jackie Robinson was an outstanding athlete who opened the door to professional sports for other black athletes. Robinson joined the Brooklyn Dodgers in 1947 and became the first black player in modern major league baseball. Robinson went to high school in Pasadena, California, where he was a star in track, football, and baseball. He attended the University of California at Los Angeles on a football scholarship and, in 1939, gained more yards than any other college player. After service in World War II, Robinson joined the Kansas City Monarchs and played for $400 a month in the Negro American League. When Dodgers general manager Branch Rickey signed Robinson, he warned him to expect acts of prejudice from other players and the fans. During the ten years he played for the Dodgers, Robinson batted .311 and helped the team win six National League championships and a World Series in 1955.

SPOTCHECK 12-3

1. Correct
2. were worn
3. thought they were
4. were taking

5. started
6. Correct
7. commissioned
8. Correct

SPOTCHECK 12-4

1. ~~you~~ they
2. ~~one~~ we
3. ~~you~~ he
4. ~~you~~ we
5. ~~you~~ one gets

SPOTCHECK 12-5

1. No ticket is needed to attend the Blue Rodeo concert.
2. Diners at Shopsey's Restaurant feel they get their money's worth.
3. I was glad to see Ralph again.
4. Foreign travel helps one understand one's own country.
5. A person driving 100 kilometres per hour would take 171 years to travel the 149.6 million kilometres to the sun.

SPOTCHECK 12-6

1. mistaken
2. attractive
3. exciting
4. danced
5. dollars

DOUBLECHECK 12-1

1. person
2. time
3. tone
4. Correct
5. person
6. time
7. tone
8. person
9. time
10. tone

SPOTCHECK 12-7

1. 2, 1, 3
2. 2, 1, 3
3. 3, 1, 2
4. 2, 3, 1

SPOTCHECK 12-8

1. First. . . . Then. . . . Now. . . .
2. Across the street. . . . To the right. . . . Farther on. . . .
3. At first. . . . Meanwhile. . . . As a result. . . .
4. First of all. . . . Moreover. . . . Finally. . . .

SPOTCHECK 13-1

1. Leah bought a new handbag <u>with a silk lining</u> at a downtown store.
2. A cowboy's 10-gallon hat holds <u>only</u> 1½ gallons of water.
3. <u>Driving home from work</u>, Min saw an accident.
4. Gloria likes her new baby <u>even</u> when he cries.
5. The average marriage in Canada lasts <u>only</u> 12.4 years.

SPOTCHECK 13-2

1. Growing careless, the clerk entered the wrong name.
2. Although I was 21 years old, my father . . . .
3. Able to bend steel bars with ease, Mighty Mo filled me with awe.
4. Vacation rushed to an end as we played tennis. . . .
5. Solomon took a photo of the cows contentedly eating grass.

SPOTCHECK 13-3

1. wrong
2. dirty
3. having a lot of money
4. how to get along with people
5. lazy
6. recreational opportunities are greater

SPOTCHECK 13-4

1. Because she was hungry, she ate a late-night snack.
2. Her family is pleased when Sally gets a raise.
3. Although sunshine is forecast, Rocky has his umbrella.
4. A good sale makes me happy.

SPOTCHECK 13-5

1. Polly is a lot smarter than Victoria.
2. The trees are greener in the spring than in the fall.
3. A Jeep Comanche looks better and goes faster than a goat cart.
4. The summers in Victoria are hotter than those in Vancouver.

SPOTCHECK 13-6

1. P
2. A
3. P
4. P
5. A

SPOTCHECK 13-7

1. Two customers saw the holdup.
2. The teacher praised Carrie.
3. The company notified all employees of the layoffs.
4. The store offered discounts to people over 65.
5. Students wrote all the essays.

DOUBLECHECK 13-1

1. D	3. B	5. A	7. D
2. C	4. E	6. B	8. E

SPOTCHECK 13-8

1. Its
2. it's
3. It's
4. its
5. its

SPOTCHECK 13-9

1. their
2. They're
3. Their, there
4. There, their
5. they're, their, there

SPOTCHECK 14-1

1. The ripe apple fell with a crashing sound.
2. Lucinda and Martin washed dishes.
3. Martin washed dishes without complaining.
4. Martin washed and dried the dishes.
5. The happy baby smiled and gurgled in the bathtub.

SPOTCHECK 14-2

1. . . . 600,000, and Edmonton. . . .
2. . . . voice, so today. . . .
3. . . . clumsy, but it. . . .
4. . . . homework, for he. . . .
5. . . . fishing, or he. . . .
6. . . . swim, for almost. . . .

SPOTCHECK 14-3

1. while one American died on-screen in *Rambo*
2. unless his sales decline
3. who owns two Dobermans
4. although many young baseball players are signed to professional contracts
5. because their pitching staff is strong

SPOTCHECK 14-4

1. The dentist was upset <u>when</u> Sean. . . .
2. Lia was nervous <u>because</u>. . . .
3. Yousuf Karsh is a great photographer <u>who</u> photographed Winston Churchill.
4. <u>After</u> gambling was legalized in Windsor, the crime rate. . . .
5. That is the bus driver <u>who</u> returned. . . .

SPOTCHECK 14-5

1. When the floor of the house shook, Jack knew. . . .
2. If the bank will give you a loan, you. . . .
3. Although Yolanda got many Christmas gifts, she. . . .
4. Because Claudette enjoys nature, she. . . .
5. Kimberly began giving money to friends after she. . . .

DOUBLECHECK 14-1

1. S
2. C
3. X
4. X
5. S

SPOTCHECK 14-6

1. Are, our, or	3. hear	5. than	7. Where, were	9. here
2. have	4. here	6. too	8. You're	10. Then

DOUBLECHECK 14-2

1. too	6. have
2. It's	7. your, its
3. our	8. then
4. too	9. than
5. there's	10. There's

SPOTCHECK 15-1

1. With grease all over his face, the mechanic looked. . . .
2. . . . picture of Marie on page 34.
3. . . . hid between two boulders.
4. After a hectic day, Mrs. Farnaby. . . .
5. In the tree's highest branches, crows were. . . .

SPOTCHECK 15-2

1. terrified at the dog's barking
2. Singing in the rain

3. taught to him by his mother
4. Finished with his homework
5. Searching for a route to Asia

SPOTCHECK 15-3

1. Played in India in the sixteenth century
2. Enjoyed by the emperor Akbar the Great
3. Moving from bush to bush in the garden
4. determined by the throw of shells
5. changing the Indian name *pacisi* to *Pachisi*

SPOTCHECK 15-4

1. Exhausted from his hike, Paul wanted. . . .
2. Having saved 10 percent of their salaries for ten years, the Selvadurais were finally. . . .
3. Excited at the victory, the players held. . . .
4. Pleased with her garden, Mrs. Ward gave. . . .
5. Playing volleyball in the gym, Richard met. . . .

SPOTCHECK 15-5

1. a fifteenth-century Romanian prince
2. "Bluebeard"
3. Elizabeth Goose
4. "Mary Had a Little Lamb"
5. inventor of the phonograph

SPOTCHECK 15-6

1. Elizabeth Kenny, an Australian nurse, developed. . . .
2. The quartet played bebop, a style. . . .
3. Elvis Presley, the "King" of rock 'n' roll, died. . . .
4. Alice Munro wrote Open Secrets, a collection of short stories.
5. The Toronto SkyDome, an arena with a retractable roof, can hold. . . .

DOUBLECHECK 15-1

1. Prep	3. Ap	5. Part	7. Ap
2. Ap	4. Part	6. Part	8. Part

SPOTCHECK 15-7

1. moving	5. satisfying
2. controlled	6. hoping
3. silliest	7. occurred
4. regrettable	8. happier

SPOTCHECK 15-8

1. deceived
2. vein
3. field
4. relieved
5. friends
6. weight
7. believe
8. received

SPOTCHECK C-1

1. N-1
2. V-1
3. N-6
4. N-4
5. N-2

SPOTCHECK E-1

1. conscience
2. advice
3. all right
4. may
5. as

SPOTCHECK E-2

1. pleasant
2. except, accepted
3. fewer
4. imply
5. desert, desserts
6. an occasion when

SPOTCHECK E-3

1. morale
2. lose
3. passed, almost
4. Tony and I
5. know
6. peace

SPOTCHECK E-4

1. quite
2. was that
3. supposed
4. whether, women
5. sit, try to

ACKNOWLEDGEMENTS

Care has been taken to trace ownership of copyright material contained in this text. The publishers will gladly take any information that will enable them to rectify any reference or credit in subsequent editions.

Bissoondath, Neil. "Traditions," from *Chatelaine,* December 1992. Reprinted with permission of the author.

Burton, Ian. "Individual Actions Can Have Huge Consequences," from *The Globe and Mail,* 1990. Reprinted with permission of the author.

Guy, Ray. "Outharbor Menu." Reprinted with the permission of Breakwater Books Ltd, from *That Far Greater Bay.* Copyright by the author.

Johnston, Lonn. "Road Warriors." Copyright, July 1987, *Los Angeles Times.* Reprinted by permission.

Kogawa, Joy. "Evacuees in Alberta," from *Obasan.* Penguin Canada, 1991. Reprinted with permission of the author.

Landsberg, Michele. "Beauty Myth Preserves Male Dominance," from the *Toronto Star.* Reprinted with permission—the Toronto Star Syndicate.

Marchand, Philip. "Nasty Canadians," from the *Toronto Star,* January 1995. Reprinted with permission—the Toronto Star Syndicate.

Mineko, Anna. "Lack of English, Not Good Will, Is the Culprit," from the *Toronto Star,* February 1994. Reprinted with permission of the author.

Posner, Michael. "The Roots Boys," from *Toronto Life,* October 1993. Copyright 1993. Adapted with permission of the author.

Quarrington, Paul. "Home Ice." Copyright November 1990. Adapted with permission of the author.

Robinson, Laura. "Feminine Finesse Versus Brute Force," from *The Globe and Mail,* 1994. Reprinted with permission of the author.

Tavender, Kate. "Earth to Generation X: Quit Whining," from *The Globe and Mail,* September 1994. Reprinted with permission of the author.

Van Gorder, Erika. "Let's Get Realistic about Teenage Drinking," from the *Toronto Star,* 1995. Reprinted with permission of the author.

Wiebe, Rudy. "Speaking Saskatchewan." Copyright 1990 by Jackpine House Ltd. Reprinted by permission of the author.

Wood, T. "When Talk Turns to Old Haunts," from *The Globe and Mail*. Reprinted by permission of the author.

INDEX